Perfect Da...

C000143966

BARCELONA

Travel with
Insider
Tips

MARCO ⊕ POLO

Contents

For chapters: see inside front cover

TOP 10

Not to be missed!

Our top hits – from the absolute No. 1 to No. 10 –

help you plan your tour of the most important sights.

1 BARRI GÒTIC ➤ 48
The magnificent architecture in the Gothic Quarter (left) is testimony to Catalonia's golden age as a Mediterranean power.

2 LA SAGRADA FAMÍLIA ➤ 104
This cathedral with its gigantic towers winding their way sky-wards – which is still under con-struction today – has become the world famous symbol of Barcelona.

3 LAS RAMBLAS ➤ 52
The famous promenade teems with a mix of tourists, theatregoers and pickpockets, culture vultures and vendors, elegant opera patrons and harried waiters. The Ramblas is a non-stop human spectacle.

4 PALAU DE LA MÚSICA CATALANA ➤ 78
A flamboyant art nouveau con-cert hall – a lavishly decorated monument to Catalan Modernisme. The curved dome of the stained-glass skylight is uniquely beautiful.

5 PARK GÜELL ➤ 111
Doric columns, serpentine figures, crooked arcades: it is no wonder that even Salvador Dalí admired Gaudí's fairytale park with the breathtaking view over Barcelona.

6 CASA MILÀ ➤ 114
Gaudí's strangest, and most famous, residential building has a remarkable rooftop landscape and a panoramic view.

7 MANZANA DE LA DISCÒRDIA ➤ 117
Three of the main figures in Modernisme have created monuments next door to each other. The Casa Batlló, designed by Gaudí, is especially striking.

8 MUSEU PICASSO ➤ 80
Housed in five medieval palaces on the elegant Carrer Montcada, Barcelona's most popular museum provides an unforgettable im-pression of the artist's work.

9 MUSEU NACIONAL D'ART DE CATALUNYA (MNAC) ➤ 136
Catalonia's art under a single roof – from the Romanesque period to the present day. The collection of Romanesque frescoes is un-paralleled worldwide.

10 SANTA MARIA DEL MAR ➤ 84
Catalan Gothic in its purest form: the unique house of worship be-came famous all over the world through Ildefonso Falcones' best-seller "Cathedral of the Sea".

THAT
BARCELONA

Find out what Barcelona is all about and savour its unique flair (almost) like a native.

RUMBA CATALAN-STYLE

The infectious melange of flamenco, Afro-Caribbean music and rock 'n' roll is all the rage. Originating in the Catalan *gitanos* neighbourhoods, the Rumba Catalana (www. calarumba.com) is considered modern Barcelonan folklore and even those who never dance will find it hard to resist. Live concerts take place in the Rumba Club of the Sala Plataforma (✚ 203 E3, Nou de la Rambla 145, tel: 9 33 29 00 29).

COOL MIDSUMMER NIGHT'S DREAM

Mediterranean nights are not only long, they are also frequently hot. And then Barcelona's night owls make their way to the city's spectacular late-night rooftop terraces, in many of the design hotels, to have a cool drink under the stars. The terraces of the Hotel Pulitzer (✚ 200 B1, Carrer Bergara 8), the Grand Hotel Central (✚ 204 C3, Via Laietana 30) and the Hotel Majestic (✚ 200 B3, Passeig de Gràcia 70) are just three of the most popular chill-out places with views of the glittering city lights.

IN THE "BELLY OF BARCELONA"

There is plenty to see and even more to eat in the Mercat de la Boquería (► 54): you will be almost overwhelmed by the colours, aromas, sounds and all the tempting delicacies. Marvel at the artistic towers of figs, mushrooms and pepperoni, the hams hanging from the ceiling and the mountains of freshly caught fish and seafood. Go with the flow of the morning market hustle and bustle and when you feel peckish try some of the produce from the stalls. Two of the most famous places for excellent food are El Quim and Pinotxo.

APPETIZING TRADITION

Barcelonans think of bars as public living rooms – a place to meet friends, colleagues, or just to relax for a few moments over an *aperitivo* – particularly after work and on Sunday mornings.

FEELING

Meeting for an aperitif is part of the Spanish way of life

That Barcelona Feeling

The traditional vermouth, a small beer (*caña*) or a glass of wine along with something to nibble: olives, chips, anchovies… Tapas are also considered an aperitif as long as they don't take the place of a meal. The top spots include the Quimet & Quimet (➤ 148) and Bar Calders (➤ 127).

BARCELONA'S HUMAN TOWERS

Building *castells* is a popular Catalan sporting activity where young men climb on each other's shoulders to make human towers – sometimes ten men high. You can watch them training at the Union of Castellers de Barcelona (www.castellersdebarcelona.cat). And, if you are brave enough, you can even join in – free of charge. Good luck!

WEEKENDS IN THE PARK

Especially at the weekend, the Parc de la Ciutadella (➤ 86) is the place to go to get a feel for the way Barcelonans spend their leisure time: families enjoy a picnic, go boating or play football, young people laze on the grass, others train on a slackline or try their hand at juggling, drummers let off steam and there are long lines in front of the kiosks – calm before the storm on Monday.

CURIOSITIES AND BARGAINS

Every Sunday morning, Barcelona's flea market fans flock to the Sant Antoni indoor market (✚ 203 E3, Carrer Comte d'Urgell 1) to hunt down books, art catalogues, comics, films, old postcards and computer games. If you see a group of locals putting their heads together, don't think that they are doing anything suspicious; they are just collectors swapping their treasures. The market hall is being renovated and the flea market will be held in a tent annexe – probably until 2015.

SNACK IN THE MILK BAR

If you get a waft of the aroma of hot chocolate and *xurros* (doughnuts) then you know that the next *granja* is not far away! Enjoy a Catalan *merienda* in the afternoon. The La Pallaresa (✚ 204 B4, Carrer Petrixol, 11, 9am–1pm and 5–9pm) is one of the most traditional: mountains of whipped cream, neon lighting and waiters balancing gigantic trays – a delicious treat!

Boating in the Parc de la Ciutadella

The Magazine

Catalan CAPITAL

Catalans, especially Barcelonans, will often tell you that Catalonia and its capital city are not Spanish. The region in the northeastern Iberian Peninsula has clung fiercely to its unique culture for centuries, despite attempts to eradicate it.

A Spanish-Catalan state existed as early as 878, when Wilfred "The Hairy" (► panel, page 13) succeeded in uniting several northeastern counties, creating the basis for a future Catalan nation. He named himself the first Count of Barcelona, founding a dynastic line that was to rule a powerful nation for several centuries before it was eventually absorbed into an expanding Spain in the 15th century.

The Spanish-Catalans were suppressed by Castilian rule until 1635, when Spain and France were at war, and Catalans on both sides of the border revolted and declared themselves an independent republic. The uprising was soon quashed. Barcelona surrendered to the Spanish army in 1652 and Spain lost control of the border districts of France. The Treaty of the Pyrenees, signed in 1659, split the historical lands of Catalonia.

The Renaixença

During the 18th century, Catalonia began to re-emerge, thanks to a steady growth in agriculture, the export of wine and increased shipping. Following the Napoleonic Wars, the region experienced such an industrial boom that Barcelona became the fastest-expanding city in Spain. This pre-empted the Catalan *Renaixença* (Renaissance) of the mid-19th century. The Catalan language has never died out, despite being banned in public life, and, as Catalan literature began to flourish once more, the language was revived in bourgeois circles. With the cultural "renaissance" came the Modernista movement (the Catalan response to art nouveau) which, together with the creation of the Eixample district (➤ 26), totally changed the face of Barcelona.

Both Spanish and Catalan flags fly above the Palau de la Generalitat

Magnificent buildings from several different centuries characterize Catalonia's capital

The Magazine

Spanish Civil War

The outbreak of the Spanish Civil War in 1936 marked the start of one of Spain's darkest periods and, under the dictatorship of General Franco, Catalan national identity was totally suppressed. Catalan language was banned once more in schools, churches and public life. But despite the decades of cultural, commercial and political repression that ensued, Catalonia managed to cling onto its identity: the Catalan Church retained its independence; artists and writers continued to work; and Barcelona emerged as a major publishing centre. Not until Franco's death in 1975 and the new Spanish constitution of 1977 did Catalonia regain a measure of self-government. Eventually, in 1979, Catalonia became an Autonomous Community within Spain.

The Catalan Capital

A strong Catalan identity has emerged in the aftermath of Franco's rule. The province is the wealthiest part of Spain, producing 20 % of the country's GNP, and for a long time held the balance of power in the Madrid parliament. To the Catalan people, who account for 11 per cent of the country's population, Barcelona is not so much Spain's second city as the capital of Catalonia. No other European city has reinvented itself as splendidly as Barcelona. It emerged after a massive facelift, prior to the 1992 Olympics, as a chic, cosmopolitan metropolis, and is once more a leading centre of fashion and design. It has an undeniable vibrancy and a sense of pride – the result of Catalan refound self-confidence. Catalans will try to convince you that Barcelona, not Madrid, is Spain's premier city, and they could well be right.

SPEAKING "CATALÀ"

The resurgence of *català* (the Catalan language) is perhaps the most obvious manifestation of Catalan identity. Catalan is currently one of the fastest-growing languages in the world. Throughout the region, Catalan has returned as the everyday language with Catalonian schools teaching in Catalan with no more than two hours a week in Castilian Spanish. Although another Romance language, Catalan displays many differences from Castilian, and its vocabulary has more in common with French and Italian. Grammatical rules differ considerably, as do various pronunciation rules: for instance, the unstressed "a" and "e" sounds are almost swallowed in Catalan but clear in Castilian Spanish, and the soft lisped Castilian "z" and "c" sounds don't apply in Catalan, so it's "Barcelona" not "Barthelona". Any effort to speak either language will be appreciated, but don't get too upset if locals mistake your attempt at Catalan as mispronounced Spanish!

Nationalist artists expressed Catalan identity through a variety of media

LOCAL HEROES

WILFRED I "THE HAIRY" (*c.* 860–98)

Count Guifré "el Pilós", founder of the Catalan nation, met an early death in battle against the Saracens. It is said that, in recognition of his heroism, the Emperor dipped his fingers into Wilfred's wounds then ran them across his golden shield, so creating the four red stripes on yellow of today's Catalan flag – the Quatre Barres (Four Bars) – the oldest national flag in Europe. What nobody seems to know, though, is why or in what way he was so hairy!

JAUME I DE ARAGON (1213–76)

Jaume I was one of the most successful Catalan kings. Not only did he establish the Corts (Catalonia's first parliament) and the Generalitat (a governing committee of the Corts), he also encouraged economic development and established Barcelona as a great Mediterranean power, by retaking the Balearic Islands from the Moors. His reign was a time of great prosperity, and impressive new buildings sprung up – including the cathedral, Santa Maria del Mar and the Drassanes shipyards – which radically changed the appearance of the city.

Celebrating Catalan style: Corpus Christi procession (left), spectacular fireworks during La Mercè in September (middle) and a *castell* (or human tower) during the Sant Joan holiday in mid-June (right)

FIESTA TIME

Barcelonans take their fiestas very seriously. Many festivals are religious in origin, but rural traditions and historic events make their mark too. Here are some of the highlights.

January
Reis Mags (6 Jan) The Three Kings arrive by boat at Port Vell (the evening before, on 5 January), then their cavalcade tours the city showering the crowd with sweets.

February
Carnestoltes A week of pre-Lenten celebrations ending on Ash Wednesday in Sitges (➤ 169).

March/April
Setmana Santa Religious services, processions and celebrations for Easter week are lower key in Barcelona than much of Spain.

April
Sant Jordi (23 Apr) St George's Day is celebrated in conjunction with International Book Day. Traditionally men give red roses and women give books. The Ramblas, Rambla de Catalunya and the Passeig de Gràcia become a huge outdoor bookshop.

May
Corpus Christi Parades of giants and papier-mâché *capgrossos* (big-heads). The fountain in the Catedral's cloister is the site of the traditional *ou com balla*, when an empty egg is balanced on the jet of water, symbolizing water and birth.

June
Sant Joan (24 June) The public holiday on the eve of St John's Day when the city is overrun by fireworks.

August
Festa Major de Gràcia (starts 15 Aug) During this popular fiesta whole streets in Gràcia are decorated thematically, there are concerts, processions and dancing.

September
Diada de Catalunya (11 Sep) Catalunya's sombre National Day marks the taking of the city by Felipe V in 1714.
La Mercè (24 Sep, with celebrations all week) This is the biggest *fiesta* of the year – dancing in the streets, parades of devils, dragons, giants and big-heads, dramatic *castellar* (human tower) displays and musically choreographed fireworks.

December
Santa Llúcia (13 Dec) The unveiling of the life-size nativity scene outside the Catedral and opening of a craft fair (13–23 Dec) mark St Lucy's Day.

La Cuina
CATALANA

Catalonia has one of the richest gastronomic traditions in Spain, drawing upon Moorish, French, Sicilian and Levantine influences.

Pork forms the cornerstone of the Catalan diet, but lamb, chicken, duck, beef, snails and game also figure prominently, often prepared *a la brasa* (on an open charcoal grill) and served with *allioli* (a garlicky mayonnaise). *Botifarra* (spicy black and white puddings) and *fuet* (long, thin salami made from dried meat) are also staples of Catalan country cuisine.

Meat is commonly combined with fruit: *conill amb prunes* (rabbit with prunes) and *pollastre amb peres* (chicken with pears), for example. But, it is the unique *mar i muntanya* (sea and mountain) combinations that differentiate *la cuina catalana* from other regional Spanish cuisines: *mar i cel* ("sea and sky"), made with sausages, rabbit, shrimp and fish, and *sípia amb mandonguilles* (cuttlefish with meatballs) are especially tasty.

Fish dishes range from grilled sardines to hearty *sarsuela* (seafood stew) and a wide variety of fish soups. Look also for *bacallà* (salt cod), *arròs negre* (rice blackened with squid ink), *arròs amb llamàntol* (rice with lobster) and *fideuà* (a local variant of paella using pasta instead of rice).

Sauces and Side Dishes

Dishes rely heavily on garlic, tomatoes, olive oil, peppers and herbs which, when blended, form *samfaina*, a delicious sauce served with many dishes. Other popular sauces include *picada* (parsley, nuts, bread, garlic and saffron), *romesco* (ground almonds, tomatoes, spicy red peppers, garlic and oil) and *sofregit* (a simple sauce of tomatoonion and garlic).

Seasonal accompaniments include white asparagus in summer, wild mushrooms in the autumn and *calçots,* elongated spring onions, roasted and served with spicy *romesco* sauce in springtime.

The Adrià Phenomenon

Barcelona-born chef Ferran Adrià is the revolutionary face of Catalan cuisine. He broke down the essentials of gourmet food to build it up again with sensational tastes and textures, like oysters with foamed carrot or melon caviar. His world-famous Costa Brava restaurant, El Bulli, closed its doors in July 2011. However, the gourmet restaurant lives on in the form of the tapas restaurant, Tickets Bar on Avinguda del Paral.lel 164 (m.ticketsbar.es).

BARCELONA'S BEST FOOD MARKETS

La Boqueria, La Rambla 89; www.boqueria.info This is the most popular, the most visited and the most famous of the city's markets and easily lives up to all the hype (► 54).

Santa Caterina, Avinguda Francesc Cambó 16; www.mercatsantacaterina.net La Ribera's market (► 96) was rebuilt to a stunning design by Enric Miralles – its multi-hued tiled roof is a highlight. Inside the market hall you can enjoy a tasty and cheap meal in the popular Bar Joan (stall number 108–110).

La Concepció, Carrer d'Aragó 311 bis The Dreta de l'Eixample, the easternmost portion of the Eixample, is served by the calm Concepció market, housed in a revamped Modernista structure.

Gràcia, Carrer de Pi i Margall 73–75; Plaça de la Llibertat 27 The little Mercat Abaceria Central is overshadowed by the fantastic Mercat de la Llibertat, now opened after a tasteful refurbishment.

Barceloneta, Plaça de la Font 1 Barceloneta market (► 88), with natty concrete exterior decoration, is the perfect place to pick up a picnic for the beach.

NEW TRADITIONS

Careful innovation and commercial savvy have put Catalan wines at the forefront of a revolution in winemaking, without losing sight of the old traditions.

Winemaking in Catalonia, as elsewhere in the Mediterranean, has a long history, with indications of vineyards dating from the 5th century BC and documentation of Roman merchants exporting Catalan wines around the Mediterranean. Wine production flourished under the many religious communities here in the Middle Ages. In the 19th century, an injection of new money from the Americas led to the development of country estates and a rise in profile of winemaking, which was marked by the commissioning of stunning Modernista buildings, dubbed "cathedrals of wine". Over the past 50 years experimentation and new techniques have steered the region's output towards classy modern wines.

Sparkling Wines

A huge diversity of grapes grow in Catalonia's varied terrain and climate and wines range from velvety reds to light, fruity whites and the region's flagship sparkling wine, cava. In 1872 the French "champenoise" method was applied to local grape varieties and a phenomenon was born. Production of this sparkling wine is still centred on the town of Sant Sadurní d'Anoia, just south of Barcelona (▶ 172). The largest producer is Freixenet, and other good labels include Codorníu, Juvé & Camps, Torelló and Parxet.

WINE TASTING

Tips: For serious (although expensive) urban wine tasting – or *cata* – head for:

- **Monvínic**: Carrer de la Diputació 249, tel: 9 32 72 61 87; www.monvinic.com
- **Terrabacus**: Carrer de Muntaner 185, tel: 9 34 10 86 33; www.terrabacus.com
- **La Vinoteca Torres**: Passeig de Gràcia 78, tel: 9 02 52 05 22; www.lavinotecatorres.com

Red or White?

Using a combination of both domestic and foreign grapes, Catalan reds are mainly smooth, full-bodied wines. The complex bold negres of the Priorat are perhaps the region's top wines of the moment, while the Penedès area (► 172), home to Bodegas Torres, Catalonia's most successful winery, continues to dominate the export market. The Costers del Segre region is making a name for itself as a centre of innovation, with Bodegas Raimat leading the way. There are also many more rich, bold wines from the Empordà, Montsant and Montblanc. Although historically still white wine production has been relatively low-key in comparison with cavas and reds, the region again lends itself to great diversity. Look out for whites from Alella and Pla de Bages elaborated from the traditionally aromatic pansa blanca grape or the light fruity pica-poll. There is also a strong tradition of smooth warm dessert wines from the Empordà and Montsant regions. Good rosés – both cava and still wines – are also produced, often using the indigenous trepat grape. Equally importantly, many quality Catalan wines are available at pocket-friendly prices.

Caves Codorníu in Sant Sadurní d'Anoia, where cava was first produced

VINEYARD VISITS

- **Alella Vinicola Can Jonc**, Rambla Àngel Guimerà 62, Alella (tel: 9 55 40 38 42; www.alellavinicola.com)
- **Caves Codorníu** (► 172)
- **Caves Freixenet** (► 172)
- **Torres**, Fina el Maset, Pacs del Penedès (tel: 9 38 17 74 87; www.torres.es)

Barcelona's BARRIS

The patchwork of districts, or *barris*, which give central Barcelona its fascinating, multifaceted character, jostle together, vying for your attention.

Delightful Plaça del Pi in the Barri Gòtic, the medieval heart of the city

Ciutat Vella

The Old Town is made up of seven different neighbourhoods, which over the centuries were gradually absorbed by the city. The Barri Gòtic, at its heart, is a tangle of mainly pedestrian-only streets, which lead up from Port Vell, the old port. Across the Ramblas is El Raval, an area once occupied by convents and monasteries just outside the city walls. In more recent memory it was the city's red-light district. The other side of the Barri Gòtic lies La Ribera, an old mercantile district where you'll probably return many times.

Barri Gòtic

Built over the Roman city of Barcino, the Barri Gòtic (➤ 48) is the very centre of the city, home to the medieval cathedral (➤ 57) and the Ajuntament, or City Hall, as well as the regional government in the Palau de la Generalitat. The winding alleyways shelter the city's old Jewish quarter, as well as the lovely Santa Maria del Pi church (➤50) and several stunning squares, including Plaça Reial (➤67) and Sant Felip Neri.

El Raval

The Raval neighbourhood across the Ramblas from the Barri Gòtic is an edgy, multifaceted and multicultural area. The shiny MACBA gallery (➤63) and CCCB arts centre (➤64) are surrounded by trendy shops, bars and restaurants, while La Boqueria (➤54), the city's most famous

Architect Richard Meier's controversial MACBA gallery, part of the revitalized El Raval

market, draws residents and visitors in their droves. But nearer the water, the dingy alleyways and stone lanes are witness to a level of poverty and destitution, most obvious in the prostitute-lined streets, at odds with the city's reputation as a playground for all.

La Ribera

La Ribera incorporates the districts Sant Pere, Santa Catalina and Born. It was cut off from the Barri Gòtic at the beginning of the 20th century when the main thoroughfare, Via Laietana, was driven through it. It's an up-and-coming neighbourhood in an attractive maze of stone alleyways and cobbled streets, with some of the best shopping, dining and barlife in the city, not to mention the Palau de la Música Catalana (➤78), the Museu Picasso (➤80) and the beautiful Santa Maria del Mar (➤84). Bordering the other side of the district is the Parc de la Ciutadella (➤86).

The Magazine

Montjuïc

Rising to the south, topped by Barcelona's castle, this wonderful oasis offers spectacular views and is home to two of the city's best galleries – the Fundació Joan Miró (➤ 144) and the MNAC (➤ 136). There is also a cable car, plus jogging routes, Olympic swimming pools and 🎠 children's play-grounds galore. At the foot of the hill the Pavelló Mies van der Rohe (➤ 146) is a magnet for architecture fans and CaixaForum (➤ 147) is a good rainy-day option for all.

WHERE TO FIND

- Modernista or art nouveau buildings: L'Eixample
- Beaches: Barceloneta, Port Olímpic
- Shopping: L'Eixample, La Ribera, Barri Gòtic
- Fresh air: Montjuïc
- Football: Les Corts
- Medieval Barcelona: Barri Gòtic, La Ribera
- Art and design: El Raval, Montjuïc, L'Eixample, La Ribera

L'Eixample

Stretching up from Plaça de Catalunya, L'Eixample is the 19th-century extension of the city, packed with the iconic Modernista buildings that make Barcelona so famous. A huge grid of streets designed by Ildefons Cerdà to solve the overcrowding in the Old Town, it linked the city centre to surrounding villages, including Gràcia and Sants. Just off Avinguda Diagonal, the wide avenue that cuts a swathe through the neighbourhood, in the business district of Les Corts, stands Camp Nou (➤ 164), the home of FC Barcelona.

CaixaForum, the work of Japanese architect Arata Isozaki

Gràcia retains its village-like atmosphere and is a great place to take a stroll

Satellite Villages

Gràcia (► 120) is proud of its village status. Being linked by the Passeig de Gràcia to the centre of Barcelona at the beginning of the 20th century hasn't taken the soul out of this attractive little nucleus of narrow streets, cafe-lined squares and local shops. Head on your way up to one of Gaudí's masterpieces, Park Güell, to the north.

Barceloneta (► 88) was built on mud flats in the mid-18th century to house fishermen and port workers. Traditionally known for its fish and seafood restaurants, the area was given a new lease of life by the regeneration of the waterfront for the 1992 Olympic Games. Beyond the waterfront the narrow, run-down streets of the old fishing and working-class neighbourhood still survives (as does its problems) with a good helping of maritime charm.

The unpretentious Poble Sec neighbourhood (► 147) nestles under the hill of Montjuïc, and its newly trendy main street, the Carrer de Blai, has a number of good bars and restaurants. Otherwise you might visit one of the bars or the summer Festival del Grec (► 150).

Plaça de la Font, Barceloneta

ON THE

In keeping with a city that made its fortune from the sea, Barcelona's waterfront is one of its highlights.

Although still a prosperous port, the city revamped its waterfront prior to the 1992 Olympic Games. Old factories and warehouses were removed from the sands and the mercantile activity and booming cruise ship harbour shifted a little round the coast to the south. Port Vell, the old port, at the foot of the Ramblas, was transformed as a complex of marinas, sailing clubs and the flagship Maremagnum shopping mall were built. From here you can tour the harbour on one of the famous Golondrinas boats (➤ 187) or be whisked up to Montjuïc on the cable car (➤ 187).

Summer and sunny weekends see visitors and residents alike flocking to the beaches, which have repeatedly won EU blue-flag status for their water quality and facilities. The Barceloneta promontory has seven swimming bays lined up one after another: Sant Sebastià, Barceloneta, Nova

XIRINGUITOS – BEACH BARS
From spring to autumn, the beaches are punctuated with beach bars – or *xiringuitos (chiringuitos* in Spanish) – serving drinks and snacks from 10am until midnight, seven days a week. They all have different personalities – some specializing in fresh fruit juices, others in live DJ sets or mojitos – and are a great place for a snack or drink during the day.

WATERFRONT

Icària, Bogatell, Mar Bella, Nova Mar Bella and Platja Llevant. Closest to the centre of town, Barceloneta is understandably the busiest, backed by traditional paella restaurants and stylish new bars.

The section around Port Olímpic is also very popular, not least because it's close to a metro station. On Bogatell, the area around the bar Vai Moana is one of the most fashionable parts of the sands, and Mar Bella has a small nudist section. Barceloneta and Bogatell are firm favourites with ⚑ families, as the sands do not shelve too steeply. Unfortunately, there are increasing numbers of pickpockets on the beaches and in the bars – so be alert!

Beach Activities

On windy days Sant Sebastià and Barceloneta beaches are bobbing with wind- and kitesurfers. This is also the area for board surfing, although new breakwaters have tamed the waves a little too much for some tastes. Equipment is available for rent from various outlets around here.

Novice sailors can take to the waters at the Centre Municipal de Vela at the Port Olímpic, and the open-air pool at Sant Sebastià, Club Natació Atlètic-Barceloneta, is heated year-round and has unrivalled views across the waters. The promenade backing the beach is popular with joggers, rollerbladers and cyclists or you can join in a game of volleyball on Barceloneta or Nova Icària beaches. There's a muscle gym on Barceloneta beach and you'll always find somewhere simply to lay your towel.

Opposite: Rambla de Mar, Port Vell. Above: Hotel Arts and Torre Mapfre, Vila Olímpica

Setting an
EIXAMPLE

Few cities in the world can beat Barcelona for Modernist art and architecture. Yet this radical new style initially met with mixed reactions. For some the daring creations of Gaudí and his peers heralded a second Catalan "Golden Age", for others it was *l'època de mal gust* – the epoch of bad taste.

For over a century Barcelona has been a world leader in town planning and modernity. The city took the lead in Spanish industrial development, becoming a centre of art and design, nurturing such Modernists as Gaudí (► 29), Picasso and Miró. A period of economic growth coincided with a wave of optimism, and from 1860 onwards an extension of the city beyond the medieval walls was built to reflect Catalonia's new-found prosperity – the Eixample.

The Eixample was the brainchild of engineer Ildefons Cerdà. A 9sq km (3.5sq-mile) *barri* (district) of geometric uniformity, based on a grid pattern of 550 symmetrical square blocks (known as *illes*, meaning "islands"), each with their corners cut off, it is a visionary example of urban planning unique in Europe, with the aptly named Avinguda Diagonal cutting through the rectilinear blocks at 45 degrees to add a touch of originality. Unfortunately though, the utopian features of Cerdà's plan – gardens in the middle of each block and buildings on only two sides – were not respected, and some today scorn the district for its monotony.

Modernisme

Just as Barcelona was building its new *barri*, Modernisme arrived in the city, bringing with it artistic geniuses who were to endow the district with architectural jewels to rival those of any city in Europe. The leading exponent of the movement in Barcelona was, without doubt, Antoni Gaudí, but he was by no means the only Modernist at work in the city. Local architects Lluís Domènech i Montaner and Josep Puig i Cadafalch created such marvels as Palau de la Música Catalana (► 78), Casa Lleó Morera (► 117) and

The magnificent skylight in the main auditorium of the Palau de la Música Catalana

the Hospital de la Santa Creu i Sant Pau (► 124), which is set defiantly at 45 degrees to the street grid.

Domènech i Montaner is considered by many to be the father of Modernisme. He was the first to give art nouveau ideals "Catalan" expression, by drawing on the region's glorious past (in particular, its rich Romanesque and Gothic traditions) for inspiration in his designs. Unlike his pupil Puig i Cadafalch, or Gaudí, he frequently worked with entire artisan teams – architects, sculptors, glass- and metal-workers and ceramicists – to create dazzlingly ornate yet always highly functional buildings, a contrast to the more idealistic, fanciful creations of Gaudí.

Revitalization

In the late 1990s, the Eixample received a facelift. Today, the Eixample is a *barri* for gazing not only at the masterpieces – such as La Sagrada Família (► 104), one of the great architectural wonders of the world, with its cloud-piercing, mosaic-clad spires – but also at the smaller details: the twisted wrought-ironwork of town-house balconies and the ornate shop facades, right down to the doorknobs of hundreds of back-street buildings. Look closely as you walk around and you will be richly rewarded.

The undulating rooftop and shard-encrusted chimney stacks at Casa Milà (La Pedrera)

The Genius of Gaudí

No visit to Barcelona would be complete without paying homage to Antoni Gaudí i Cornet, one of Spain's most brilliant architects. Even his first work – the simple lamp posts in Plaça Reial – revealed a distinctive architectural personality. A nonconformist, he conceived his buildings as "visions" and developed an idiosyncratic, organic style that reached a peak in the sinuous Casa Milà (➤ 114) and his neo-Gothic master-piece, La Sagrada Família (➤ 104).

Other well-known Gaudí creations include the Palau Güell (➤ 60), Park Güell (➤ 111) and Casa Batlló (➤ 118). No other architect had

---

LESSER-KNOWN GAUDÍ SIGHTS

- **Pavellons de la Finca Güell** (➤ 156)
- **Casa Bellesguard** (Carrer Bellesguard 16) – fantasy town house evoking a medieval past, built between 1900 and 1902 (Carrer Bellesguard 20, Winter: Mon–Sat 10–4, Summer: 10–7).
- **Casa Calvet** (Carrer de Casp 48) – an apartment block (1898–1900) with a conventional exterior but a refined interior typical of Gaudí. It has some features of the original castle of 1410 and houses a restaurant.

The Magazine

Casa Batlló, Passeig de Gràcia

ever made such expressive use of stone and iron, and nobody else had ever gone to such painstaking lengths to embellish their buildings with ceramics, glass, wood and wrought iron. La Sagrada Família soon became his obsession. For the last years of his life (1908–26), he lived in a hut on the site and, having spent his entire finances on the project, he went begging from door to door through the streets of Barcelona so that work could carry on. Work continues today although the original plans were lost in a fire.

A Love-Hate Relationship

During his lifetime Gaudí was considered a crank by many Catalans, and it was only after his death that his genius was acknowledged. In 1926, aged 74, he was knocked down by a tram and died in a hospital for the poor. He was recognized by the chaplain and given a public funeral in the Sagrada Família. All Gaudí's buildings are listed as UNESCO World Heritage Sites; he is the first artist since Fra Angelico to be beatified by the Vatican; and his buildings have brought pleasure to millions. Perhaps it's more than mere coincidence that *gaudi* in Catalan means "delight".

WHAT IS MODERNISME?

Modernisme emerged at the turn of the 20th century with the aim of breaking away from the past through new art forms. Architecture throughout Europe had developed into an empty routine and a mishmash of uninspired styles. Artists longed for a regeneration of art and architecture based on curves rather than symmetry, and a new feeling for design was sweeping the continent, led by Belgian Victor Horta and Englishman William Morris. Flowers, foliage and oriental patterns were increasingly used for ornamentation, and each material (most notably iron, ceramics and stained glass) was exploited to the full. These ideals gave rise to such movements as French art nouveau and German Jugendstil. Modernisme was their Catalan equivalent – albeit a somewhat quirkier, longer-lasting version. And, largely thanks to Gaudí, Catalan Modernisme had the biggest impact, influencing all forms of art, architecture, literature and theatre.

Finding Your Feet

First Two Hours

Barcelona's airports are well connected to the city centre by fast, efficient bus links. The main train station is conveniently linked to several metro lines.

Airports

Barcelona's airport, **Aeroport del Prat** (www.aena.es) lies 12km (7.5 miles) south of the city centre. There are two international terminals: Terminal 1 south (A1) and Terminal 2 north (A2), linked by shuttle bus.

Some no-frills flights use **Girona** and **Reus** airports, 50km (31 miles) and 100km (62 miles) respectively from Barcelona. Flights are met by direct coaches to Barcelona. The Girona bus comes into the Estació del Nord and the Reus bus arrives at Estació de Sants.

Airport Transfers

By Taxi

A cab to the city centre will cost around €30. The journey takes 30 minutes, except in rush-hour jams.

■ **Use only official taxis**, easily recognizable by their **black-and-yellow paintwork**. Wait for these at the official stations outside each terminal.
■ **Taxi drivers use their meters**, so there's no need to agree on a fare in advance. Each piece of luggage costs €1 extra.

By Bus

The spacious, convenient **Aerobús** (tel: 9 02 10 01 04) connects all three terminals to Plaça de Catalunya, stopping en route at Plaça d'Espanya, Gran Via de les Corts Catalanes (at the corner of Carrer del Comte d'Urgell) and Plaça de la Universitat. The cost for a single ticket is €5.90.

■ At the airport, **bus stops** are clearly marked from the Arrivals area.
■ You buy **tickets** from the driver. A discount pass for travel on the Aerobús, metro and city buses is available (➤33).
■ The **journey** takes about 30 minutes, and buses run every 7–15 minutes, between 6am and 1am. At rush hour the journey takes longer.
■ On the **return to the airpor**t, the bus leaves from Plaça de Catalunya (opposite El Corte Inglés), stopping at Sants-Estació (Sants station).

By Train

The regular **Renfe Cercanías** train service (tel: 9 02 24 02 02) runs from the airport station at Terminal 2 to Sants-Estació in about 20 minutes and to Passeig de Gràcia in 24 minutes. It is less convenient if you are travelling with luggage.

■ A bus shuttle links terminals A1 and A2 and the **airport station**.
■ You must buy your **ticket** before boarding. Tickets cost just over €3.80, but you can use a cheaper multiple-journey **T-10 city transport card** (➤34) for the bus and underground.
■ Trains **run daily** between 6am and 11:30pm, every 30 minutes.

Barcelona-Sants-Estació (Train Station)

Most **international and national trains** stop at Sants station. Though the station is a fair distance from downtown Barcelona, **Line 3** (green) of the metro (➤33) gets you to the Ramblas (Liceu station), central Plaça de Catalunya and Passeig de Gràcia (where some mainline trains also stop) in a few minutes. Look for direction "Trinitat Nova" on the signs.

Getting Around

The modern metro system and air-conditioned buses provide good transport links in the city. Cable cars and funicular railways (► 187) can also help you get around. Tickets are integrated and valid for 75 minutes for up to four changes on any combination of metro, buses, tram and FGC trains.

The Metro

The metro is the best way to travel where longer distances are involved. It is fast, frequent, quite modern and most trains are air-conditioned.

- Six central lines make up the **TMB metro network**, which covers much of the city. The system is supplemented by the **Ferrocarrils de la Generalitat de Catalunya (FGC)** run by the Catalan government. The FGC line most likely to be of use is U7, from Plaça de Catalunya up to Tibidabo. Free maps are available from metro stations.
- Both the **metro** (www.tmb.cat) and **FGC** (www.fgc.net) run from 5am to 11pm, starting and stopping slightly later on Sundays, and running till 2am on Fridays and the day before a public holiday, and all night on Saturdays. Try to avoid **rush hours**: roughly 7:30–9am and 6–8pm.
- Although improving, **accessibility is poor** for wheelchairs and strollers with infinite steps and changes of levels. You can also expect long walks between lines.

How to Use the Metro

- **Lines** are identified by colours, while directions are denoted by the end-stations clearly marked on the metro map.
- Individual **tickets** must be pushed through the slot in the turnstile and retrieved – there are frequent ticket checks, but you don't need the ticket again to get out. A number is printed on **multiple tickets** (► 34) showing how many journeys you have left.
- Have enough **change ready** for ticket machines, in case the ticket offices are closed, which is often the case at night or on Sundays.

Buses

Like the metro, buses are air-conditioned and comfortable. Useful routes take you where the metro can't. Bus numbers are given throughout this guide, but free maps showing all the routes are available from the Tourist Information Offices (► 35) and transport information offices in the major stations (Universitat, Diagonal, Sagrada Família, Sants-Estació, Catalunya).

- In general, **metro fares and times** apply to the city buses, and single tickets can be bought from the driver, who gives change.
- Special **night buses** (Nitbus) run regularly from 11pm to 3am or 5am on selected routes.
- The **Bus Turístic** also provides a hop-on, hop-off service. Open-topped double-deckers serve three interlinked circular routes (colour coded red, blue and green) that take in the city's main sights. **One- or two-day tickets** (discounts for children) can be bought at tourist offices (also at www.barcelonabusturistic.cat) or on the bus.

Discount Passes

Passes can be bought from ticket offices and automatic machines at all stations, from kiosks and lottery shops, and from Servi-Caixa machines (► 42). The ones most likely to be of interest are listed below.

Finding Your Feet

- The **T-10** or **T-50** is valid for 10 and 50 trips respectively on all three networks and can be shared (pass it through the stamping machine once per passenger).
- **T-Dia** provides unlimited 24-hour travel for one person. **2 Dies**, **3 Dies**, **4 Dies** and **5 Dies** passes are available, which are valid for two, three, four and five days respectively.
- The **Bus Turístic** fare (➤ 33) also entitles you to a booklet of discount vouchers for various attractions along the route.
- One-, two- and five-day **Barcelona Cards** (available at Tourist Information Offices) entitle you to unlimited metro and bus travel and reductions at most museums, plus some restaurants and shops across the city.

Taxis
Official taxis have distinctive **black-and-yellow** paintwork. A **Lliure/Libre** sign in the window and a green light on the roof indicate that a taxi is available for hire. Prices are set by meters with various supplements clearly displayed on the rear side windows in English. These include airport, station, weekend and late-night supplements, plus €1 for each piece of luggage.
- **Barna Taxi** (tel: 9 33 22 22 22) and **Fono Taxi** (tel: 9 33 00 11 00) are two reliable phone-cab companies.

Driving
Driving in Barcelona can be tiresome and parking expensive. If you bring a car, the best advice is to leave it in the hotel garage.

Car Rental
The major companies have desks at the airport and city-centre offices, but local companies can work out a lot cheaper.
- **Pepecar:** tel: 8 07 41 42 43; www.pepecar.com
- **Vanguard:** tel: 9 34 39 38 80; www.vanguardrent.com

Mopeds
If you want to rent a moped, simply bring a driving licence, then don the helmet provided. Rental costs just over €40 for 24 hours, including insurance, with a cash or credit card deposit of around €250.
- **Barcelona Cooltra:** tel: 9 32 21 40 70; www.cooltra.com
- **Mondorent:** tel: 9 33 01 13 17; www.mondorent.com
- **Barcelona Sweetrent:** tel: 9 33 01 56 24; www.barcelonasweetrent.com

Bicycle Rental
The cycle lanes on the seafront, the pedestrian-only roads in the Old Town and the wide avenues of the Eixample are great places to explore by bicycle. Many companies rent out bikes by the hour or day (around €15).
- **Classic Bikes:** tel: 9 33 17 19 70; www.barcelonarentbikes.com
- **Barcelona by Bicycle:** tel: 9 32 68 21 05; www.bicicletabarcelona.com
- **Barcelona Biking:** tel: 65 63 56 300 mobile; www.barcelonabiking.com

Tours
- English-speaking drivers at **Trixitours** bike taxis (Mar–Nov; tel: 9 33 10 13 79; www.trixi.com) can take you on any tour that takes your fancy. The rate is €6 for 15 minutes.
- **GoCar** (tel: 9 02 30 13 33; www.gocartours.es) provides GPS-guided, convertible mini cars that can take you on English-speaking tours around town, or you can wander at will. Rental costs around €35 per hour.

Tourist Information Offices

Main Office
✚ 200 B1 ✉ Plaça de Catalunya (under the square, opposite El Corte Inglés)
☎ 9 32 85 38 34; www.barcelonaturisme.com
🕐 Daily 8:30–8:30 🚇 Catalunya

Ajuntament (City Hall)
✚ 204 B3 ✉ Carrer de la Ciutat 2
🕐 Mon–Fri 8:30–8:30, Sat 9–7, Sun and holidays 9–2 🚇 Jaume I

Barcelona-Sants train station
✚ 198 C3
🕐 Daily 8–8 🚇 Sants-Estació

Catalonia Tourist Office
✚ 200 B4
✉ Palau Robert, Passeig de Gràcia 107
☎ 9 32 38 80 91; www.gencat.cat/palaurobert
🕐 Mon–Sat 10–7, Sun 10–2. Closed holidays
🚇 Diagonal

Accommodation

Accommodation in the city caters for all tastes and budgets. Most of the city's luxury hotels are very expensive, but since the city has become a year-round venue for trade fairs and conferences, more mid-range hotels have appeared. Quality budget accommodation and decent singles are still hard to find, but there are some good-value *hostals* (akin to an inexpensive hotel) and a new breed of hostels, plus a profusion of holiday apartments suitable for longer stays.

Districts

The least expensive hotels tend to be around the **Barri Gòtic**, in the heart of the old city, and many of Barcelona's first hotels were built along the Ramblas. Areas become seedier the closer you get to the port and you should take care when returning to your hotel late at night. Noise, especially near the Ramblas and in the Barri Gòtic, may also be a problem.

There is an extensive choice of hotels in the **Eixample**, particularly mid-range hotels, although even these can be quite expensive. Be aware, though, that sometimes modern amenities take second place to Modernisme style. Beyond the Avinguda Diagonal is the neighbourhood of **Gràcia**, easily reached by public transport, although farther away from the main attractions.

Reservations

Barcelona's booming popularity has put increasing pressure on hotel rooms. **Advance booking** is strongly recommended, but it's worth knowing that the hotel reservations office at the airport (daily 9am–9pm) will book you a place to stay on arrival. The **tourist office** in Plaça de Catalunya (tel: 9 32 85 38 34; www.barcelonaturisme.com) is very helpful, but may request a deposit. **Barcelona Allotjament** (Carrer de Pelai 12, pral B, tel: 9 32 68 43 57; www.barcelona-allotjament.com) charges a commission, but can find a wide range of accommodation ranging from B&Bs with local families to whole apartments. Other agencies include **Oh-Barcelona** (Carrer de Roger de Llúria 50.1, tel: 9 34 67 37 82; www.oh-barcelona.com).

Prices

The financial crisis has meant a drop in Spanish hotel rates but despite this nights in popular hotels remain quite expensive, especially during trade fairs and congresses. Many hotels offer online discounts for early bookings

Finding Your Feet

or have last minute offers but check that the mandatory 10 per cent VAT is included in the price. Catalonia also charges a tourist tax from 0.50–€2.50 per person per night. Breakfasts and parking are usually extra.

Apartments

Many of Barcelona's small Old Town flats have been turned into self-catering apartments and they can be a great way of accommodating a family or a small group. Check what's included and beware of all-night noise in the Old Town's narrow lanes. Four of the many online rental companies are:

- **Friendly Rentals:** www.friendlyrentals.com
- **Rent a Flat in Barcelona:** www.rentaflatinbarcelona.com
- **Rent9Days:** www.rent9days.com
- **Habitat Apartments:** www.habitatapartments.com

Hostels

Slick, well-conceived hostels, with en-suite doubles and triples, as well as the usual small dorms, provide a competitive alternative to budget hotels; age doesn't matter and there are often extras like free WiFi and outside terraces. Rooms get snapped up so book ahead, especially in summer.

- **Alberg Mare de Déu de Montserrat €** (Passeig de la Mare de Déu del Coll 41–51, tel: 9 32 10 51 51; www.hihostels.com), the official YHF youth hostel, is in a splendid Modernista building but it has an institutional feel and is quite a way from the centre, behind Park Güell.
- The **Equity Point** chain (www.equity-point.com) operates the smart **Centric Point** on the Passeig de Gràcia, the more spartan **Sea Point** in Barceloneta and **Gothic Point**, an old-style backpackers place in the Barri Gòtic.
- Small en-suite rooms are bright and fresh in both **Gat Xino €** (Carrer de l'Hospital, 155, tel: 9 33 24 88 33) and at its sister *hostal*, **Gat Raval €** (Carrer de Joaquin Costa, 44–1°, tel: 9 34 81 66 70).

Accommodation Prices
Expect to pay per double room, per night

€ under €100	€€ €100–€150	€€€ €151–€230	€€€€ over €230

The 5 Rooms €€€

This is an intimate place in the very centre of town. Choose from one of the impeccable rooms or apartments and enjoy the informal, friendly atmosphere in this Modernista apartment building.

➕ 200 C1 ✉ Carrer de Pau Claris 72, 1°
☎ 9 33 42 78 80; www.thefiverooms.com
Ⓜ Catalunya, Urquinaona

Casa Camper €€€

This boutique hotel, found in El Raval and owned by the Camper shoe company has the same re-laxed, stylish feel as their footwear. Rooms are comfortable, each with its own small sitting room. There's a rooftop terrace and a 24-hour snack bar.

➕ 204 A4 ✉ Carrer d'Elisabets 11
☎ 9 33 42 62 80; www.camper.com
Ⓜ Catalunya, Liceu

Chic & Basic Born €€ *Insider Tip*

Creative, cosmopolitan, cool – this hotel is housed in a renovated medieval building in the trendy La Ribera district. An unconventional design and some surprising lighting ideas. Friendly service.

➕ 204 C3 ✉ Carrer Pincesa 50 ☎ 9 32 95
46 52; www.chicandbasic.com 🚇 Jaume I

Ciutat Barcelona €€

This slick, colourful hotel is steps
away from the Museu Picasso in
the inviting La Ribera neighbourhood. The soundproofed rooms
are spacious and the service very
friendly, but even better is the
rooftop terrace with plunge pool.

➕ 204 C3 ✉ Carrer de la Princesa 33–35
☎ 9 32 69 74 75; www.ciutatbarcelona.com
🚇 Jaume I

H10 Racó del Pi €€€

The hotel is perfectly located in the
old quarter, close to the attractive
Plaça del Pi. The 37 rooms are
tastefully furnished, the breakfast
expensive, but delicious. A welcome
glass of champagne sets the tone
plus free coffee and cakes during
the day.

➕ 204 B3 ✉ Carrer del Pi 7
☎ 9 33 42 61 90; www.h10.es 🚇 Liceu

Hostal Goya €€

In an Eixample town house, the
Goya is a charming place. Original
floor tiles work well with the tastefully decorated, comfortable rooms,
some with balconies. The owners
couldn't be more helpful.

➕ 204 C5 ✉ Carrer de Pau Claris 74
☎ 9 33 02 25 65; www.hostalgoya.com
🚇 Catalunya, Urquinaona

Hostal-Residencia Oliva €

A delightfully antiquated lift takes
you up to the fourth floor of this
friendly, family-run *residencia*
overlooking the Passeig de Gràcia.
Most of the rooms are light and
airy, and some have a balcony.
Not all, however, have bathrooms.
It's great value given the location.

➕ 200 B2 ✉ Passeig de Gràcia 32
☎ 9 34 88 01 62; www.hostaloliva.com
🚇 Catalunya/Passeig de Gràcia

Hotel 54 €€€

The only hotel in Barceloneta is
a slick new option with fine views
over the yachts at the Port Vell
marina. The 28 bright rooms are
well soundproofed from the restaurants in the street below. You
can even choose your own lighting
scheme.

➕ 204 C1 ✉ Passeig Joan de Borbó
☎ 9 32 25 00 54; www.hotel54barceloneta.com
🚇 Barceloneta

Hotel Arts €€€€

This towering world-class hotel is
one of the few on the waterfront
and offers spectacular views from
its giant picture windows. Although
deals are often available it's as
pricey as you would expect, with
its own fitness centre, pool and.

➕ 205 E2 ✉ Carrer de la Marina 19–21
☎ 9 32 21 10 00; www.hotelartsbarcelona.com
🚇 Ciutadella

Hotel Axel €€€

Calling itself "heterofriendly",
this stylish hotel, in a converted
Modernist corner house, targets
gay clients, attracted by the heart-
of-Gayxample (➤ 129) location.
A cocktail bar, a restaurant with
weekly drag shows, a boutique and
fitness club are added attractions.
Rooms are spacious, with eye-
catching details such as Kenzo
fabrics and Alessi furniture. Some
rooms have mini-conservatories.

➕ 200 A2 ✉ Carrer d'Aribau 33
☎ 9 33 23 93 93; www.axelhotels.com/
barcelona 🚇 Passeig de Gràcia

Hotel Banys Orientals €€

Its cool greys and whites are in
stark contrast with the adjoining
Senyor Parellada (➤95), but
this hotel maintains the same impeccable quality and is famously
good value. Each of the 43 rooms
in this historic building is slightly
different – some have four-poster
beds – but all are extremely comfortable and stylish, with beautiful
bathrooms.

➕ 204 C3 ✉ Carrer de l'Argenteria 37
☎ 9 32 68 84 60; www.hotelbanysorientals.com
🚇 Jaume I

Finding Your Feet

Hotel España €€

The public rooms of this popular hotel in El Raval are a showcase of Modernist design. The comfortable, spacious bedrooms have a more modern appearance, and many overlook a bright, interior patio.

🔲 204 A3 ⊠ Carrer de Sant Pau 9–11
☎ 9 33 18 17 58; www.hotelespanya.com
🚇 Liceu

Hotel El Jardí €€

You have to book well ahead to get a room overlooking the square, one of the Old Town's prettiest. These rooms tend to be better furnished than the interior ones, but they are also more expensive. Rooms are plain and simple, though all have adjoining bathrooms.

🔲 204 B3 ⊠ Plaça de Sant Josep Oriol 1
☎ 9 33 01 59 00; www.eljardi-barcelona.com
🚇 Liceu

Hotel Jazz €€

Part of a reliable local chain, the cool, fashionable Hotel Jazz, just off Plaça de Catalunya, could not be more central. The spacious, relaxing, designer-decorated rooms are soundproofed: this is not a quiet part of town. The views from the rooftop swimming pool and deck are simply fabulous.

Insider Tip

🔲 204 B5 ⊠ Carrer de Pelai 3
☎ 9 35 52 96 96; www.hoteljazz.com
🚇 Catalunya

Hotel Mesón Castilla €€

The combination of quiet, charming rooms in a central location at reasonable prices is hard to beat. This well-run, mid-range hotel has a wealth of art nouveau detailing and some of the comfortable rooms open onto large terraces. A generous breakfast buffet is served in the small dining room or on the patio. There are several rooms that are suitable for families (there are up to four beds in each).

🔲 200 A1 ⊠ Carrer de Valldonzella 5
☎ 9 33 18 21 82; www.mesoncastilla.com
🚇 Universitat

Hotel Neri €€€€

If you want to stay in the historic centre, this is the place to go. A Gothic palace sumptuously converted into a boutique hotel, the Neri is tasteful, charming and utterly comfortable. While the library is reserved exclusively for guests, the small restaurant is open to the public for lunch and dinner. The luxurious rooms, some of them suites, are equipped with flatscreens and CD players. On the roof you can use the small sundeck and pool.

🔲 204 B3 ⊠ Carrer de Sant Sever 5
☎ 9 33 04 06 55; www.hotelneri.com 🚇 Liceu

Hotel Omm €€€€

On the outside it looks like a post-modernist pastiche of the wavy and scaly Casa Milà, just around the corner. Inside the overriding feeling is of spaciousness and the very latest in design. Every part of the hotel grabs your attention with sleek lines and luxurious blends of wood, glass and textiles. Rooms are generously sized, with bathrooms that will make you want to have one just like it at home. The Moo Restaurant serves an outstanding selection of wines and haute cuisine in the coolest of settings, while Ommsession in the basement, is one of the city's most fashionable nightclubs (➤ 130).

🔲 200 B3 ⊠ Carrer del Rosselló 265 ☎ 9 34 45 40 00; www.hotelomm.es 🚇 Diagonal

Hotel SixtyTwo €€€€

Facing the Manzana de la Discordia, this elegant hotel has spacious rooms and suites, some with large balconies. The soothingly minimalist interior, with fashionable details such as rectangular porcelain washbasins, is enhanced by top-quality linens, furnishings and fittings. Special touches include Nespresso coffee machines, iPod stations, Bang & Olufsen TVs and wine-tasting sessions every Wednesday.

🔲 200 B3 ⊠ Passeig de Gràcia 62
☎ 9 32 72 41 80; www.sixtytwohotel.com
🚇 Passeig de Gràcia

Food and Drink

The enjoyment of good food and eating is considered one of life's priorities in Barcelona.

Catalan cooking is at its finest here, both traditional and innovative. There's also a strong French presence, as well as a considerable number of foreign restaurants. There is some of the best seafood in the country, and an unusually high number of vegetarian eating places.

When to Eat

Be prepared either to eat late or to dine in an otherwise empty restaurant. Most people eat **lunch** at around 2pm, but many places serve food until about 4pm. **Dinner** does not usually start until 8:30pm and food can be served up until midnight.

Table Tips

■ Good restaurants always get fully booked, especially at the weekend, so make a **reservation** to avoid disappointment. Many places are also closed on Sunday evenings as well as on the evening of a holiday, so those that are open tend to get very crowded. It's worth checking national holiday dates (➤ 192); many restaurants close for Easter and during August.

■ Those who eat neither fish nor meat will usually find plenty of **vegetable, salad and egg dishes** on most menus. In Barcelona, unlike many other cities in Spain, the number of vegetarian and vegan restaurants is growing. In ordinary restaurants, look for Catalan dishes such as *espinacs a la catalana* (spinach with raisins and pine nuts), *escalivada* (chargrilled vegetables) and, in early spring, *calçots* (➤ 17).

■ In most restaurants, should you wish to leave a tip, €2–€3 is perfectly acceptable. Many locals just leave a token sum, if at all. **IVA** (VAT) at 10 per cent is nearly always included in the prices shown on the menu. It should say on the menu if you have to pay the tax on top.

■ Don't be surprised to see napkins, toothpicks and olive stones just being dropped on the floor of old-fashioned tapas bars; however, this may not be acceptable in other places. **Take your lead** from the way locals behave.

■ There are **different sets of prices** depending on whether you choose to stand at the bar to eat or sit at a table. Prices will be even more expensive if you decide to sit out on a terrace.

Cheap Eats

■ Fill up at breakfast time on *croissants*, *torrades* (toasted rolls with butter and jam), *truita* (omelette) or *xocolata amb xurros* (delicious doughnuts with thick drinking chocolate).

■ Throughout the day, you can get *bocadillos* or *entrepans* (sandwiches), **tapas** (➤ 6) and **pizza slices** at bars and shops all over the city.

■ *Llesqueries* specialize in open sandwiches of cheese, meat, particularly ham, anchovies or vegetables on a base of *pa amb tomàquet* (toasted slices of bread rubbed with garlic, the pulp of very ripe tomatoes, salt and olive oil). To sample this typical Catalan snack, try La Bodegueta (➤ 116).

■ Try *ensaimades* (pastry spirals) and cakes from the city's excellent bakeries and pastry shops, or indulge in some hot *buñuelos*, doughnuts bought from a street-seller and eaten dusted with sugar.

Finding Your Feet

- **Fast food** is as ubiquitous in Barcelona as it is in other major cities and there are plenty of familiar burger chains around town. You'll also find falafel and kebab outlets, especially in the Old Town.
- The *menú del dia*, the daily set menu, usually three or four courses and wine, always provides great value for money in Barcelona. The cheapest set menus are usually available at lunchtime only, but many decent restaurants have a good-value set menu in the evening.
- Several budget restaurants offer a *plat combinat*, a combined plate of something like chicken and salad with bread and a drink included.

Good-value Chains

You'll find branches of the following good-value restaurants at strategic locations throughout the city.

- **Fresc & Co** Enjoy a full meal for around €10–€12 in a bright cafe environment. Help yourself to salad, then return to the soup, hot plate or dessert as often as you like. Children dine free at weekends.
- **Origins** This very popular group of restaurants serves mainly organic Catalan specialities. Service is often slow.
- **Taller de Tapas** You'll find outlets of this reliable chain of tapas restaurants at all the prime spots in Barcelona.

What to Drink

There is little difference on the whole between a bar and a cafe, although it's worth noting that *cellers* are really wine bars. Unlike many restaurants, most bars and cafes stay open throughout August.

- Most people **drink wine with their meals** and it is usually very inexpensive, especially house wine. Catalonia produces a variety of excellent wines (➤ 18). To sample the year's new wine, ask for *vi novell*.
- *Xampanyeries* specialize in champagne and cava, the traditional sparkling wine of Spain. You can sample a range of house cavas by the glass, either the sweetish *brut* or drier *brut nature*.
- *Cerveseries* serve mostly beers such as San Miguel, Estrella, Voll-Damm, local Moritz and draught *cerveza negra* – bitter, black, fizzy lager.
- *Orxateries* and *granjas* serve *orxata*, an unusual but popular non-alcoholic, cold milky drink made from tiger nuts, *granissats* (refreshing iced fruit drinks), coffee, cakes, milkshakes and *suissos* (hot chocolate topped with whipped cream).

Best Orxateries and Granjas

- **Dulcinea** (➤ 70) is the place to head for *suissos* (hot chocolate topped with whipped cream) and *melindros* (sugar-coated biscuits). ✚ 204 B3
- **La Pallaresa** is famous for its *suissos*. ✚ 204 B3 ✉ Carrer de Petritxol 11.
- **Orxateria-Gelateria Sirvent** is one of the best places in the city to try *orxata*. ✚ 203 F3 ✉ Ronda Sant Pau 3 🚇 Paral.lel.
- **El Tío Che** was founded in 1912 and is famous for its malt-flavoured *granissat*. ✚ 206 C3 ✉ Rambla del Poble Nou 44.
- **La Valenciana** (➤ 123) is one of the last places in the city to serve traditional malt-flavoured *granizado*. ✚ 204 A4

Restaurant Prices

Expect to pay per person for a three-course meal, excluding drinks:

€ under €25   €€ €25–€50   €€€ over €50

Shopping

Shops in the city range from old-fashioned little businesses and trendy boutiques to glitzy shopping centres and large department stores selling just
about anything you might want.

Where to Go

- The Eixample harbours the city's densest concentration of fashion
  emporia (➤ 128). The **more exclusive establishments**, and star designers,
  be they Catalan, Spanish or international, line the **Passeig de Gràcia** and
  other **Eixample** streets.
- **Portal de l'Angel** and the northern reaches of the **Ramblas**, just off **Plaça
  de Catalunya**, are lined with national and international chain stores,
  specializing in clothes and shoes.
- **Avinguda Diagonal** is the third major commercial axis, with shopping
  malls every couple of kilometres. Head up to **L'Illa** (➤ 166) for leading
  international names, a good food hall and a branch of El Corte Inglés.
- If you're looking for **jewellery**, **glassware**, **textiles**, **prints** and **paintings**,
  the labyrinthine streets of La Ribera and, increasingly, El Raval, should
  come up trumps. Gràcia and the Barri Gòtic are also worth investigating.
- **Shoe shops** Camper, Tascón and Casas have branches across the city.
- Several of Barcelona's **museums** have shops attached. The best are at
  the Fundació Joan Miró (➤ 144), MACBA (➤ 63), CCCB (➤ 64),
  Fundació Antoni Tàpies (➤ 123), Museu d'Història de la Ciutat (➤ 64)
  and Casa Milà (➤ 114).
- If you want to put together a picnic to remember, the city's many colourful
  food markets (➤ 17) are the best places to stock up. **Mercat de la Boqueria**
  (➤ 54) in particular shouldn't be missed.
- Several **specialist food shops** will tempt you with local specialities that
  travel well, including wine and olive oil, salt cod and hams, *torró* (Catalan
  nougat) and honey. Supermarkets are often a better-value alternative –
  try the Ramblas branch of **Carrefour** (La Rambla 113) or the basement
  of **El Corte Inglés** in Plaça de Catalunya.

Opening Hours

- Bigger stores tend to stay open from 9am to 9pm. Smaller shops **close
  during the siesta** (usually 2–4:30pm), early on Saturdays, stay shut on
  Mondays and frequently pull down the shutters for the whole summer.
- Most shops are closed on **Sundays**, there are only a few Sundays of the year
  when shops may open. Some exceptions to this rule are *fleques* (bakeries)
  and *pastisseries* (cake shops) and the shops in the **Maremagnum** mall in
  Port Vell and branches of **OpenCor**, the chain of convenience stores run
  by El Corte Inglés. These sell a selection of toys, gifts and decent (although
  pricey) food and are open seven days a week until late.

Etiquette

- In most shops **customer service is laid back**, though you may be
  approached in exclusive boutiques. However, prodding fruit and
  vegetables is not appreciated.
- Old-fashioned stores and groceries have **cashiers *(caixa)*** who you pay
  to get a ticket to be exchanged for your purchase. In small shops and
  markets, other customers often ask who's last in line *"Qui es l'últim?"*,
  answered by *"Soc jo"* (me).

Entertainment

True to fame, Barcelona really does offer every possible form of evening entertainment, from bars and clubs to quality concerts and cutting-edge theatre.

Information

On Fridays, *La Vanguardia* newspaper has a good cultural supplement in Catalan, but the best listings magazine is the Catalan-language *Time Out*, which comes out on Thursdays; also available online at www.timeout.cat.

Clubs

- Many of the better clubs are located in the lanes of the Old Town, particularly **El Raval**, **Barri Gòtic** and the **Born**, although **Gràcia** also has some local favourites. Glitzier places can be found in the **Port Olímpic** and the **Eixample**, while **Montjuïc** offers the old favourite in the Barcelona clubbing scene, La Terrrazza (➤ 150).
- Most clubs open around midnight and close at 3pm. In less residential areas, like Montjuïc and the Port Olímpic, they **stay open later**.
- Some of the fancier establishments in the Eixample and by the coast impose a **dress code**. Though scruffiness is definitely out, in the summer skimpiness is de rigueur. Many clubs allow women in free.
- Barcelona's hip clubs are free to those on the guest lists, so sign up with one such as www.shazguestlist.com. Be aware that the invitation is only valid for the specified time, latecomers have to pay!

Opera and Music

- The **Gran Teatre del Liceu** (➤ 64) is one of the world's most celebrated opera houses. The **Palau de la Música Catalana** (➤ 78 and 97) offers spectacular architecture as well as high-quality music, while the city's **L'Auditori** (➤ 97) hosts the world's leading musicians.
- **Jazz** and **rock**, **pop** and **salsa**, **flamenco** and **folk** are all on offer at a variety of haunts around the city.

Theatre, Dance and Cinema

- Most shows are in Catalan, however, there are some international guest performances in the Mercat de les Flors, in the Teatre Lliure and especially during July and August when the annual **Festival del Grec** (➤ 150) is held.
- A couple of great **art-house cinemas** regularly screen English-language films. Among the best are Verdi (➤ 130) and Verdi Park (➤ 130).

Tickets

Two rival savings banks, La Caixa (de Pensions) and CatalunyaCaixa, sell tickets for theatres and other entertainment venues, including the Teatre Nacional, Liceu and Festival del Grec. These services are called **Servi-Caixa** (www.servicaixa.com) and **Tel-entrada** (tel: 902 10 12 12; www.telentrada.com), respectively. You can order by phone or via the internet and pick up the tickets at the venue. **Servi-Caixa** also has special machines next to La Caixa's ATMs, which print the tickets out. **Tel-entrada** is operated out of most of CatalunyaCaixa's branches and at a special desk at the Plaça de Catalunya **tourist office**. The **Palau de Pa Virreina** (Rambla 99) box office sells tickets half-price, cash only, three hours before performances.

Las Ramblas & Either Side

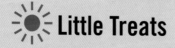 Little Treats

In Hemingway's footsteps

The legendary Boadas bar, where Hemingway drank mojitos, is on the corner of Carrer dels Tallers and the **Rambla de Canaletes** (➤ 52).

Traditional hand-sewn footwear

La Manuel Alpargatera (➤ 72) in Carrer Avinyó in the **Barri Gòtic** (➤ 48) have been making espadrilles for generations.

Picturesque oasis

Just a few steps from the Ramblas is **El Jardí** (➤ 70), a bar tucked away in a Gothic courtyard lined with orange trees.

Getting Your Bearings

There are few city streets in the world as well trodden as the Ramblas, one long thoroughfare divided into five distinct sections. As you saunter down the tree-lined avenue from Plaça de Catalunya, Barcelona's main square, towards the Mediterranean, you'll be drawn into the ceaseless flow of pedestrians.

On your left is the magnificent Barri Gòtic (Gothic Quarter), where the cathedral towers over one of the world's best-preserved sets of medieval palaces and churches. Beyond, at Port Vell (Old Port), the colourful harbourside, one of the major draws is a huge aquarium, nestling among modern shops and multiscreen cinemas. Off the tail-end of the Ramblas, Antoni Gaudí's castle-like Palau Güell sits uneasily in the sleazy lower side of El Raval – a jumble of medieval streets, dingy alleyways and dead-ends. By contrast, El Raval's increasingly gentrified upper reaches are dominated by the gleaming white hulk of the Museu d'Art Contemporani (MACBA), Barcelona's contemporary art museum set amid stylish restaurants and art galleries galore.

Yachts moored at Port Vell, the city's harbour

The Ramblas extend 1 km (0.6 miles) from the harbourside to Plaça de Catalunya

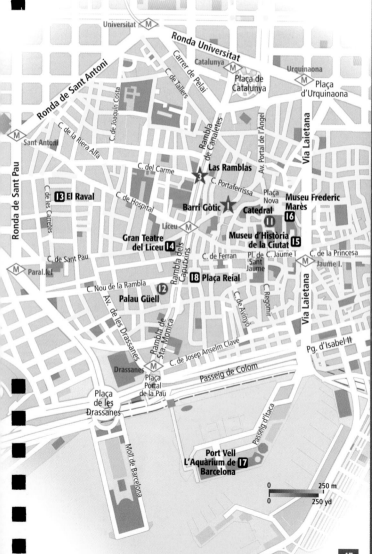

The Perfect Day

If you're not quite sure where to begin your travels, this itinerary recommends a practical and enjoyable day around the Ramblas, taking in some of the best places to see. For more information see the main entries (➤ 48–67).

🕘 9:00am

Make an early start, amble down 🔢 **Las Ramblas** (➤ 52) from Plaça de Catalunya, which at this time of day will be fairly quiet, as far as the **🔢 Gran Teatre del Liceu** (➤ 64). The Carrer Casañas leads to the Gothic church of **Santa María del Pi** (➤ 50). Treat yourself to a coffee on the **Plaça del Pi** and soak up the atmosphere of the charming Old Town square.

🕙 10:00am

Visit the **🔢 Catedral** (➤ 57) – best approached along delightful Carrer la Palla. After touring the cathedral and its cloisters, take the lift to the rooftops and survey the whole of the ⭐ **Barri Gòtic** (below, ➤ 48).

🕚 11:00am

After a short visit to the historic Plaça de Sant Jaume, with the City Hall and the Palau de la Generalitat (➤ 49), you should definitely stop by the medieval **Plaça del Rei** (➤ 48). Then you can explore Barcelona's origins at the Roman ruins in the **🔢 Museu d'Historia de la Ciutat** (➤ 64) and walk up the royal guard tower.

🕜 1:30pm

It's early for a midday meal in Barcelona, but you'll be sure of a table. Go to **La Boqueria** (➤ 54) and head for one of the popular stands before

the locals arrive to stake their claim, or find a table at the **Pla del Àngels** (➤ 69) restaurant.

⏰ 3:00pm

From the El Jardí bar (➤ 70), in the courtyard of the Antic Hospital de la Santa Creu, you can enjoy your coffee with a view of the former hospital's Gothic walls and arches. Then head to **⑫Palau Güell** (➤ 60).

⏰ 5:30pm

Your next stop is **⑰Port Vell** (➤ 66). After a stroll around the marina, you can have an aperitif at one of the cafes on the **⑱Plaça Reial** (above ➤ 67), your best bet is Café Glaciar.

⏰ 8:00pm

Wind up a perfect day with dinner in the trendy Raval district, and maybe a drink on the lovely rooftop terrace of the Hotel Pulitzer(www. hotelpulitzer.es). Or if you'd prefer a romantic meal to remember, the stylish ambience of **Pla** (➤ 69) or **Cometacinc** (➤ 68) would be the answer. If you are in luck you may have managed to get last minute tickets for an opera at the opulent **Gran Teatre del Liceu** (➤ 64).

Barri Gòtic

A maze of dark, twisting medieval streets and sunny squares lined with venerable churches and lavish palaces huddles around the cathedral. The Barri Gòtic (Gothic Quarter), a part of the city once overlooked by visitors, was extensively restored in the 1920s and has now regained much of its former splendour. A couple of the city's finest museums flank the medieval Plaça del Rei, while the magnificent Ajuntament (City Hall) and Palau de la Generalitat (Government Palace) face each other across Plaça de Sant Jaume, the monumental, historic heart of old Barcelona.

Plaça del Rei

Tucked away to the north of the cathedral is the Plaça del Rei, flanked by the stately buildings of the Palau Reial, the former royal palace. In medieval times, the square served as a market-place where hay and flour were sold; later locksmiths plied their trade here, making so much noise that the royal court moved out.

The mid-16th-century **Mirador del Rei Martí** (King Martin's Watchtower), a curiously modern-looking building distinguished by five storeys of stone arches, and the svelte turret of the 14th-century **Capella de Santa Agata** (the royal chapel) tower over the square. They can be investigated as part of a visit to the Museu d'Història de la Ciutat (▶ 65). To your left as you look towards the Mirador is the stern **Palau del Lloctinent** (Lieutenant's Palace), built in 1549 as the official residence for the Viceroy of Catalonia. Among the pigeons and street musicians, you'll see **Topo** (1985), an abstract sculpture by Basque artist Eduardo Chillida. The work's enigmatic B-shapes may (or then again may not) stand for Barcelona.

The beautiful medieval Plaça del Rei

Plaça de Sant Jaume

Nearby **Plaça de Sant Jaume**, the historical and political heart of the Old City, is spacious and imposing, where Plaça del Rei is intimate and secluded. The square was a crossroads even in Roman times and today busy Carrer de Ferran slices through it. Two ancient rivals, the **Casa de la Ciutat** (or **Ajuntament**) and the **Palau de la Generalitat** face each other across the flagstones. The former is home of the left-wing city council, the latter the official head-quarters of the firmly conservative Catalan government. Both buildings have been added to piecemeal over the centuries, with the extravagant neoclassical facades a 19th-century addition.

Both the Ajuntament and Palau de la Generalitat are worth visiting. Outstanding work in the Ajuntament includes Josep Maria Sert's 1928 murals depicting great moments from Catalan history in the **Saló de les Cròniques** (Hall of the Chronicles); Sert later decorated New York's Rockefeller Center. In the Palau de la Generalitat, the frescoes of classical allegory by J Torres-Garcia typify the Noucentisme movement. The Generalitat's highlight, though, is undoubtedly the Gothic inner courtyard, the raised **Pati de Tarongers** (Courtyard of the Oranges), with fine Renaissance columns and sweet-scented orange trees.

The Generalitat is joined to the **Casa dels Canonges**, a set of 14th-century cathedral canons' houses where the Catalan prime minister now has his official residence, by a bridge

The Bridge of Sighs was part of Barcelona's 1920s Gothic revival

across Carrer del Bisbe. It may look Gothic from a distance but beware of appearances; the bridge, modelled on the Bridge of Sighs in Venice, was in fact built in the 1920s, when all things medieval were in vogue and this area of the city first became known as the "Barri Gòtic".

Pati de Tarongers, the serene inner courtyard of the Palau de la Generalitat

Santa Maria del Pi

The 14th- to 15th-century church of Santa Maria del Pi, a squat yet sumptuous Gothic masterpiece, lies just off the Ramblas. The interior is almost disconcertingly simple and empty, with a wide single nave without aisles. The gigantic rose window, however, is magnificent, filling the church with multicoloured light.

The church is surrounded by three delightful little squares (**Plaça del Pi**, where you'll find the church's main entrance, **Plaça de Sant Josep Oriol** and **Placeta del Pi**), and strolling between them gives you a chance to survey the church's sober exterior. At weekends and during the summer the squares are filled with artists and musicians. Choose one of the many cafe terraces from which to enjoy

Plaça de Sant Josep Oriol, one of three pretty squares surrounding Santa Maria del Pi

The church of Sant Felip Neri, in the secluded Plaça de Sant Felip Neri

the spectacle of street life. Cheeses, sausages and other local produce are sold at makeshift stalls on the first Friday of the month.

TAKING A BREAK

Bar del Pi (Plaça de Sant Josep Oriol 1, tel: 9 33 02 21 23) gets crowded, so pick a table outside in the lovely medieval square and be entertained by street performers. The tapas selection is limited but good.

➕ 204 B4
🚇 Jaume I, Liceu

The Ajuntament
➕ 204 B3
🕐 Sun 10–1:30
🎟 Free

Palau de la Generalitat
Guided tours only by appointment, by telephone or better still by email: visitespalau.presidencia@gencat.cat
➕ 204 B3
☎ 93 4 02 47 75
🕐 2nd and 4th Sun of every month, Aug 23, Sep 11 and 24, 9:30–1
🎟 Free

INSIDER INFO

■ If you want to immerse yourself further in Gothic architecture, follow the **Barri Gòtic** walk (➤ 176).

■ The **Museu Diocesà** (Diocesan Museum, ➕ 204 C3, Avinguda de la Catedral 4, tel: 9 33 15 22 13, Tue–Sat 10–2, 4–8, Sun and holidays 11–2, €6) is housed in a patchwork of Roman, Renaissance and later buildings, capped with some 20th-century elements. Occasionally, interesting exhibitions of mostly sacred art are staged here.
Albeit chaotic, the permanent display offers some gems of Catalan religious sculpture and painting, including an altarpiece or two by Bernat Martorell – look for his Retable of St John the Baptist.

■ The **Museu del Calçat** (Footwear Museum, ➕ 204 B3, Plaça de Sant Felip Neri 5, tel: 9 33 01 45 33, Tue–Sun 11–2, €2.50) is something of a curiosity. Many famous people, including Catalan cellist Pau Casals, have donated their shoes to the museum. One oddity is a shoe big enough for the Columbus statue.

 Las Ramblas

Once just a dried-up river bed, the Ramblas are now flooded with people 24 hours a day. The avenue, flanked by flaky-trunked plane trees, acts as a long magnet, attracting crowds who flock to watch or add to its never-ending ferment. People chat, buy flowers, catch up on world news, have a drink, observe the ever-more inventive human statues or simply join the flow of other people who wander up and down during the early-evening *paseo* (stroll) and on week-end afternoons. Not only the best-known street in Barcelona, the Ramblas are also a non-stop human spectacle, and you can have it all for free – unless you toss the street entertainers a coin or two.

The Ramblas funnel you from Plaça de Catalunya, the city's main square, to the harbourside, where the Monument a Colom (► 55) stands like the full stop finishing off an enormous exclamation mark. The total distance is little over a kilometre, but there are so many diversions that you need to allow plenty of time. This has been a popular promenade since the 18th century, when the walls that once protected the Barri Gòtic were torn down and the first street lamps were put up. Although it has seen many changes since, the present character of the Ramblas owes most to the 19th century, when the opera house, market and cast-iron flower stalls were built.

The Ramblas attracts a never-ending stream of people

Rambla de Canaletes
Although people often walk it as one continuous promenade, the street is divided into five fairly distinct sections.

Street entertainers perform along the Ramblas, helping to create a lively atmosphere

Starting at the top end, adjoining Plaça de Catalunya, is the Rambla de Canaletes, named after a black-and-bronze **drinking fountain** – if you quench your thirst here, so the legend goes, you're bound to return to Barcelona. For a small fee you can sit on one of the rickety seats and watch the world stroll by, or listen to the elderly men who gather here to talk about politics or football.

The fountain is the traditional focus of celebrations when FC Barcelona wins a match. Also along this stretch are news kiosks selling papers and magazines from all around the world, plus everything from postcards to hard-core DVDs.

Rambla dels Estudis

The character of the Ramblas changes several times as you continue down towards the port. After the first crossroads, you enter the Rambla dels Estudis, also known as the Rambla dels Ocells (*ocell* is Catalan for bird). A dozen or so stands sell canaries, budgies and prize parrots, distressingly cooped up in cages, while pathetic goldfish and rabbits stare out from an assortment of cramped abodes.

Església de Betlem, at the corner of Carrer del Carme, is a splendid baroque church; its once glorious interior was destroyed during the Civil War. It dates from the late 17th century, before the Ramblas became Barcelona's main thoroughfare, which is why its severe facade and majestic doorway are actually on a side street. Busy Carrer de Portaferrissa, on your left, runs straight to the Catedral (➤57) and the Barri Gòtic (➤48).

Rambla de Sant Josep

Next comes the Rambla de Sant Josep, nicknamed the Rambla de les Flors on account of its colourful **flower stalls**. Impressive displays of cut flowers, pot plants,

Las Ramblas & Either Side

shrubs and even huge palms brighten up the street along this stretch. At No 99, on your right, is the late 18th-century **Palau de la Virreina**, built by the Viceroy of Peru for his wife Vicereine Maria Francesca. The story goes that she was due to marry his nephew, but when the Viceroy saw the bride-to-be dressed up for her wedding, he fell in love with her and declared that he would have married her himself if he had not been too old. She replied that she lived in a very old convent, which pleased her greatly; he took the hint and married her after all, leaving the nephew somewhat in the lurch. Later, the Viceroy made his fortune in Lima, kept a famous mistress, and built this palace to placate his wife when she found out (forgetting that she preferred older things). The palace now houses the city's Culture Institute called the **Centre de la Imatge**, with good-quality photographic exhibitions, many of them free.

A little way farther down on the right lies the **Mercat de la Boqueria**, Barcelona's central market. Although it's officially called the Mercat de Sant Josep, everyone knows it as La Boqueria (meaning "the butchery"). The market, housed in an airy iron-and-glass structure, with token Modernist touches at the Ramblas entrance, is where the city's top chefs come to buy their ingredients. It is a great place to pick up picnic ingredients such as cheeses, olives and tomatoes, or to wander around the mouthwatering displays of hams, Catalan sausages, seafood, vegetables, herbs and dried fruits.

Across the street at No 82, **Casa Bruno Quadros** (1883–85), now a bank, occupies a former umbrella shop. The facade is decorated with ornate

Insider Tip

> ### WHAT'S IN A NAME?
> The word *rambla* is now accepted in Spain as the word for a main city promenade, but it is actually derived from the Arabic *raml*, meaning "river bed". It originally referred to the gullies running through most Catalan towns, which were dry for most of the year and only filled with water after heavy rains. It has even given rise to a tailor-made Catalan verb, *ramblejar*, meaning "to wander up and down the Ramblas".

The parasols decorating Casa Bruno Quadros on the Rambla de Sant Josep are a legacy from its days as an umbrella shop

Joan Miró's 1976 pavement mosaic at Pla de l'Os

parasols, part of a theatrical, oriental design of dragons and lanterns. Criminals were once hanged on this site in the Middle Ages.

Rambla dels Caputxins

Pla de l'Os, on the central walkway, marks the halfway point of the Ramblas and the start of the Rambla dels Caputxins. It also offers a rare opportunity to walk over a work of modern art: Joan Miró's colourful mosaic (1976) is crying out to be trampled on. The next stretch of the street is always one of the liveliest, with 🎭 **street musicians** and **magicians** competing for attention with **human statues** coated in large quantities of gold paint. The **Gran Teatre del Liceu** (➤ 64), Barcelona's opera house, extends between Carrer de Sant Pau and Carrer Unió. To the right, a short distance along Carrer Nou de la Rambla, is **Palau Güell** (➤ 60) and, immediately opposite, **Plaça Reial** (➤ 67).

Rambla de Santa Mònica

Performance artists give way to portrait painters as you reach the Rambla de Santa Mònica, the final stretch of the Ramblas at its seaward end. As you might expect in a port city, this area is decidedly seedy. Drug-dealers and prostitutes still ply their trade here after dark (sometimes even in daylight). Although some people find the atmosphere on this section of the Ramblas threatening, it is generally safe for streetwise visitors – just hang on to your valuables. This is also where you will find the **Centre d'Art Santa Mònica**, an avant-garde art gallery housed in a converted convent.

Monument a Colom

At the bottom of the Ramblas, in the middle of the busy Plaça del Portal de la Pau, stands the **Monument a Colom**, erected for the 1888 Universal Exhibition. From the top of the 60m (200ft) Corinthian column, a statue of Christopher Columbus points out to sea, while at his feet is a viewing platform that offers a panorama of the city and its harbour. Pigeons appear to treat the statue with utter contempt, providing the great explorer with a permanent white wig.

To enjoy the views up the Ramblas and along the harbourfront, you have to take the lift up. It's a shame about the inevitable X-loves-Y graffiti scratched onto the glass.

The Monument a Colom stands at the end of the Ramblas overlooking the harbour

TAKING A BREAK

Food comes no fresher than at the numerous bars and food stalls in **La Boqueria**, the city's famous food market. Don't worry about language barriers: many of the stallholders speak English or you could always just point at what you want. Open breakfast and lunchtimes only.

➕ 204 A2–B4
🚇 Catalunya, Liceu, Drassanes, FGC Catalunya

Palau de la Virreina/Centre de la Imatge
➕ 204 B4
☎ 9 33 16 10 00; www.bcn.cat/virreinacentredelaimatge
🕐 Tue–Sun noon–8 🎫 Exhibitions free 🚇 Liceu

Mercat de la Boqueria
➕ 204 A4
☎ 9 33 18 25 84 🕐 Mon–Sat 8am–8:30pm 🚇 Liceu

Monument a Colom
➕ 204 A2
☎ 9 33 02 52 24 🕐 Daily 8:30–7:30 🎫 €4 🚇 Drassanes

INSIDER INFO

- Light years away in terms of atmosphere is the **Rambla de Catalunya**, which slices through the Eixample above Plaça de Catalunya, at the top end of the Ramblas proper. Here the cafes are costlier and the shops unashamedly chic (➤ 128). This is the Rambla for you, though, if madding crowds drive you crazy – and it's ideal for a late afternoon stroll.

- The heaving crowds, the distraction of the entertainments and the large numbers of foreign visitors mean that **petty crime is a problem**. Don't let the mostly harmless but very light-fingered pickpockets who congregate here spoil your stay. Keep your hands firmly on all belongings, especially valuables, at all times; don't be distracted, and watch out for suspicious behaviour.

In more depth However enticing the advertisements or the attendant dishing out flyers at the door, you're better off giving the **Museu de l'Eròtica** (Rambla de Sant Josep 96, €9) a miss. Avoid the terrace bars and restaurants on the Ramblas – tourists are usually fleeced there.

⑪ Catedral

Barcelona's great cathedral, at the spiritual and physical heart of the splendid Barri Gòtic, is a beautiful example of Catalan Gothic architecture. Its shady cloisters are a delight, and from the rooftops you can admire the impeccably preserved medieval buildings spread out below.

The cathedral's elaborate 19th-century facade

While the cathedral's facade is impressive at first glance, a closer look reveals that it is a late 19th-century neo-Gothic addition. Compared with more typically plain Catalan churches, such as the Basílica de Santa Maria del Mar (►84) or Santa Maria del Pi (►50), this facade, with its detailed stone carving and slender pinnacles, looks rather more northern European than southern. That said, at sunset, when the stone glows coppery brown, or at night, when the building is illuminated, it can be mesmerizing. At times, however, the pollution-damaged exterior is under wraps for cleaning.

The Interior

Inside, the building dates back to the 14th century. The huge space is divided into two broad aisles, nearly as wide as the cavernous central nave, that soar heavenwards. Immediately to your right after you enter is the **baptistery**, where, as a plaque records, the six Native Americans brought back from the New World in 1493 by Christopher Columbus were christened.

But your eye is quickly drawn to the central enclosed **choir** (separate entrance fee), where there are exquisitely carved 14th-century stalls. This is where the Chapter of the Order of the Golden Fleece, a kind of early European summit meeting, was convened by Emperor Charles V

and attended by England's King Henry VIII and a host of European monarchs in 1519. Look at the royal coats of arms, including that of Henry VIII, painted on the backs of the stalls. The intricate wooden **pulpit** of 1403 and Italianate Renaissance **choir-screen** (1519–64) also stand out as masterpieces.

Your entrance fee to the choir entitles you to descend to the **crypt** where, among other relics, you'll find a gorgeous alabaster sarcophagus (1327) thought to contain the remains of Santa Eulàlia, Barcelona's patron saint (along with the Virgin of Mercy). The 4th-century martyr converted to Christianity at the age of 13 and was subjected to unspeakable tortures at the hands of Roman governor Dacian.

Soaring heights are a typical feature of Catalan Gothic architecture

The Cloisters

The cloisters, for many visitors, are the best part of the cathedral. Orange and medlar trees, glossy magnolias and shaggy palms held up by trapeze wires blend in beautifully with the lush floral motifs of the Flamboyant Gothic iron- and stonework, some dating back to the 14th century. In the middle of the garden, a mossy green **fountain**, sheltered by a stone tabernacle decorated with a carving of St George (Catalonia's patron saint) and the Dragon he killed, tinkles into an emerald pond. Here you'll find a 🕑 **half-dozen gaggle of geese** – a nice change for the children. There were originally 13, one for every year of St Eulàlia's life. Legend has it that they either hark back to Barcelona's Roman past (geese guarded the Roman

Capitol in ancient times), or that their pure white feathers symbolize the martyr's virginity.

Leading off the other side of the cloisters is the simple but beguiling late Romanesque **Capella de Santa Llúcia** (13th century). A closer look at the chapel reveals intricate carvings above the main doorway, featuring plants believed to cure eye ailments. St Lucy is the patron saint of the blind. If you leave the cathedral on this side, you'll be facing the handsome **Casa de l'Ardiaca**, a renovated 15th-century palace now housing the city archives. Within the tiled courtyard stands a spindly palm, but the palace's special feature is on the outside wall: a Modernist letter box carved with a tortoise and swallows.

From the cathedral's bell tower you can enjoy a bird's-eye view of the Barri Gòtic

From the Rooftops

Before leaving the cathedral, don't forget to 🎫 take the lift to the rooftops for a bird's-eye view of the medieval district and a closer look at the beautiful late 19th-century bell towers; the lift entrance is beyond the choir, to the left as you look at the main altar.

TAKING A BREAK

Pablo Picasso's first paid commission was to design the menu cover at **Els Quatre Gats** (➤ 69), once the popular meeting place of bohemian Barcelona. Now smartly restored, the cafe is an animated spot for coffee, snacks and traditional Catalan meals.

➕ 204 B3
✉ Plaça de la Seu ☎ 9 33 42 82 60
🕐 Mon–Sat 8–12:45, 1–5, 5:15–7:30, Sun 8–1:45, 2–5, 5:15–7:30; cloisters and choir open slightly later and close earlier 💶 Cathedral: noon €6, morning and afternoon: free; Choir: €2.80; roof: €3
🚇 Jaume I, Liceuv

INSIDER INFO

- Try to come on **a sunny day**, when the light filters through the stained-glass windows into the nave and through the lush canopy of palms and shrubbery into the cloisters.
- Every Sunday, from noon to 2pm, you can watch the *sardana*, Catalonia's national folk dance, on the cathedral square. The dancers are accompanied by an instrumental group *(cobla)*.
- Look for the **stone carvings** around the door overlooking the Plaça de Sant Iu – these are the oldest feature of the exterior.

In more depth The Museu de la Catedral, in the 17th-century chapter house off the cloisters, charges extra for a glance at some rather dull religious paintings. However, from 1–5 the museum entrance is included in the cathedral ticket – so go then and save!

⑫ Palau Güell

Chimney-pots decorated with glazed tiles crown the Palau Güell, Gaudí's glorious exercise in discreet opulence. The marvellous interior remains more or less as it was when it was built in 1890, thanks to painstaking restoration.

When wealthy industrialist Eusebi Güell i Bacigalupi and his aristocratic wife decided to move into Carrer Nou de la Rambla to be near his parents' home on the Ramblas, Barcelona society drew gasps of amazement. Not only was everyone else moving out to fashionable addresses in the Eixample, the new residential district on the outskirts of the city, but the Güell's new home was on the edge of El Raval's red-light district, opposite Eden Concert, a notorious cabaret-cum-brothel (now a multi-storey car park). This insalubrious neighbourhood and the cramped plot of land would have posed almost insurmountable challenges for most architects, but Gaudí turned these

Trencadí **(tile fragments) decorate Palau Güell's chimneys**

restrictions to his advantage and produced a masterpiece.

Not What it Seems

Don't be daunted by the austere **facade**; the cold limestone, portcullis-like grilles and wrought-iron dragons were meant to ward off undesirables. The Gothic, fortress-like windows, parabolic arches and doorways concealed behind metalwork – later to become decorative hallmarks of all Modernist architecture – provided privacy and safety. Gaudí used many other architectural tricks. In the inner courtyard, the tiles may look like stone but they are actually made of Scots pine, which muffled the noise of horses' hoofs; and in the interior, false windows create an illusion of space. Other devices include protruding bay windows and oriels, mezzanine minstrel galleries, hidden chapels and secret passages (including one linking the house to Güell's parents' home).

Gaudí's genius at work: part medieval fortress, part mischievous fantasy

The Interior and the Roof

The palace was donated to the city authorities in the early 20th century and underwent a series of renovations, the latest taking more than seven years. Since May 2011 the entire building, restored to its original splendour, has once again been made accessible to the public. Despite being used as a detention centre during the Civil War and later by the Centre of Drama Studies, most of the palace's **interior** has survived intact and even some of Gaudí's original furniture remains.

Start your visit – allowing at least an hour – in the cellars, stables and kennels, which are reached by a spiral ramp from the courtyard. Mushroom-shaped brick columns support the ceiling, creating a cave-like atmosphere. Back on **ground level**, you can admire the grand granite staircase with a red-and-yellow glass screen depicting the Catalan flag above it.

On the **main floor** are the reception hall, the dining room and private apartments, all more or less as they were when the Güells lived here. The central feature of the house is a galleried salon, rising up three storeys to a perforated dome, which looks rather like the roof of a Turkish bath.

Las Ramblas & Either Side

Throughout the palace, it is the attention to detail and the quality of the materials (supplied in large part from the stone quarries, metalworks and glass and ceramics factories owned by the Güell family) that is so impressive. Beech and ebony, walnut and teak are just some of the dozens of different woods used for the ceilings and windows, the lattice-work screens and furniture. Polished granite, alabaster and blood-red marble were used for the floors and the delicate columns.

Finally, you come to the **roof**, with its spectacular profusion of chimneys, ventilators and turrets coated in *trencadí* (a mosaic of multicoloured ceramic-tile fragments). The views of the city and its surroundings from here are wonderful.

GLOVE AT FIRST SIGHT?

Gaudí's patron and publicist, Eusebi Güell i Bacigalupi commissioned several projects that bear his name. It is said that Güell first came across Gaudí's work when he spied a glass cabinet for gloves that he was making for the 1878 Universal Exhibition in Paris.

Insider Tip

TAKING A BREAK

Les Quinze Nits (Plaça Reial 6, tel: 9 33 17 30 75) offers a winning combination of low prices, modern and traditional Catalan and Mediterranean food and elegant surroundings. No advance reservations.

Craftsmanship and attention to detail characterize Gaudí's work at Palau Güell

🚩 204 A3
✉ Carrer Nou de la Rambla 3–5 ☎ 9 34 72 57 75; www.palauguell.cat
🕐 Apr–Sep Tue–Sat 10–7; Oct–Mar 10–4:30 💶 €12 🚇 Liceu

INSIDER INFO

- You must first buy your ticket at the ticket office along Las Ramblas. Join the queue to enter – **only 100 visitors** are allowed in at any one time.
- Notice the **iron bat weathervane** on top of the middle tower on the roof, an unusual decorative subject.

At Your Leisure

🔟 El Raval

Geographically, El Raval is a mirror image of the Barri Gòtic, a warren of narrow streets and alleyways to the west of the Ramblas. For centuries this was an insalubrious part of Barcelona, but the city authorities are now trying to shake off its seedy reputation with an extensive programme of renovation and rebuilding. In the lower, portside fringes of the neighbourhood (roughly beyond Carrer de l'Hospital), the seamier side of city life is more in evidence.

By contrast, in the upper reaches of the district – especially around the Museum of Contemporary Art (MACBA) and the new Rambla del Raval boulevard – gentrification is well advanced. This is reflected in modern workshops and art galleries, bars, lively cafes and refined restaurants.

Museu d'Art Contemporani de Barcelona (MACBA)

Towering over the skateboarders who congregate below, the brilliant white, glass-fronted museum dominates the Plaça dels Angels. After opening in 1995, American architect Richard Meier's startling building received mixed reactions: many local people felt that the ostentatious design was inappropriate in such a run-down area and, furthermore, the exorbitant construction costs had left no money in the coffers to stock the gallery with worthwhile exhibits. However, continuing investment in the area has meant that the exhibition rooms are now filled with works by major artists such as Brossa and Tàpies, Fontana and Dubuffet, Calder and Klee, while the regular temporary exhibitions of internationally acclaimed painters, sculptors, photographers, video artists and avant-garde performance artists are increasingly successful.

MACBA, in El Raval, part of a programme of regeneration begun in the 1990s

MUSEU D'ART CON

Las Ramblas & Either Side

🕂 204 A4
✉ Plaça dels Angels 1
☎ 9 34 12 08 10; www.macba.es
🕐 Jul–Sep Mon, Wed–Fri 11–8, Sat 10–8, Sun 10–3; Oct–Jun Mon, Wed–Fri 11–7:30, Sat 10–8, Sun 10–3. Guided tours in English: Mon, Wed–Fri noon and 6pm; Spanish tours: Mon, Wed–Sun 1 and 6pm 💶 €9
🚇 Catalunya, Universitat, FGC Catalunya

Centre de Cultura Contemporània de Barcelona (CCCB)

Behind MACBA, across a rather stark playground area, is the Centre de Cultura Contemporània de Barcelona. Piñón and Viaplana, a duo of local architects transformed an early 19th-century workhouse – the Casa de la Caritat – into this impressive arts centre. The high-quality exhibitions you can see inside range from architecture to design, fashion and photography. The tile-lined courtyard, where the cityscape and harbour are reflected in plate-glass panels, is used for theatre, dance and other performance arts.

🕂 204 A4 ✉ Carrer del Montalegre 5
☎ 9 33 06 41 00; www.cccb.org
🕐 Tue–Sun 11–8. Special opening times 24–26, 31 Dec, 5, 6 Jan till 3pm. Guided visits (Spanish) Sat 11:30 💶 €5
🚇 Catalunya, Universitat, FGC Catalunya

🔢 Gran Teatre del Liceu

Tragedy struck Barcelona's prestigious opera house in 1994 when a spark from a welder's blowtorch set alight the stage curtains, and the whole theatre went up in flames. After a campaign led by local diva Montserrat Caballé, the Liceu was restored to its former glory. The theatre, one of the world's largest, complete with modern extensions and the original understated facade (which survived the inferno), occupies a huge chunk of land along the Ramblas.

As you go inside, a marble staircase sweeps up to the Salon of Mirrors, lavishly decorated with mirrors, columns and chandeliers.

Gran Teatre del Liceu, restored to its original glory following a fire in 1994

The huge gilded auditorium, which can seat 2,334, was rebuilt to the design of the 19th-century original with improved acoustics and sight-lines and a larger stage. Local designer Antoni Miró produced an incredibly lavish velvet curtain, and avant-garde Catalan artist Perejaume decorated the ceiling. Behind the scenes, state-of-the-art machinery and electronics bring the theatre into the 21st century. Even if you don't make it to a performance – but do try, it's the experience of a lifetime – you can admire all these splendours on a tour.

🕂 204 A3 ✉ La Rambla 51–59
☎ 9 34 85 99 00; www.liceubarcelona.cat
🕐 Daily 11:30am–1pm. Half-hourly guided tours in English and Spanish, longer tours in English and Spanish at 10am
💶 €11.25 🚇 Liceu

🔢 Museu d'Història de la Ciutat

The main body of the museum of the city's history is housed in a 15th-century mansion, the Casa Padellas, which was moved here stone by stone in the 1930s. During the work, Roman city foundations were discovered and these are now beautifully laid out and lit.

A museum ticket also includes entry to three of the highlights of the Catalan royal palaces on the Plaça del Rei (➤ 48). The first is the divine royal chapel, **Capella de Santa Agata**, where the bare stone walls set off one of the most highly acclaimed works of Catalan Gothic art, the exquisitely painted 15th-century altarpiece by Jaume Huguet. From there you can climb the maze of passages and staircases to the top of **Mirador del Rei Martí** (King Martin's Watchtower) and peer down onto the square through the dark arches – you'll also be face to face with the grotesque gargoyles. The vistas of the cathedral and surroundings from the top are superb. You'll also be allowed into the staggering **Saló del Tinell**, a huge barrel-vaulted banqueting hall, where, it is claimed, Christopher Columbus was feted by Ferdinand and Isabella when he got back from the Americas. Temporary exhibitions of a historic nature are held here.

🕂 204 C3
✉ Plaça del Rei/Carrer del Veguer 2
☎ 9 32 56 21 00; www.museuhistoria.bcn.cat
🕐 Tue–Sat 10–7, Sun 10–8
🖐 €7; free Sun after 3pm 🚇 Jaume I

16 Museu Frederic Marès

Frederic Marès i Deulovol (1893–1991) was a prolific sculptor and magpie-like collector who acquired all manner of curios during his long life. The museum houses his eclectic collection with row upon row of wooden Virgins and perfume bottles, labels and coins, fans and playing cards, photographs and crucifixes – you name it and there will be at least four-score-and-ten varieties of it. Jaume Huguet's moving *Christ on his Way to Calvary*

Statues of the Virgin, part of the eclectic collection at Museu Frederic Marès

(15th century) in the Gothic painting gallery is one of the museum's highlights.

The collection is fascinating, i only for the sheer number of exhibits, and will provide avid collectors with an excuse never to throw anything away again. Equally, it can be overwhelming, particularly as the artefacts lack any explanation. For some visitors, the cafe-terrace in the beautiful courtayard may come as a welcome relief.

🕂 204 C3 ✉ Plaça de Sant Iu 5–6
☎ 9 32 56 35 00;
www.museumares.bcn.cat
🕐 Tue–Sat 10–7, Sun and holidays 11–8
🖐 €7. Free first Sun of the month and every Sun after 3pm
🚇 Jaume I
🍴 Café d'Estiu Apr–Sep 10–10

Las Ramblas & Either Side

The Rambla de Mar footbridge links the Ramblas to the shopping and entertainment complex at Moll d'Espanya

17 Port Vell

The regeneration of Port Vell (Old Port) prior to the 1992 Olympics transformed the once neglected waterfront into a polished pleasure port, with the commercial harbour banished to the far-off Zona Franca.

You can admire luxury yachts as you saunter around the marina, along the Moll d'Espanya (Spanish Wharf), and over the wooden-planked swing-footbridge known as the Rambla de Mar – an extension of the Ramblas.

At the end of the Moll d'Espanya, the Maremagnum, a shiny complex of aluminium and plate-glass designed by controversial local architects Piñón and Viaplana, is home to shops, bars, eateries and a multiscreen cinema. Next door is the acclaimed L'Aquàrium de Barcelona and a state-of-the-art IMAX cinema. From the end of the jetty you can look across to the circular hulk of the World Trade Center. At the end of the port's other main pier, Moll de Barcelona, is the functional Estació Marítima, used by ferries plying to and from Mallorca, Ibiza, Menorca and Genoa. A little further south is where the fleets of cruise ships that visit the city dock; over the last few years Barcelona has become the leading cruise-ship harbour in Europe.

Alternative ways to see the harbour are either to take the **18 Transbordador Aeri** cable car that swings across from the Torre de Sant Sebastià at Barceloneta to Montjuïc (Miramar) via the Torre de Jaume I on the Moll de Barcelona, or to board the little double-decker boats known as Golondrinas that run trips into the harbour and along the coast (more information: ► 187).

19 L'Aquàrium de Barcelona

Twenty-one mini-aquariums on the lower floor of the building re-create the environments of different marine habitats, from the Ebro Delta near Barcelona to the Red Sea, Australia's Great Barrier Reef and the coral reefs of Hawaii.

Palau Güell ⑫

C. de Ferran

Pl. de Sant Jaume

⑱ **Plaça Reial**

C. Regomir

C. de Avinyó

C. Nou de Sant Francesc

Rambla de Sta. Mònica

C. de Josep Anselm Clavé

Ⓜ **Drassanes**

Plaça Portal de la Pau

Passeig de Colom

Dàrsena Nacional

Port Vell L'Aquàrium de ⑰ Barcelona

the top floor. There are also great harbour views from the terrace.

🕂 204 B2

✉ Moll d'Espanya

☎ 9 32 21 74 74;
www.aquariumbcn.com

🕐 Sep–Jun daily 9:30am–9pm;
Jul–Aug 9:30–11pm

💶 €20. Free under 4s

Ⓜ Drassanes, Barceloneta

🚌 14, 19, 36, 40, 57, 59, 64, 157

⑱ Plaça Reial

Francesc Molina, architect of La Boqueria (► 54), the city's central market, designed this square in the 1840s. The tall palm trees, Gaudí's tree-like lamp posts, and the much-copied **Three Graces** fountain, cast by the French ironworks Duresne in the 19th century, combine to give the square its tropical feel. Although the area became synonymous with drugs and drunkenness in the 1970s and 1980s, a permanent but fairly discreet police presence has turned things around, and the square's benches and cafe-terraces (notably Glaciar at No 3) are now pleasant places to linger. A couple of good restaurants and unmissable night-spots occupy opposite corners of this lively square.

🕂 204 B3 Ⓜ Liceu

The aquarium's highlight is the 80m (260-foot) glass tunnel containing a moving walkway that plunges you into the silent universe of the Oceanarum, where sharks and stingrays slink past, over or towards you. Many of the exhibits are interactive, with some good child-oriented installations on

Close encounters of the fishy kind: the glass tunnel at L'Aquàrium de Barcelona

Where to...
Eat and Drink

Prices

Expect to pay per person for a three-course meal, excluding drinks:

€ under €25   €€ €25–€50   €€€ over €50

Bar Cañete €€ *Insider Tip*

This small restaurant, a few steps away from the tourist traps on the Ramblas, is a real gem where you can enjoy a feast. All the dishes are made with regional ingredients, fresh from the market. They serve traditional tapas and simple dishes, either at the long bar or at one of the few tables. Daily lunch menus.

➕ 204 A3 ✉ Carrer de la Uniò, 17
☎ 9 32 70 34 58; http://barcanete.com
⏰ Bar: Mon–Sat 1–midnight and restaurant: 1–4 and 8–midnight 🚇 Liceu

Biocenter €

This is one of the largest and best-known vegetarian restaurants in Barcelona. Its walls are hung with artworks created by the owner and his friends. There is a good specials menu, a wide choice of seasonal vegetable casseroles, pizzas, couscous and an extensive salad bar. A selection of vegan dishes is also served, as well as a wide range of organic drinks and juices.

➕ 204 A4 ✉ Carrer del Pintor Fortuny 25
☎ 9 33 01 45 83; www.restaurantebiocenter.es
⏰ Daily 1–11:15pm 🚇 Liceu

Cafè de l'Acadèmia €€

Although you can have breakfast or just a coffee here, the main attraction is the great-value special lunchtime menu, which packs the place with the city's civil servants. Beamed ceilings and bare stone- and brickwork create an appealing setting. Try the terrine with goat's cheese followed by lamb stuffed with pears and mushrooms. Salt

cod is a house speciality, served in a variety of ways; try it with chickpeas or a green pepper sauce.

➕ 204 B3 ✉ Carrer dels Lledó 1
☎ 9 33 19 82 53 ⏰ Mon–Fri 9–noon, 1:30–4, 8:45–11:30 🚇 Jaume I

Can Culleretes €€

Can Culleretes in the Barri Gòtic has the distinction of being the oldest restaurant in Barcelona. Founded in 1786 as a pastry shop, it retains many of the original architectural features. The three rambling dining rooms are decorated with tiles and wrought-iron chandeliers, and the walls display signed celebrity photographs. The lengthy menu includes traditional Catalan dishes such as wild boar stew, *canelons* (pasta) and paella. Game is a speciality in season. Reservations are recommended at weekends.

➕ 204 B3 ✉ Carrer Quintana 5
☎ 9 33 17 30 22; www.culleretes.com
⏰ Tue–Sat 1:30–4, 9–11, Sun 1:30–4 🚇 Liceu

Cometacinc €€€

At this small, elegant restaurant in the Barri Gòtic you can enjoy creative dishes of fresh seasonal produce ranging from ravioli stuffed with scallops to Basque black pudding. Expect wooden tables and lots of glass and white linen. Staff will help you find your way round the good wine list. Vegetarians are well catered for.

➕ 204 B3 ✉ Carrer del Cometa 5
☎ 9 33 10 15 58; www.cometacinc.com
⏰ Wed–Mon 6pm–1am 🚇 Jaume I

Dostrece €€

This funky little restaurant just round the corner from MACBA and La Boqueria market has a handful of tables outside opposite a children's playground and a chill-out lounge downstairs where you can wind down to DJ sessions from Thursday to Sunday. The light Mediterranean cooking might include couscous, a tasty salad, fresh fish or pasta.

➕ 204 A4 ✉ Carrer del Carme 40
☎ 9 33 01 73 06; www.dostrece.net
🕐 Daily 10am–midnight 🚇 Liceu

Organic €

The corner tapas bar is the newest outlet of this small chain, with a larger refectory restaurant down the road at Junta de Comerç 11 and a takeaway stand at the back of La Boqueria market. The fresh, organic produce is locally sourced and there's an imaginative selection of vegan and vegetarian dishes, including plenty of salads. It's just the place to head to when you can't face eating any more deep-fried seafood.

➕ 204 B4 ✉ Carrer d'En Xuclà 15
☎ www.antoniaorganickitchen.com
🕐 Daily noon–nidnight 🚇 Liceu

Peimong €

Peruvian cooking makes a change from Catalan. If you're in the mood to experiment with *ceviche* (marinated raw fish) or duck stewed with peas, potatoes and white rice, this is the place to come.

➕ 204 B3 ✉ Carrer dels Templers 6–10
☎ 9 33 18 28 73 🕐 Tue–Sat 1–4:30, 8–11:30,
Sun 1–4:30 🚇 Jaume I

La Pineda €

A charming and authentic charcuterie and deli where you can buy (and taste) typical Catalan delicacies: sausages, Iberian ham, cheese, wine or cava. The few bistro tables are often taken as the shop is popular with both visitors and locals alike.

➕ 204 B4 ✉ Carrer del Pi, 16
☎ 9 33 02 43 93
🕐 Mon–Sat 9–3, 6–9:30, Sun 11–3 🚇 Liceu

Pla €€

This is an excellent place for a romantic meal in the Barri Gòtic. With candlelit tables for two and gentle music, Pla is usually full every night. Dark walls, mock-medieval chandeliers and a sweeping archway give this split-level restaurant its atmosphere. There are interesting salads dressed with mint or grapes, fish dishes such as the smoked wild salmon with glazed radish or the confit of cod, and the delectable 18 hour lamb shoulder.

➕ 204 B3 ✉ Carrer de Bellafila 5
☎ 9 34 12 65 52 🕐 Sun–Thu 7:30pm–
midnight, Fri–Sat 7:30pm–12:30am 🚇 Jaume I

Pla del Àngels €€

Effectively the MACBA's canteen, this little place is very popular with artists and art-lovers alike, especially the outside tables. Attractively decorated with brightly painted walls and with some fun details, it specializes in a trio of impeccably seasoned carpaccios: duck, octopus and salmon. The portions may be dainty but the food is tasty.

Insider Tip

➕ 204 A4 ✉ Carrer de Ferlandina 23
☎ 9 33 29 40 47 🕐 Daily 7:30pm–midnight
🚇 Universitat

Els Quatre Gats €€€

The walls of "The Four Cats" were once hung with works by Picasso and other great artists of the day, and this legendary restaurant and meeting place has preserved its art nouveau look well. As you eat unpretentious market-fresh Catalan cooking in the large, lively inner dining room, imagine this as the setting for poetry readings, piano recitals and impassioned cultural and political debates.

➕ 204 B4 ✉ Carrer de Montsió 3
☎ 9 33 02 41 40; www.4gats.com
🕐 Daily 1–1 🚇 Catalunya

Las Ramblas & Either Side

El Salón €€

The interior of this informal restaurant is decorated in an appealing mix-and-match style. The well-judged world cuisine with a Spanish twist is equally eclectic; dishes include marinated cod salad with langoustines and ox carpaccio with goats' cheese and rocket. Outside, in the shadow of Roman walls, there are a few tables in the sunny, quiet little square.

➕ 204 B4 ✉ Carrer de l'Hostal d'en Sol 6
☎ 9 33 15 21 59 🕐 Mon–Sat 1:30–4, 8:30–11:30 🚇 Jaume I

BARS AND CAFES

Café de l'Opera €€

Café de l'Opera remains one of the most popular and fashionable places in town. The coffees, drinks and snacks don't come cheap, but it's worth coming here at least once to enjoy the late 19th-century decor and savour the atmosphere. Splash out on a table on the Rambla and enjoy one of the best people-watching spots in the city. Alternatively, take a seat upstairs to watch the busy street below.

➕ 204 B3 ✉ La Rambla 74
☎ 9 33 17 75 85; www.cafeoperabcn.es
🕐 Daily 8:30am–2am 🚇 Liceu

Dulcinea €

You can indulge in delicious cakes or milkshakes at Dulcinea, but it is the *suissos* (hot chocolate) that steals the show here. Established in 1941 and a favourite ever since, this is the most famous place in the city to come for hot chocolate. The gorgeous, thick drink, topped by an avalanche of whipped cream, is served by super-fast, white-coated waiters in traditional surroundings. *Melindros* (delicious sugar-topped biscuits) are traditionally dunked into the chocolate.

Insider Tip

➕ 204 B4 ✉ Carrer de Petritxol 2
☎ 9 33 02 68 24; www.granjadulcinea.com
🕐 Daily 9–1, 5–9. Closed late July to mid-Aug
🚇 Catalunya, Liceu

Granja M Viader €

Down a tiny side street just off the Ramblas is one of the dwindling number of authentic *granjas* left in the city (▶ 40). Granja M Viader specializes in dairy products – the milkshakes are legendary and there's a counter of fresh cheeses and home-made yoghurts on one side. Come for breakfast, an afternoon coffee or to nurse one of their fabulous hot chocolates on a colder day. The pace of service and the decor in this historic place, however, are from another era.

➕ 204 B4 ✉ Carrer d'En Xuclà 4
☎ 9 33 18 34 86; www.granjaviader.cat
🕐 Mon–Sat 9–1, 5–9 🚇 Liceu

El Jardí €€

Tucked into the corner of the picturesque courtyard of the Antic Hospital de la Santa Creu (now housing the Biblioteca de Catalunya) this laid-back cafe-bar is a great place to stop for a drink when you want a break from sightseeing. Tapas and simple snacks are also available, whether you want a breakfast croissant or some nibbles with your evening drink.

➕ 204 A3 ✉ Carrer de l'Hospital 56
☎ 9 33 29 15 50; www.eljardibarcelona.com
🕐 Mon–Sat 10am–11pm 🚇 Liceu

Schilling €

This trendy – check out the ceiling – gay-friendly bar in the Barri Gòtic is a stylish place to stop for a cup of tea or coffee and serves good *entrepans* (sandwiches). If you can, try to get one of the sought-after window tables, which offer great views of the passing crowds. When you eventually get a seat (it's always full) you won't be hurried to leave.

➕ 204 B3
✉ Carrer de Ferran 23
☎ 9 33 17 67 87, www.cafeschilling.com
🕐 Mon–Sat 10am–2:30am, Sun noon–2:30am
🚇 Liceu

Where to…
Shop

The Ramblas are lined with all kinds of shops, from classy *patisseries* to tacky souvenir outlets. You'll also find the unmissable La Boqueria food market (➤50) here. Boutiques and specialist stores cluster in the Barri Gòtic and El Raval, while Plaça de Catalunya and pedestrian-only Portal de l'Àngel and the surrounding streets are home to many of the major department and chain stores.

DEPARTMENT & CHAIN STORES

El Corte Inglés (Plaça de Catalunya 14, tel: 9 33 06 38 00, Metro: Catalunya), Spain's ubiquitous department store, crams a tantalizing variety of goods, from fashion to food and wine into this massive building that overflows into an annexe on nearby Avinguda del Portal de l'Àngel.

On the other side of the huge square, the **El Triangle** complex (Metro: Catalunya) is home to the French megastore **Fnac** (tel: 9 33 44 18 00), good for foreign-language magazines, books, films and music, as well as the cosmetics temple **Sephora** (tel: 9 33 01 14 63), and several small branches of national clothing chains. Branches of home-grown chains like **Zara** and **Mango** jostle for attention with **H&M** along Portal de l'Àngel.

Down by the sea at Port Vell, **Maremagnum** (Moll d'Espanya, tel: 9 32 25 81 00, Metro: Drassanes) is a fun place for window-shopping or snapping up souvenirs, especially on a Sunday when the other shops are closed. Football fans invariably make a beeline for the official merchandise at its **Botiga del Barça**. There are two more branches, one at the top left corner of Plaça de Catalunya at Ronda Universitat 37, and another at Carrer de Jaume I 18. The largish branch of **Carrefour** (La Rambla dels Estudis 113, Metro: Liceu) is a good place to head if you need to do food shopping, but gets very busy in the early evening.

GIFTS

The gift shops in the city's galleries and museums offer a wide variety of appealing objects to take home, as well as attractive publications on the city; those at MACBA (➤63), CCCB (➤64) and the Museu d'Història de la Ciutat (➤64) are good examples. For traditional candles, try **Cereria Subirà** (Baixada de la Llibreteria 7, tel: 9 33 15 26 06, Metro: Jaume I), or for something more innovative **Cereria Abella** (Carrer dels Boters 5, tel: 9 33 18 08 41, Metro: Jaume I).

Try **Germanes Garcia** (Carrer Banys Nous 15, tel: 9 33 18 66 46, www.germanesgarcia.com, Metro: Liceu) for its selection of traditional wicker goods. You can watch the craftspeople at work. For a rather bizarre present to take home check out **Pi 4** (Carrer del Pi 4, tel: 9 33 17 48 89, Metro: Liceu). The entire contents of the shop are items for hanging things up – coathangers, hooks and more.

Italian stationers **Il Papiro** (Plaça de Sant Josep Oriol 3, tel: 9 33 42 43 30, Metro: Liceu) sells handmade marbled papers and stationery accessories. **Raima** (Carrer Comtal 27, tel: 9 33 17 49 66, Metro: Urquinaona) and **Papirum** (Baixada de la Llibreteria 2, tel: 9 33 10 52 42, Metro: Jaume I) offer ranges of beautiful stationery with a Barcelona theme, plus elegant photo albums.

FOOD AND DRINK

For those with a sweet tooth, the humbugs at **Papabubble** (Carrer Ample 28, tel: 9 22 68 86 26, www.papabubble.com, Metro:

Drassanes) will appeal. **Escribà** (La Rambla 83, tel: 9 33 01 60 27, www.escriba.es) is one of the finest cake and chocolate makers in town. The florentines are amazing – perfect with a cup of coffee on the tiny terrace. Many locals claim that **Planelles Donat** (Portal de l'Àngel 7 and 25, tel: 9 33 17 29 29, www. planellesdonat.com, Metro: Catalunya) has some of the best *ortxata* and *torrons* (nougat). **Caelum** (Carrer de la Palla, tel: 9 33 02 69 93, www.caelumbarcelona. com, Metro: Liceu) sells traditional confectionery and liqueurs sourced from the country's convents and monasteries. Sample some of the *yemas de Avila* in the genteel tea-rooms. Just next door, **Orolíquido** (Carrer de la Palla 8, tel: 9 33 02 29 80; www.oroliquido.es) has a selection of fine olive oils. The knowledgeable staff at **La Catedral dels Vines i Caves** (Plaça de Ramon Berenguer El Gran 1, tel: 9 33 19 07 27, Metro: Jaume I) will help you navigate your way through a variety of vintages from Catalonia and the rest of Spain.

FASHION AND ACCESSORIES

For footwear, there's a branch of **Camper**, next to the company's designer hotel at Carrer d'Elisabets 11 (▶ 36), and **Casas** (Portal de l'Àngel 40, tel: 9 33 17 90 40, Rambla de Catalunya, 109, La Rambla, 125, Metro: Catalunya). Hand-sewn espadrilles are avail-able in every possible hue at **La Manuel Alpargatera** (Carrer d'Avinyó 7, tel: 9 33 01 01 72, www.alpargata-barcelona.com, Metro: Liceu). **Almacenes del Pilar** (Carrer de La Boqueria 43, tel: 9 33 17 79 84, Metro: Liceu) is a shawl and mantilla specialist, while **Mil Barrets i Gorres** (Carrer de Fontanella 20, tel: 9 33 01 84 91, Metro: Catalunya) has provided lavish hats for the rich and famous since 1850.

Where to...
Go Out

The Liceu opera house, the *grande dame* of Catalan culture, stands proudly on the Ramblas while on all sides quirky cafes, slick cocktail lounges, touristy pubs and dingy dives offer a myriad choice for bar-hoppers.

CLASSICAL MUSIC

The programme at the **Gran Teatre del Liceu** (▶ 64) includes classical ballet and modern dance, along with contemporary opera. Tickets are like gold dust, but sometimes there are returns on the night.

Classical concerts are also held at the cathedral and the churches of Santa Maria del Pi, Sant Felip Neri and Santa Anna. Ask at Tourist Information for details.

NIGHTLIFE

For flamenco head to **Los Tarantos** (Plaça Reial 17, tel: 9 33 19 17 89; www.masimas.com, Metro: Liceu), where good-value *tableaux* are programmed along-side other Latin rhythms.

At 1am, the club joins with the legendary jazz club **Jamboree** next door to become one big nightclub, although you'll need to pay again. **Moog** (Carrer de l'Arc del Teatre 3, tel: 9 33 01 72 82, Metro: Drassanes) has electronic music down-stairs and R&B in a small upstairs room.

A great option for a fusion of jazz, flamenco and blues is the **Harlem Jazz Club** (Carrer de la Comtessa de Sobradiel 8, tel: 9 33 10 07 55; www.harlemjazzclub.es, Metro: Jaume 1).

La Ribera, Port Olímpic & Poblenou

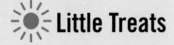 **Little Treats**

Cava at rock-bottom prices
The rustic Can Paixano bar, just around the corner from the **Museu d'Història** (➤87), serves their own inexpensive Catalan sparkling wine.

Fideuà with a sea breeze
In the Xiringuito Escribà on **Playa Bogatell** (➤91) the Catalan dish is particularly good and it comes with a fantastic beach view.

Wooden benches in a courtyard cafe
Escape the hustle and bustle around the **Palau de la Música** (➤78) in the enchanting garden of L'Antic Teatre – right next door.

Getting Your Bearings

La Ribera has been regenerated since the 1990s and its handsome medieval streets buzz with tapas bars, wine bars and boutiques in Gothic palaces and ancient warehouses. Developed for the 1992 Olympic Games, Port Olímpic is a prime piece of real estate on the seafront, also full of bars and restaurants, along with a yacht marina and outdoor sculptures.

La Ribera is reached from the Barri Gòtic by crossing busy Via Laietana. The northern part of the medieval district, known as Santa Catarina and Sant Pere, is home to the Modernist masterpiece Palau de la Música Catalana, as well as the attractive market hall of Santa Caterina.

South of Carrer Princesa, you enter the Born, a warren of narrow streets which was an important centre of the textile trade in the 14th century. Merchants wealthy from Barcelona's thriving sea trade built their palaces along Carrer Montcada, now a showcase of art galleries and museums, among them the Museu Picasso. The surrounding lanes are full of creative fashion, design and arts and crafts shops.

There is also were you will find the Santa María del Mar cathedral, a masterpiece of Gothic architecture. A waterfront walk leads from La Ribera past the Port Vell marina to the fishing village of Barceloneta with its small restaurants and pubs.

North of Port Olímpic you encounter some quieter beaches, and the regenerated area of Poblenou and the new Diagonal Mar neighbourhood. The district, known locally as *El Manchester Català* (Catalan Manchester) grew rapidly during the industrial era. The factories have since moved further out towards the periphery, and the district has evolved to a chic residential and business district.

Gehry's bronze, the towering Hotel Arts and Torre Mapfre dominate the waterfront at Port Olímpic

Plaça de les Glòries Catalanes

28 Torre Agbar

29 Media Tic

Carrer de Pere IV

SANT MARTÍ

Avinguda Diagonal

MARESME

Carrer de Llull

Parc Diagonal Mar

Torre Telefónica **Diagonal ZeroZero** **30**

Passeig del Taulat

Av. d'Icària

31 Edifici Fòrum

26 Vila Olímpica

Ronda Litoral

27 Platja Nova Icària

27 Platja del Bogatell

27 Platja de la Nova Mar Bella

| 0 | | 500 m |
| 0 | | 500 yd |

Perfect Days in...

The Perfect Day

If you're not quite sure where to begin your travels, this itinerary recommends a practical and enjoyable day in La Ribera and Port Olímpic, taking in some of the best places to see. For more information see the main entries.

🕙 10:00am

Be at the ⭐ **Palau de la Música Catalana** (left, ► 78) for the first guided tour of the day (best to reserve online) which takes almost an hour. While you are here, maybe try to get tickets for an evening performance of Bach, Bartók or Bernstein.

🕚 11:00am

Have a coffee or pick up a snack at the inspiring Santa Caterina market (► 96), before making your way along Carrer de l'Argenteria to ⭐ **Santa Maria del Mar** (► 84). The impressive interior of this Gothic masterpiece is beautiful in the morning light.

Palau de la
Música Catalana

**Museu
Europeu d'Art
Modern** ⭐

Disseny Hub
(DHUB) 20 19 8

Santa María
del Mar ⭐

Museu d'Història 22
de Catalunya

24 25 Torre
Marenostrum

Barceloneta 27

Platja 27
de Sant Miquel

Museu
Picasso

Sant Pere & 23
Santa Caterina

21 Parc de la
Ciutadella

27 Platja de la
Barceloneta

Platja
Nova Icària 27

28
Torre Agbar

29
Media Tic

26 Vila Olímpica

27 Platja del
Bogatell

Torre Telefónica
Diagonal ZeroZero

30
31
Edifici
Fòrum

27 Platja de la
Nova Mar Bella

🕐 12:00 noon
You should by now be prepared for one of the city's cultural highpoints, the ⭐ **Museu Picasso** (below, ➤ 80), reached after a short walk up Carrer Montcada. The museum's collection of ceramics, paintings and drawings is breathtaking.

🕐 2:30pm
Once you have finished your museum visit, tuck into lunch in one of the restaurants and tapas bars in the area, such as Euscal Etxea (➤ 94) or the Bar del Pla (Carrer Montcada, 2).

🕐 4:30pm
By now you may want to slow the pace. Head down Passeig Joan de Borbó and wander around the lively streets of nearby **24 Barceloneta** (above, ➤ 88) for a real flavour of the seaside. In the summer this is exactly the right time to chill out on the beach.

🕐 7:00pm
Round off the day with sole or squid at Cal Pintxo (➤ 93) or a *paella* Les Set Portes (➤ 95), or attend a concert in the opulent surroundings of the Palau de la Música Catalana, if you picked up tickets in the morning. The choice is yours.

⭐4 Palau de la Música Catalana

The Palau de la Música Catalana (Palace of Catalan Music) is a fantastic venue for choral, chamber and symphonic music, and attracts a galaxy of classical music maestros. It is also a temple to Catalan tradition and history, testifying to the splendour of Barcelona's art nouveau movement.

The stupendous concert hall was built in 1908 as the headquarters of the Orfeó Català choral society by Lluís Domènech i Montaner, one of the leading exponents of Modernisme (➤ 27). The building is a masterpiece and was declared a World Heritage Site in 1997. Even if you don't make it to a concert (there are 300 each season), you can take a guided tour (in English, Catalan or Spanish) for a chance to see this stunning concert hall.

The Exterior

Before going inside, take a good look at the **facade**, complete with mosaic-coated columns, busts of Bach, Beethoven, Palestrina and Wagner, and across the upper storey, allegorical mosaics depicting a Catalan choir, with the jagged peaks of Montserrat in the background. On the corner of the building, a sugary sculpture symbolizing Catalan popular song trickles down from a Moorish turret. Crowning it all is a mosque-like **dome**, decorated with the Catalan flag and St George shields. In 1989, local architect Oscar Tusquets added the brick-and-glass extension to the palace, as well as updating some of the facilities inside.

The lavish interior of the main auditorium shows the work of architect Domènech i Montaner at its very best

Floral motifs are used in much of the Palau's interior decoration

The Interior

In the entrance hall and staircase, the prolific decoration continues. The theme of much of the work is floral; roses, lilies and fanciful blooms picked from Montaner's fertile imagination climb up pillars and trail across the ceilings and stained-glass windows. As always with Modernist design, there is a profusion but never an excess of detail.

The climax of the tour, however, is the magnificent **concert hall** on the upper floor. Ethereal stained-glass windows flank the great organ, and below it, behind the stage, are muse-like figures with mosaic-tile bodies and terracotta statues for heads. On either side of the stage rise marble sculptures by local artists Didac Masana and Pau Gargallo, representing the cityfolk's taste in music: to the right, Richard Wagner's Valkyries ride over a stern bust of Beethoven, while to the left a tree of traditional song casts its leafy shade over 19th-century Catalan composer Anselm Clavé. The gorgeous blue-and-gold stained-glass **skylight** by Antoni Rigalt is encircled by 40 women's heads, representing a heavenly choir.

Now, imagine concerts by the likes of Richard Strauss, Pau Casals or Mstislav Rostropovich, all of whom have performed here, and the experience will be complete.

TAKING A BREAK

The majestic atmosphere of the air-conditioned foyer makes it a great spot for a drink at any time of day. If you're feeling peckish choose from the selection of Basque-style canapés.

🕂 204 C4
✉ Carrer de Sant Pere Més Alts
☎ Ticket office 9 02 47 54 85; Palau 9 32 95 72 00; www.palaumusica.org
🎫 Daily 10–3:30; Holy Week and Aug 10–6. Closed holidays J €17
🚇 Urquinaona 🚌 17, 19, 40, 45, N8v

INSIDER INFO

- Tickets for the **hour-long tours** (every hour) are sold online and at both Les Muses del Palau gift shop across Plaça de Lluís Millet, just off the Via Laietana, and at the ticket office located in the modern extension.
- The Palau's strongest musical tradition is **choral music**, so try to attend a concert by the Orfeó Català (▶ 97 for box office details). **World music** concerts, however, including the likes of Wilco, Malú and the Alabama Gospel Choir, are also frequent.
- Bring binoculars to scrutinize the fine details. The **columns** at the top of the side balconies inside the concert hall fan out along the tiled ceiling like peacock tails, and **ceramic roses** stud the ceiling.

Insider Tip

⑧ Museu Picasso

Barcelona is where Picasso learned to paint, so it is appropriate that the city has one of the greatest repositories of his art. The collection, housed in not one but five handsome, medieval mansions on the elegant Carrer Montcada, traces the artist's career through ceramics, paintings, drawings and lithographs; it has a particularly fine collection of early works.

Picasso's family moved to Barcelona in 1895, when Pablo was just 13 years old, after his father got a job teaching art at the city's School of Fine Arts. An amazingly early starter, Picasso began studying at the same school, La Llotja, in the autumn of the same year. After a year away in Madrid attending classes, he returned to Barcelona in 1898, by which time he had produced an incredible number of touching self-portraits, many of which are on display at the Museu Picasso.

Picasso never lost his affection for the city, despite decades of living in France. He effectively initiated the collection when he donated *The Harlequin* (1917). More generous donations followed, including a sizeable collection of his early paintings and a pledge to give Barcelona a copy of every print he produced until he died. When **Jaume Sabartés**, Picasso's lifelong friend and personal secretary, died in 1968, he bequeathed his private collection of Picasso's works to the city authorities. Picasso paid tribute to him by matching his donation painting for painting.

The museum's collection is housed in five beautifully converted medieval palaces on Carrer Montcada

Science and Charity (1897), painted when Picasso was just 15, is one of the principal works in the collection

The Permanent Collection

The circuit begins upstairs, and the works are arranged chronologically. In **Rooms 1–9** Picasso's earliest etchings and academic drawings, nudes and doodles, including some delightful miniature seascapes, are on display. Before Picasso reached the age of 20, he had produced a vast number of powerful studies, realistic landscapes and promising still lifes, and even one or two mocking self-portraits. At the far end of **Room 8** you'll see *Science and Charity* (1897), a huge, forceful work, portraying an old woman on her sick bed. Painted when Picasso was only 15, it is early proof of his immense talent.

In 1900 Picasso spent a few months in Paris, scouring its avant-garde galleries, cafes and cabarets. The experience greatly influenced the young painter, as is clearly visible in the colourful, Fauvist-influenced paintings such as *The Embrace* (1901) and *Margot* or *The Wait* (1901), both in **Room 10**.

A clutch of paintings in **Rooms 11** and **12** represents work from the Blue Period. Picasso, profoundly affected

---

THE MUSEUM BUILDINGS

Aguilar, Baró de Castellet and Meca, three of the medieval palaces in which the museum is housed, are well worth seeing in their own right. Opened in 1982, after years of painstaking renovation work that joined the three seamlessly together, they represent some of the world's finest domestic architecture from the 13th and 14th centuries. Built to fashionable styles influenced by Italian *palazzi*, each of these aristocratic homes was more beautiful and lavish than the previous one, testifying to the rivalry among the city's merchants. The museum was extended in the 1990s by converting two more fine medieval buildings, the Casa Mauri and Palau Finestres; the extra space is used to display the museum's top-notch temporary exhibitions, usually devoted to Picasso's contemporaries or particular aspects of his own work, such as linocuts or sculptures.

by the suicide of close friend Carles Casagemas, turned to a more limited palette dominated by cold blue tones. Look for *Dead Woman* (Barcelona, 1903).

In the **Sala Sabartés**, Picasso's irreverent painting of his friend, *Portrait of Sabartés Wearing a 16th-century-style Ruff and Hat* (1939) is given prominence, along with a series of caricatures of his assistant. Some minor Cubist works from 1917 are shown in **Rooms 13** and **14**. Most of Picasso's work from the interwar years, however, went to

Margot (1901) was influenced by the Fauvist artists Picasso met in Paris

collections in Paris, Madrid and New York. In **Rooms 15** and **16**, you'll find the museum's real highlight, a set of Cubist reinterpretations of *Las Meninas,* a monumental 17th-century painting by Spanish master Diego Velázquez. Picasso broke the original composition up into its components, in a set of 44 canvases, reinterpreting the scene from different perspectives. The centrepiece is a mind-boggling monochrome reworking of the whole work in **Room 15**, painted in 1957. Nine versions of *The Pigeons*, inspired by the dovecote he installed at his Cannes studio in the 1950s, are displayed in **Room 17**.

The circuit is rounded off by an exquisite set of boldly painted ceramic plates and vases (**Rooms 18** and **19**), mostly fashioned in the 1950s and donated by Picasso's widow, Jacqueline, in 1982, just in time for the museum's opening. A portrait of Jacqueline (1957), plus a handful of the artist's final works, adorn the walls of these two rooms.

TAKING A BREAK

There is a good cafeteria in the museum. Alternatively, try **La Bàscula** (Carrer del Flassaders 30 bis, tel: 9 33 19

GALLERY HIGHLIGHTS

- *Portrait of the Artist's Mother* (1896) Room 3
- *Science and Charity* (1897) Room 8
- *Margot* or *The Wait* (1901) Room 10
- *Roofs of Barcelona* (1902 and 1903) Room 11
- *The Harlequin* (1917) Room 12
- *Las Meninas* (1957) Rooms 15–16
- *Ceramics* Rooms 18–19

98 66) in an old candle factory behind the museum, which serves tasty vegetarian dishes and wonderful cakes and crêpes.

Much of the museum's collection of ceramics was donated by Picasso's widow

➕ 204 C3 ✉ Carrer Montcada 15–23
☎ 9 32 56 00 00; www.museupicasso.bcn.cat
🕐 Tue–Sun and holidays 10–8. Guided tours in English Thu 6pm, Sat 12 noon (tel: 9 32 56 30 22)
✋ €11, first Sun of every month and Sun after 3pm free
Ⓜ Jaume I
🍴 Cafe and bookshop

INSIDER INFO

- Try to go on a **Sunday afternoon** or the **first Sunday of the month**, when admission is free.
- Always **get there early** (or time your visit during the afternoon siesta) as the museum is invariably busy.
- Don't forget to look up at the marvellous **painted ceilings** in some of the rooms.
- A great place to linger a while and catch your breath is the sumptuous **19th-century neoclassical hall**, in the Palau del Baró de Castellet, next to the Sala Sabartés. The hall is a mix of baroque and classical elements and drips with sculpted cherubim, crystal chandeliers and gold-leaf decorations.

Insider Tip

⭐ 10 Santa Maria del Mar

Like all great stars, Santa Maria looks beautiful from every angle. Slim, tall and elegant, it represents the high point of Catalan architecture of the 14th centuryand is remarkable for its simplicity and purity of style.

In medieval times, La Ribera was the centre of a thriving shipbuilding and fishing industry. As the Catalan empire grew, trade flourished, creating great wealth among a growing middle class. The wealthy citizens wanted to build a magnificent church, to keep in with God as well as Mammon. The resulting cathedral, built with funds collected to celebrate Catalonia's conquest of Sardinia, was completed within 55 years, which accounts for its astonishing architectural unity.

The **facade** is robust with decorative flourishes, typical of the Catalan Gothic style. Slender, pencil-like towers soar on either side of a plain curtain wall, and it is easy to see why it has been likened to a mantelpiece with a pair of candlesticks. Before going inside, take a good look at the wood and bronze doors – the two little brass workmen carrying heavy loads on their backs are very finely crafted.

The facade is typical of the Catalan Gothic style

The Interior

Baroque and neoclassical additions and heavy decoration inside the basilica were destroyed by fire during the Civil War, leaving only the Gothic shell. But what a shell. The narrow **nave** accentuates the basilica's length and height, creating an effect of great elegance. Eight octagonal pillars punctuate the side aisles, off which side chapels radiate. Another eight pillars form an arcade behind the main altar.

Fire destroyed the basilica's interior decoration, leaving only the Gothic shell

From the altar, look back at the **rose window**, which depicts the Virgin's Coronation. It was installed in 1458 after an earthquake shattered the original. Finally, leave by the strangely angled door on Carrer del Born; the carving of the Virgin Mary over the doorway is by Frederic Marès (►65).

TAKING A BREAK

Choose one of the shady tables at **La Vinya del Senyor** (►95). Look for the special selection of wines, cavas and sherry. The tapas are good, especially the Iberian ham, cheeses and slices of *coca*, rather like pizza.

✚ 204 C3 ✉ Plaça de Santa Maria ☎ 9 33 10 23 90
🕔 Daily 9–1:30, 4:30–8, Sun and holidays free after 10:30 💷 Free 🚇 Jaume I

INSIDER INFO

- Concerts, **mostly classical**, are held in the basilica from time to time, which bring the place to life. Ask at the basilica for details.
- The best time to **view the interior** is in the morning light.
- **Fossar de les Moreres** (Mulberry Graveyard) is a small square along Carrer de Santa Maria shaded by mulberry trees. A granite slab inscribed with lines of verse and an eternal flame on a giant metal sculpture mark the graveyard of the Catalan martyrs killed fighting against the Spanish in 1714.

At Your Leisure

🔟 Museu Europeu d'Art Modern (MEAM)

Figurative and contemporary art is rather rare in Barcelona's cultural scene which makes this museum all the more surprising. It is housed in the Palau Gomis, a magnificently restored baroque palace. Only a few steps away from the Museu Picasso, the collection offers three floors of international temporary exhibitions and modern fine art from the late 19th century to present day. Concerts are held on Fridays and Saturdays.

➕ 204 C3 ✉ Barra de Ferro 5
☎ 9 34 17 93 60; www.meam.es
🕐 Tue–Sun 10–8
💶 €7 🚇 Jaume I

🔟 Disseny Hub (DHUB)

The Disseny Hub combines the collections of three museums: the Textile and Clothes Museum, the Ceramic Museum and the Museum of Decorative Arts. The new building on Plaça de les Glòries was designed by the award-winning Catalan architect Oriol Bohigas. Scheduled to open in early 2015.

➕ 206 B5
✉ Pl. de les Glòries Catalanes 37–38
☎ 9 32 56 67 13; www.museudeldisseny.cat
🚇 Glòries

THE SPANISH CITADEL

The Parc de la Ciutadella occupies the site of the citadel built in the early 18th century by Felip V following the Spanish defeat of the Catalans. A symbol of Spanish oppression, it was eventually demolished and the park created.

🔟 Parc de la Ciutadella

A leafy haven of tranquillity, the Parc de la Ciutadella is a great place to take a shaded walk, stop for a leisurely picnic, or for children to let off steam.

The park was the site of the Universal Exhibition of 1888, and several Modernist buildings constructed for the exhibition remain. The **Arc de Triomf**, an unusual Moorish-style arch on Passeig de Lluís Companys outside the park proper, formed the main entrance. Inside the park, look for the red-brick Castle of Three Dragons, a stupendous mock medieval fortress designed by the Modernist architect Lluís Domènech i Montaner as the exhibition cafe. It now houses a rather musty zoology museum (one to miss). The L'Umbracle, a fanciful iron-and-glass vivarium, and the L'Hivernacle, or winter

garden, also date from this time. Both have undergone some refurbishment.

By the lake at the centre of the park, you'll find the Cascada, a monumental wedding cake of a fountain complete with spouting griffins and sea gods. The grotto at its centre was one of Gaudí's first projects.

✚ 193 F2
🕐 Park and zoo: May–Sep daily 10–7; Oct–Apr 10–5
🚇 Arc de Triomf, Barceloneta

The Moorish-style Arc de Triomf, once the main entrance to Parc de la Ciutadella

🍴 PLACE TO PLAY

Parc de la Ciutadella (➤ 86–87) has plenty of green space, three children's play areas, table-tennis tables and row boats for rent. Most weekends there are free children's activities. The zoo is pricey and its habitats are outdated, but it has a good adventure playground for under 10s.

🔢 Museu d'Història de Catalunya

The Palau de Mar, a stunning ensemble of beautifully restored brick warehouses, dominates the northern, Barceloneta side of Port Vell. Inside, an extensive display takes you through the history of Catalonia from prehistoric times to the present day. The attractive 🍴 **exhibition is interactive** and informative, which should also make the museum interesting for older children. Highlights include a suit of armour that you can try on. Exhibits are labelled in Catalan only and non-Catalan speakers have to rely on the sketchy information given in the translated handbook issued with the ticket

Stone griffins guard the base of the vast Cascada fountain at the heart of Parc de la Ciutadella

La Ribera, Port Olímpic & Poblenou

Exhibits at the Museu d'Història de Catalunya trace the region's often turbulent past

for much of the exhibition. The top-floor Mediateca, however, does have displays in English and, in June to September, the excellent guided tours conducted on Wednesday evenings are given in English as well as Catalan.
🔢 204 C2 ✉ Plaça de Pau Vila 3
☎ 9 32 25 47 00; www.mhcat.net
🕐 Thu–Sat, Tue 10–7, Wed 10–8, Sun and holidays 10–2:30. Guided tours Wed 10pm–midnight, reservation only
💶 €4; Guided visits included in admission every Sun and holidays 12, 1.
Free first Sun of the month
🚇 Barceloneta 🍴 Cafe on fourth floor; excellent bookshop and gift shop

23 Sant Pere & Santa Caterina
The twinned neighbourhood is between Via Laietana, Carrer Pincesa and Sant Pere més and features a medieval ambience with winding alleys and atmospheric squares. The first textile mills in Catalonia were established here in the 12th and 13th centuries when area was settled by traders, craftsmen and artisans. The neighbourhood eventually fell into disrepair but was redeveloped in the 1980s. The area around the renovated **historic market hall** now has trendy restaurants and boutiques alongside well-established shops and restaurants. The Plaça Sant Agustí Vell with its wrought-iron lanterns reminds one of old Paris, while there is always something new on the **Plaça Pou de la Figuera** (also known as Forat de la Vergonya) which is designed and managed by the locals.

24 Barceloneta
Barceloneta (Little Barcelona) is a honeycomb of lively, narrow streets lined with fishermen's houses and low-rise apartments, dotted with delightful little squares and a park. The area was created in the mid-18th century when the land was drained and low-rent housing was built for workers displaced by the construction of the Spanish citadel (► panel, page 86). It is now a great place to come for a taste of Mediterranean life.

The historic focal point is the picturesque Plaça de la Barceloneta, with its cafes, the 18th-century Església de Sant Miquel del Port and fountains, where people still come for drinking water. These days all eyes are on the beach, perfect for a picnic lunch bought at the nearby market. The old *xiringuitos*, or beach-hut restaurants, on the waterfront were replaced in the 1990s by

top architect Enric Miralles (who died in 2000) and his partner, the Italian architect, Bennedetta Tagliabue, as the headquarters for Catalan gas. Miralles earned

Museu d'Història de Catalunya **22**
Estació Barcelona de França
Parc Zoològic
Torre Marenostrum **25**
24 Barceloneta
Pg. de Joan de Borbó
Ronda Litoral
Av. d'Icària
26 Vila Olímpica

permanent structures catering for a trendier crowd.
🚇 205 D2 🚇 Urquinaona and Arc de Triomf

25 Torre Marenostrum
Looking from Barceloneta towards Diagonal Mar you can't help but notice this futuristic landmark skyscraper. Its distinctive crystal shape has sections that protrude from the facade and freely float in space like a sculpture. The Torre Marenostrum was designed by the

international acclaim for his highly idiosyncratic constructions. His free form structures, often using massive (and unusual) materials and steel, are in context to – and form relationship with – the surrounding environment.
🚇 205 D2 ✉ Plaça del Gas 1
🚇 Vila Olímpica 🚌 10, 36, 45, 57, 59, 71, 92

26 Vila Olímpica
Barcelona's 1992 Olympiad bequeathed the city a chic marina, a palm tree-lined seafront promenade and a complex of modern buildings, known collectively as Vila Olímpica, just a short walk from Barceloneta. The area

Restaurants on Barceloneta's promenade

Barceloneta's beaches are an ideal place to chill out and have fun

abounds with expensive restaurants, beach bars and clubs that draw customers with parties, DJs and sun loungers that overlook the sea.

In the shadow of two twin towers, the luxury Hotel Arts and an office block, is a striking bronze sculpture of a giant fish designed by the renowned American architect Frank Gehry.

⊞ 206 A2

⊕ Ciutadella-Vila Olímpica

⊟ 10, 36, 41, 45, 57, 59, 71, 92, 157

27 ⚥ Platges

How many other big cities in the world – save for Rio and Sydney – can boast clean, sandy beaches (*platges*) on their doorstep? Barcelona enjoys almost 5km (3 miles) of them, stretching all the way from Barceloneta to Diagonal Mar, to the north. Behind them is a promenade, the Passeig Marítim, lined with palm trees. Showers, bars, shops and restaurants along the beaches make the experience all the more pleasant. The water quality is monitored, and there are lifeguards and Red Cross stations aplenty, plus buoys to keep boats and jet skis away from swimmers. All the beaches, easily accessible by public transport, have qualified for EU Blue Flag status to vouch for their safety and cleanliness.

The three beaches nearest the city, Platges Sant Sebastià, Barceloneta and Passeig Marítim, get very crowded on hot days,

so it's worth going that bit farther to Nova Icària, Bogatell, Mar Bella or Nova Mar Bella. **Insider Tip**
At the latter two beaches you can rent water-sports equipment such as sailing boats, windsurf boards and surfboards.

➕ 204 C1–208 B3

🚇 Barceloneta, Ciutadella-Vila Olímpica, Bogatell, Llacuna, Poble Nou, Selva de Mar

🚌 10, 36, 41, 45, 57, 59, 71, 92, 157

28 Torre Agbar

North of the Olympic Village the former industrial district of Poblenou has in recent years seen the development of some spectacular new buildings, making the area interesting to anyone with a passion for modern architecture, hi-tech and contemporary design. One such building is the striking office tower, Torre Agbar, head offices for Barcelona's water utility company. A postmodernist structure that protrudes 142m (465.87ft) into Barcelona's skyline the distinctive phallic shaped building was designed by Jean Nouvel.

The structure has an aluminium facade covered with 56,000 individual glass slats in more than 40 different colours, so that the building shimmers in different colours depending on the time of day. At night the city's massive new landmark is even more luminous when its exterior is illuminated by a palette of vibrant colours.

➕ 206 B5 ✉ Avinguda Diagonal 211

🚇 Glòries

29 Media Tic

Hi-tech, design and sustainability all merge in the facade of the Technology Centre Media Tic building, the work of the Catalan architect Enric Ruiz Geli, a pioneer of green architecture in Spain. The facade is covered by a membrane of triangular plastic air cushions that expand and contract (depending on the angle of the sun) and keep the building cool throughout the day. The membrane gives the facade its distinctive profile. Geli referred to his work as 'the digital Pedrera', after Antoni Gaudi's famous Casa Milà known popularly as La Pedrera (the Quarry).

➕ 206 C4

✉ Carrer Roc Boranat 117

🚇 Glòries or Poblenou

30 Torre Telefónica Diagonal ZeroZero

Another recent architectural coup is the 110m (360ft) high Torre Telefónica Diagonal ZeroZero,

Torre Agbar: Barcelona's new eye-catcher

La Ribera, Port Olímpic & Poblenou

named after the international calling code. The eccentric design is by Enric Massip-Bosch and houses the head office of the Spanish Telefónica telecoms company. In its inauguration year 2010 the building was selected as one of the top ten most beautiful skyscrapers in the world and in 2011 Massip-Bosch was awarded the prestigious international architecture prize, the LEAF Award. The diamond-shaped building dazzles like a gem in the Mediterranean sky. Its bright white exterior has a mesh-like aluminium facade giving it a constantly changing appearance, dependent on the weather and sunlight.

➕ 208 C1
✉ Avinguda Diagonal 0
🚇 Fòrum

🗐 Edifici Fòrum

Opposite the Torre Telefónica is a striking blue triangular building, the multi-award winning Edifici Fòrum construction by the Swiss design team Herzog & de Meuron. Built for the 2004 Forum of World Cultures, the front of the building seems to float above the ground. The multifunctional venue, known locally as the 'blue sponge', is one of the largest convention and exhibition centres in Europe. The building is the centrepiece of Esplanada del Fòrum, a 15ha (37-acre) artificial platform that covers a coastal ring road and a waste water treatment plant and provides public access to the sea.

➕ 208 C2   ✉ Parque del Fòrum
☎ 9 32 30 10 00   🚇 Fòrum

Plaça de les Clòries Catalanes
🗍 Torre Agbar

Media Tic 🗍

SANT MARTÍ

Avinguda Diagonal

Carrer de Llull

MARESME

Torre Telefónica
Diagonal ZeroZero
🗍

Edifici 🗐
Fòrum

The Edifici Fòrum, with the Torre Telefónica Diagonal ZeroZero in the background

Where to...
Eat and Drink

Prices
Expect to pay per person for a three-course meal, excluding drinks:
€ under €25   €€ €25–€50   €€€ over €50

Agua €€
When you long for beachfront eating head for Agua, next to the Hotel Arts (►37). The menu offers Catalan and Spanish dishes such as salt cod with sun-dried tomatoes, and wild rice with green vegetables and ginger, although pastas, hamburgers and salads are also available. House specialities are prepared in a coal-fired oven. In summer, reserve in advance.

🔢 205 E1
✉ Passeig Marítim de la Barceloneta 30
☎ 9 32 25 12 72; www.aguadeltragaluz.com
🕐 Daily 1–3:45 (4:30 on weekends) and 8–11:30 (12:30am on weekends)
🚇 Barceloneta

Bestial €€
Below the iconic bronze whale by Frank Gehry, this slick Port Olímpic beachfront restaurant serves well-judged Mediterranean food with Italian leanings in a stylish modern interior. There are tables outside on a terrace next to the laid-back bar area, which is open until late at weekends.

🔢 205 E2
✉ Carrer de Ramón Trias Fargas 2–4
☎ 9 32 24 04 07; www.bestialdeltragaluz.com
🕐 Mon–Fri 1–3:45, 8–11:30, Sat–Sun 1–4:30, 8–12:30am 🚇 Ciutadella-Vila Olímpica

Ca' la Nuri Platja €€€
This is the stylish beach branch of a classic Port Olímpic family-run restaurant. Perfectly executed fish and seafood dishes complement the rice and fideuà (noodles) favourites. Literally on the beach, the restaurant's relaxed service

and unbeatable views make this ideal for a special occasion or a long afternoon lunch.

🔢 205 E1
✉ Passeig Marítim de la Barceloneta 55
☎ 9 32 21 37 75; www.calanuri.com
🕐 Tue–Sat 1–4:30, 8–11, Sun 1–5
🚇 Ciutadella-Vila Olímpica

Cal Pep €€€
Be prepared to wait at this popular, small seafood restaurant run in idiosyncratic style by Pep himself. Grab a stool at the bar if you can and, unless you speak Catalan, simply point to any of the tapas that look good, or wait to be seated in the tiny, brick-lined restaurant. Highlights are pebrots del padró (fried green peppers), chickpeas with spinach and Catalan sausage, and crayfish with chilli sauce.

🔢 204 C3
✉ Plaça de les Olles 8
☎ 9 33 10 79 61
🕐 Tue–Sat 1:30–4, 8–11:45, Mon 8–11:45. Closed Easter, Aug, public holidays
🚇 Jaume I

Cal Pinxo €€
The beach restaurant serves spot-on traditional dishes. Crunchy chiperones (fried baby squid) are balanced by excellent ham and mouth-watering rape (monkfish), a house speciality. If the weather's not up to the outside tables, reserve a place on the first floor for unbroken ocean views.

🔢 204 C1
✉ Carrer de Baluard 124, Barceloneta
☎ 9 32 21 50 28; www.pinxoplatja.com
🕐 Daily 12:30–4, 8:30–11:30

La Ribera, Port Olímpic & Poblenou

Can Maño €

Fresh fish and seafood, prepared simply and well. This no-frills little restaurant (the decor seems straight out of the 1960s) is very popular with the locals so you need to arrive early to secure your place before it fills up.

✚ 204 C2 ✉ Carrer Baluard, 12
☎ 9 33 19 30 82 ⏰ Closed Sat dinner, Sun, Mon lunch 🚇 Barceloneta

Can Ramonet €€

A new terrace has added to the attractions of this family-run restaurant, said to be the oldest in the port area. The restaurant has a front bar with stand-up tables and a few seated tables where you can enjoy seafood tapas, beer and some regional wines. This provides a crowded but less expensive option than dining in one of the two rooms at the rear. The seafood is good, and it's worth paying the price for the spanking-fresh hake, monkfish and shellfish spectacularly displayed at the entrance. Specialities include lobster with clams, stockfish with romesco and marinated anchovies. Vegetarians can opt for braised artichokes or tortilla with spinach and beans.

✚ 204 C2 ✉ Carrer de la Maquinista 17
☎ 9 33 19 30 64 ⏰ Daily noon–midnight
🚇 Barceloneta

Can Ros €

There's a good choice of classic dishes such as paella, *suquets* (stews) and *arròs negre* (rice cooked with squid ink) at this popular, and newly renovated, Barceloneta seafood restaurant. You can nibble on a mixed platter of *peixets* (deep-fried whitebait), prawns and mussels while you wait for the main course. The weekday lunch menus are excellent value.

✚ 204 C1 ✉ Carrer de l'Almirall Aixada 7
☎ 9 32 21 50 49
⏰ Thu–Tue 1–5, 8–midnight, Mon 1–5
🚇 Barceloneta

Cuines Santa Caterina €€

Santa Caterina market provides a stylish restaurant to please everyone. Using fresh produce straight from the market, chefs in a series of open kitchens within the restaurant create dishes ranging from Catalan staples such as *botifarra amb mongetes* (sausage with white beans) to well-executed sushi, as well as excellent vegetarian options. The market is also a good option for breakfast or for a snack at the tapas bar.

Insider Tip

✚ 204 C4 ✉ Mercat Santa Caterina, Avinguda Francesc Cambó 16
☎ 9 32 68 99 18; www.grupotragaluz.com/santacaterina ⏰ Mon–Fri 1–4, 8–11:30, Sat–Sun 1–4:30, 8–12:30am 🚇 Jaume I

Euskal Etxea €€

Pintxos are the Basque version of tapas – reputedly the best in Spain. You need to get here early for the best selection, but even then you'll probably still have to stand. There is, however, a restaurant with a Basque menu at the back – but part of the fun is fighting at the bar for the laden plates of tuna chunks, crab claws and much, much more.

Insider Tip

✚ 204 C3 ✉ Placeta de Montcada 1–3
☎ 9 33 10 21 85 ⏰ Bar: Tue–Sat 8:30am–11:30pm, Sun 12:45–3.30. Restaurant: Tue–Sat 1–3:30, 9–11:30
🚇 Jaume I

Mercat Princesa €/€€

A magnificent 14th century city palace with 16 food stalls under one roof – a unique dining experience in the Born! There is a great selection of different cuisines (including Italian, Indonesian, Spanish and Catalan) and whether you opt for a salad, tapas, pizza, hamburger, wine or cocktails – everything is very well priced. Risottos are available for €4!

✚ 204 C3
✉ Carrer dels Flassaders, 21
☎ 9 32 68 15 18; www.mercatprincesa.com
⏰ Sun–Wed 9–midnight, Thu–Sat 9am–1am
🚇 Jaume I

La Paradeta €€

Choose from the array of fresh fish and seafood, decide whether you want it grilled, steamed or battered, add a salad and some wine and wait for your number to be called. This self-service restaurant is a no-nonsense place with great food, a bustling atmosphere and affordable prices. No reservations or credit cards.

✚ 205 D3 ⊠ Carrer de Comercial 7
☎ 9 32 68 19 39; www.laparadeta.com
🕐 Tue–Thu 8pm–11:30pm, Fri–Sat 8pm–midnight, Sun 1–4 🚇 Arc de Triomf

Els Pescadors €€/€€€

This former fishing tavern is now one of Barcelona's gastronomic institutions. Specialising in fresh fish and rice dishes, the restaurant also impresses with its old world maritime charm. In the summer you should definitely reserve a table out on the shady terrace.

✚ 207 D2 ⊠ Plaça de Prim, 1
☎ 9 33 30 03 03; www.elspescadors.com
🕐 Daily 1–3:45, 8–11:30 🚇 Poblenou

Senyor Parellada €€

This bright and cheerfully decorated restaurant is a modern version of the traditional Catalan *taberna*. It is housed in an elegant 19th-century manor house and the menu includes dishes typical of the region: hearty fare such as lamb with whole garlic or cod with honey.

✚ 204 C3 ⊠ Carrer de l'Argenteria 37
☎ 9 33 10 50 94
🕐 Daily 1–3:45, 8:30–11:45 🚇 Jaume I

Les Set Portes €€

If you eat only one paella in Barcelona, eat it here. The huge, historic restaurant opened in 1836, and since then has been serving a legendary selection of different paellas daily. The shellfish paella is classic, but varieties made with squid ink, rabbit or sardines are also available. There is also a wide choice of fish dishes and savoury casseroles.

✚ 204 C2 ⊠ Passeig d'Isabel II 14
☎ 9 33 19 30 33; www.7portes.com
🕐 Daily 1–1 🚇 Barceloneta

Tantarantana €€

Fashionable restaurant in the Born: small, rustic and cosy, sometimes crowded. If you steer clear of the usual local meal times, you might get a table on one of the two charming patios. Freshly prepared tapas – try the anchovies with guacamole. Light Mediterranean cuisine, good wine list.

✚ 205 D3 ⊠ Tantarantana, 24
☎ 9 32 68 24 10 🕐 Tue–Sun 1–midnight, Mon 8pm–midnight 🚇 Jaume I

La Vinya del Senyor €€

The location of this quality wine bar, set just across the cobbles from the glorious facade of Santa Maria del Mar, is hard to beat. The excellent wines are accompanied by quality tapas.

✚ 204 C3 ⊠ Plaça de Santa Maria 5
☎ 9 33 1 03 33 79 🕐 Mon–Thu noon–1am, Fri noon–2am, Sun noon–midnight 🚇 Jaume I

BARS AND CAFES

Café de la Ribera €

Sit outside on the peaceful, traffic-free square and snack on reasonably priced tapas any time from breakfast until the early hours of the morning. Lunchtimes in particular can be busy; a daily special menu is supplemented by salads and pizzas.

✚ 204 C3 ⊠ Plaça de les Olles 6
☎ 9 33 19 50 72 🕐 Mon–Sat 8:30am–1am
🚇 Barceloneta

Bodega L'Electricitat €

Loud, crowded and cheerful – this authentic Barceloneta bodega has been going for over 100 years. Wine and vermouth are dispensed from large barrels and the fluorescent strip lighting in no way detracts from the atmosphere.

✚ 204 C1 ⊠ Carrer Sant Carles, 15
🕐 Tue–Sat 8–3, 7–11:30 🚇 Barceloneta

El Xampanyet €

This tiny bar is an essential stop on any cava and tapas trail. The decor of coloured tiles has changed little since the 1930s. Cava – the rosé is particularly popular – and cider are specialities, but the draught beers are also good. Tapas include superb anchovies and tortilla. It's often standing-room only and at busy times crowds spill out on to the street.

🗺 204 C3 ✉ Carrer Montcada 22
☎ 9 33 19 70 03 🕐 Tue–Sat noon–4, 6:30–11:30, Sun noon–4. Closed Aug 🚇 Jaume I

Where to...
Shop

La Ribera bursts with irresistible showrooms, galleries and traditional little shops. Fashion boutiques, a wide range of crafts and tempting food shops are the district's main specialities.

FASHION AND ACCESSORIES

Carrer dels Flassaders is lined with stunningly stylish fashion and jewellery boutiques catering to myriad tastes; Carrer del Rec and Espateria are similar. In the showroom **Coshop** (Banys Vells, 9, www.capipotaproductions.com, Metro: Jaume I) you can purchase creative, sustainable fashion, jewellery and other items from Catalan designers. As well as the small independent boutiques, three big home-grown names also have prominent showrooms on the lanes of El Born. Bold patterns and prints are the signature look at **Custo** (Plaça de les Olles 7, tel: 9 32 68 78 93; www.custo-barcelona.com, Metro: Jaume 1), while the deliberately clashing colourful garments of **Desigual** (Carrer de l'Argenteria 65,

tel: 9 33 10 30 15; www.desigual. com, Metro: Jaume I), another Barcelona brand, are in a big industrial-effect showroom. **Vialis** (Carrer de la Vidrieria 15, tel: 9 33 19 94 91; www.vialis.es, Metro: Jaume I) has a cult following for its women's leather shoes and unisex trainers.

FOOD AND WINE

The beautifully refurbished **Mercat Santa Caterina** is a lively neighbourhood focus with its wooden beams, natural light and superb produce (Avinguda Francesc Cambó 16, tel: 9 33 19 57 40; www.mercatsantacaterina.net, Metro: Jaume I). More low-key but still wonderfully stocked, **Barceloneta market** (Plaça de la Font 1, Metro: Barceloneta) is a natural stop for anyone putting together a picnic for the beach. The bread shop, **Baluard**, opposite at No 38 (tel: 9 32 21 12 08, Metro: Barceloneta) is renowned as one of the best bakeries in town.

Down the side of Santa Maria del Mar, **La Botifarreria** (Carrer de Santa Maria 4; www.labotifarreria. com, Metro: Jaume I) is the place in town to choose your best Catalan sausages in Barcelona. **La Ribera** (Plaça Comercial 11, tel: 9 33 19 52 06; www.laribera-sa.es, Metro: Jaume I) offers an eye-popping array of olives and salted cod, as well as top-class **conservas** or tins of anchovies, mussels and the like. Complement your purchases with a bottle of something from **Vila Viniteca** (Carrer dels Agullers 7, tel: 9 32 32 77 77; www.vilaviniteca.es, Metro: Jaume I), one the city's leading wine sellers.

And at the corner, at **Bubo** (Carrer de Caputxes 10, tel: 9 32 68 72 24; www.bubo.ws, Metro: Jaume I) you can admire the most wonderful confectionery masterpieces. Displayed in sleek surroundings, the delectable little

Insider Tip

sweets and cakes found here are an artistic high point. The charming 150-year-old grocery store **Casa Gispert** (Carrer Sombrerers 23, tel: 9 33 19 7535; www.casagispert. com, Metro: Jaume I) sells roasted hazelnuts, walnuts, almonds and pistachios by the sackful. Equally aromatic is **El Magnifico** (Carrer de l'Argenteria 64, tel: 9 33 19 60 81, Metro: Jaume I), where a magnificent range of coffee beans perfumes the air.

CRAFTS AND GIFTS

Galerie Mo-Art (Carrer Montcada 25, tel: 9 33 10 31 16, Metro: Jaume I) is a space where young artists and designers sell handmade pieces – an exquisite selection of sculptures, jewellery, textile art and other items. **Ici et Là** (Plaça de Santa María 2, tel: 9 32 68 11 67, Metro: Jaume I) specializes in accessories and decorative itemsby local designers and artists.

Ivo&Co (Carrer del Rec 20, tel: 9 32 68 33 31; www.ivoandco.com, Metro: Arc de Triomf) is a fun, beautifully laid out shop offering kitchenware and other colourful retro style must-haves.

Where to...
Go Out

The Passeig del Born in La Ribera and some of the surrounding streets are lined with bars and small clubs, but if you're after glitzier venues with international DJs and chill-out zones head – dressed to impress – to the Port Olímpic. In the twinned districts of Sant Pere and Santa Catalina, a hip bar scene has recently emerged. Especially around the historic market hall and the romantic old town square of Sant Pere, in the lanes around Carrer Carders and in the lively Carrer d'Allada Vermell. Here off-beat venues and trendy bars alternate with traditional taverns and authentic old corner bars.

SPORT AND LEISURE

At the **Base Nautica de la Mar Bella** (tel: 9 32 21 04 32, Metro: Selva de Mar), at the beach of the same name, you can hire windsurfing and snorkelling equipment and small craft, and learn to sail.

Treat yourself to a spa experience at the **Aire de Barcelona** (Passeig de Picasso 22, tel: 9 02 55 57 89; www.airedebarcelona.com, Metro: Arc de Triomf). You can submerge yourself in tubs of different types followed perhaps by a massage or another special treatment.

MUSIC

The **Palau de la Música Catalana** (► 78) may not have the world's best acoustics, but a concert in its extravagant auditorium is an unforgettable experience. Try to attend a performance by the amateur **Orfeó Català** choir, the institution for which it was originally built, or by its professional cousin, the **Cor de Cambra del Palau de la Música**, or chamber choir; one or the other gives a concert at least once a week during the season. The box office (tel: 90 24 42 882) is open Monday–Saturday 10–9, and one hour before Sunday concerts. Alternatively, try ordering tickets online through Servi-Caixa (► 42).

The **OBC** (National Catalan Orchestra) plays at the modern **L'Auditori** (Carrer Lepant 150, Metro: Marina). It seats 2,300 in the Sala Simfònica, while chamber music and recitals are given in the smaller **Sala Polivalente**. It is modern, not to say clinical, in style, and some conservative concertgoers have boycotted it,

La Ribera, Port Olímpic & Poblenou

but the programming is impressive. The box office (tel: 90 21 01 212; www.auditori.org) is open Mon–Sat 3–9. The splendid interior of **Santa Maria del Mar** (➤84) also makes a stunning setting for classical concerts. Check at the basilica for details of forthcoming events.

CINEMAS

The state-of-the-art **Icària Yelmo Cineplex** (Carrer Salvador Espriú 61, tel: 9 32 21 75 85/72 56; www.yelmocines.es, Metro: Ciutadella–Vila Olímpica) in the Olympic village houses 25 screens, many of which show English-language films. Half the films on average are blockbusters, but there's also a decent programme of independent cinema. It is one of the few cinemas in Barcelona with wheelchair access.

THEATRE

Performances at the government-sponsored **Teatre Nacional de Catalunya** (Plaça de les Arts 1, tel: 9 33 06 57 00; www.tnc.cat, Metro: Glòries) are mostly in Catalan, but for non-Catalan speakers dance performances are often staged too.

NIGHTCLUBS

Sant Pere and Santa Catalina are known for their great nightlife and selection of hip venues. Just around the corner from the Palau de la Música is **El Bitxo** (Verdager i Callis 9, tel: 93 2 68 17 09 Metro: Urquinaona) with candlelight, wine and tapas. Then there is the rather quirky **Bar Pasajes** (Sant Pare més Alt, 31–33, tel: 93 3 10 55 35 Metro: Urquinaona) squeezed into a narrow alleyway where drapers used to hawk their wares. The small but trendy bar **Lupara** (Plaça Santa Catalina, 2, Metro: Jaume I) has a terrace right near Santa Catalina market and is popular with the bohemian crowd.

El Born continues to be one of the heartlands of Barcelona nightlife. Try **Magic Rock 'n' Roll Club** (Passeig de Picasso 40, tel: 9 33 10 72 67, Metro: Barceloneta), a somewhat cramped club where the music – funky and up-to-the-minute – pulls in the crowds.

Astin (Carrer Abaixadors 9, tel: 9 33 00 00 90, Metro: Jaume I) is renowned for being at the vanguard of rock. If you need rest for your eardrums and fancy a refreshing cocktail, dive into one of the many bars along Passeig del Born: **Miramelindo** (at No 15), the best, or **Berimbau** and **Trípode** (both at No 17).

Diobar (Avinguda Marquès de l'Argentera 27, tel: 9 32 21 19 39) is a small funky basement soul club just round the corner opposite the Parc de la Ciutadella. **Le Kasbah** (Plaça de Pau Vila, at the back of the Palau de Mar, tel: 9 32 38 07 22; www.ottozutz.com, Metro: Barceloneta) starts with laid-back cocktails and hots up as the evening progresses.

While the plethora of flashy discos – some downright outrageous – in the Olympic village continue to thrive, interesting nightspots have sprung up in the Poblenou district. The gigantic **Razzmatazz**, for example (Carrer dels Almogávers 122, tel: 9 32 72 09 10, Metro: Marina) hosts national and international rock bands, with plenty of room in the converted factory space for all-night weekend dancing. Back near Port Olímpic, **Catwalk** (Carrer de Ramon Trias Fargas 2–4, tel: 9 32 21 61 61, Metro: Ciutadella-Vila Olimpica), throbs to house, funk, R&B, rap, techno and hip hop; or just chill out for a drink. Not far away on the beachfront, **Shôko** (Passeig Marítim de la Barceloneta 36, tel: 9 32 25 92 03; www.shoko.biz, Metro: Ciutadella–Vila Olímpica) has a glitzy crowd dancing the night away to a mixed soundtrack.

Insider Tip

98

L'Eixample & Gràcia

 **Little Treats**

Swinging Barcelona
There is dancing in the **Plaça de la Virreina**
(► 120) on the last Sunday of each month
in the morning – and anyone can join in.

Barcelona 48hours Open House
In October you can take a closer look at art
nouveau buildings or designer hotels – for
free (www.48hopenhousebarcelona.org).

Culture and culinary delights…
…come together at **Fundació Francisco Godía**
(► 122) and **Fundació Suñol** (► 124) and the
tapas bars of Carrer d'Enric Granados.

Getting Your Bearings

Spacious and orderly where the Old City is cramped and chaotic, the district of Eixample is home to Barcelona's prosperous middle classes. At its heart is the "Quadrat d'Or" (Golden Square), a core of elegant streets studded with the most architecturally important art nouveau wonders, two of them by architect Gaudí. A magical park and the world's most innovative cathedral are thrown in for good measure.

When the city expanded beyond its medieval walls in the 1850s, the new district, the Eixample, was laid out in a perfect chequerboard pattern of square blocks (*illes* or *manzanas*) separated by wide, tree-lined streets, ideal for gentle strolling. Its main thoroughfare, the Passeig de Gràcia, offers row upon row of smart restaurants and even smarter boutiques. The most impressive block on the Passeig de Gràcia, known as the Manzana de la Discordia, is a showcase for the three greatest Modernist architects, among them Gaudí.

As the avenue slopes towards Gràcia, a bohemian village stubbornly refusing to be swallowed up into the city proper, you pass another example of Gaudí's genius, Casa Milà. On the hillside above, away from the traffic, is Gaudí's fairy-tale Park Güell. Wending your way back into the Eixample, you can see the Sagrada Família, Gaudí's unfinished masterpiece and the city's most celebrated sight.

Gràcia retains a village-like atmosphere and its shady squares are the perfect place for a relaxed drink

**Colonnaded pathway at
Park Güell**

The Perfect Day

If you're not quite sure where to begin your travels, this itinerary recommends a practical and enjoyable day in the Eixample and Gràcia, taking in some of the best places to see. For more information see the main entries (➤ 104–125).

🕘 9:00am

Stop for an early-morning cup of coffee. Choose either the Bracafé (Carrer de Casp 2), for a robust *tallat* (a small coffee with milk), or Laie Llibreria-Café (Carrer de Pau Claris 85), for a delicious cappuccino.

🕘 9:30am

Stroll up the Passeig de Gràcia to the ⭐ **Manzana de la Discordia** (➤ 117). Three very different Modernist facades make up the block. Afterwards, spend an hour or so at the nearby **34 Fundació Antoni Tàpies** (➤ 123) or **33 Fundació Francisco Godia** (above, ➤ 122), depending on whether you like contemporary or traditional art.

🕘 11:30am

Continue your gentle ascent of the Passeig de Gràcia – the extraordinary Modernist bench-cum-lamp posts are perfect for resting on while you study the ⭐ **Casa Milà**, known as La Pedrera (➤ 114). Then go inside, enjoy the views from the rooftop (opposite), and visit the temporary art exhibition on the first floor, if it's to your taste.

🕘 1:00pm

Now it's time to think about lunch in the *barrio* of **32 Gràcia** (➤ 120), with its villagey atmosphere and simple eateries. To get there, keep going up the Passeig de Gràcia until it narrows to become Carrer Gran de Gràcia. Branch off into one of the neighbourhood's little squares, such as Plaça de la Vila de Gràcia or Plaça del Sol, where the *menú del dia* should give you energy for the afternoon.

Park Güell

Gràcia 32

Hospital de la Santa Creu i 37 Sant Pau

Fundació Suñol 36

Fundació Antoni Tàpies 34

Casa Milà 6

La Sagrada Família 2

Manzana de la Discordia 7

Museu Egipci 35

Fundació Francisco Godia 33

🕒 3:30pm

From Plaça de Lesseps, at the top of Carrer Gran de Gràcia, turn along the Travessera de

Dalt and follow the signs to ⭐**Park Güell** (➤ 111), up Avinguda del Santuari de Sant Josep de la Muntanya, and along Carrer d'Olot.

Allow at least an hour to explore the park in depth and take in the wonderful views.

🕒 5:30pm

Make your way back down to ⭐**La Sagrada Família** (➤ 104) in time to see it at its best – the panoramas from its towers are remarkable as the sun goes down. You can take a taxi or use public transport. For the latter, take the No 24 bus or metro to Diagonal station, and then continue on to the Sagrada Família by metro.

🕒 8:30pm

The Eixample has plenty to offer in the evening: dinner at a fashionable restaurant, cocktails at a designer bar, a movie at an art-house cinema or all-night dancing at a *the*-place-to-be-seen nightspot. Drinking in the views with a glass of cava on the rooftop of Casa Milà is a great option on summer weekends.

★2 La Sagrada Família

Part hermit's grotto, part futuristic tower of Babel, the Temple Expiatori de la Sagrada Família (Expiatory Temple of the Holy Family) has to be seen to be believed. Salvador Dalí found the cathedral's cigar-shaped turrets as sensual as a woman's skin, French film director Jean Cocteau called it an "idea-scraper" as opposed to a skyscraper, while English novelist George Orwell described it as one of the most hideous buildings he had ever set eyes upon.

A Life's Work

In 1883 the young Antoni Gaudí took over from the original architect, Francisco de Villar, who had planned a run-of-the-mill neo-Gothic pile. Gaudí, a fervent Catholic and iconoclastic young architect, had other ideas: he envisaged a "people's cathedral", a project more ambitious and original than anything hitherto conceived. He devoted the rest of his life to the cathedral's construction and was still working on the plans when he was run over by a tram in 1926. Almost a century later, his great project is still a long way from completion. Many locals and visitors feel that the cathedral should have been left alone when Gaudí died, while others are pleased that Gaudí's vision is continuing and evolving. The jury is still out.

The Passion Facade, the work of modern Catalan sculptor Josep Maria Subirachs, serves as the main entrance to the cathedral

Gaudí intended the interior of the cathedral to be "like a forest", an effect achieved by the columns in the central nave

Grand Plans

During Gaudí's lifetime, only the crypt, apse, Nativity Facade and one of the bell towers were completed. After his death, controversy raged over whether or not the work should continue. Since 1952 the Passion Facade has been added and there are now eight towers, clad in ceramic mosaics which spell out the Latin prayer *Sanctus, Sanctus, Sanctus, Hosanna in Excelsis* (Holy, Holy, Holy, Glory to God in the Highest). The plans include **four more spires** and a colossal central tower, 170m (560 feet) tall, representing Christ. Four domes at each corner will symbolize the Evangelists, and the **nave** will be filled in, making it probably the only cathedral to be built inside-out. Finally, the **west facade**, dedicated to the Celestial Glory, will be linked by a bridge across Carrer de Mallorca to an open atrium – once an entire block of houses has been demolished to make way for it.

Nativity Facade

For the best views of the Nativity Facade, the cathedral's *pièce de résistance*, do not enter the cathedral site but cross Carrer de la Marina to reach the small park in Plaça Gaudí. The **facade** is dedicated to the birth and early life of Christ. Its **three doorways** – representing Faith, Hope and Charity – resemble those of a Gothic cathedral that has melted in a furnace. They drip with detail, more like the natural excrescences of a cave than the ornaments of a church. Above the central Nativity scene, look out for the wingless angels with their elongated bronze trumpets; they are said to have been modelled on guardsmen practising near the cathedral site. High above the doorway and nestling between the towers is the **Tree of Life**, a green ceramic cypress studded with white doves. Beneath it is an equally striking white pelican feeding its young. At least 36 different birds and 30 species of plants have been identified in the mosaic of the facade.

Passion Facade

The entrance to the cathedral is at the opposite end of the site to the Nativity Facade, facing Plaça de la Sagrada Família. It leads straight to the Passion Facade, completed

Gaudí's Nativity Facade is dedicated to the birth and early life of Jesus

Subirachs's portrayal of Peter denying Jesus for the third time, to the right of the door on the Passion Facade

in 1990 by the modern Catalan sculptor Josep Maria Subirachs. The **towers** are built to Gaudí's design, but the **statues** below (which tell the story of Christ's Passion and death, from the Last Supper to the crucifixion) are angular and rigid in contrast to Gaudí's flowing, organic style. The facade has created much controversy, with some people likening the figures to characters from a science-fiction film. Many argue, though, that Gaudí would have approved and that he always intended the cathedral to be built by different generations in changing styles.

Inside the Church

Consecrated by the Pope in 2010, the monumental church interior impresses even those critical of the continuing construction. You can see some of the plans in the **cathedral museum**, which is situated in the crypt and reached from an entrance beside the Passion Facade. In one of the chapels, dedicated to Our Lady of Carmen, **Gaudí's tomb**, a simple slab, lies at the feet of a statue of Mary, inscribed pithily in Latin: *Antonius Gaudí Cornet, Reusensis* (from Reus, the town where he was born in 1852).

TAKING A BREAK

For great views of the Sagrada Família try any of the many **bars** and **pizzerias** with a terrace along Avinguda de Gaudí. None of them stands out, but you can feast your eyes on Gaudí's most celebrated building as you snack.

✚ 201 E5 ✉ Plaça de la Sagrada Família
☎ 9 32 07 30 31; www.sagradafamilia.cat
🕐 Apr–Sep daily 9–8; Oct–Mar 9–6
💶 Basilica: €14.80, Basilica and towers: €19,30
🚇 Sagrada Família

Gaudí's Legacy

The architect Antoni Gaudí estimated that it would take approximately 20 years to build the Sagrada Família. The model on the right shows a section of the nave that has since been roofed over.

❶ Cupolas and towers: It will be a few years before the central dome and the accompanying towers are completed. The central vaulted dome is intended to symbolise Christ; two towers represent the Virgin Mary and four the Evangelists.

❷ A forest of stone: The pillars that support the Sagrada Família in the interior resemble tree trunks that are divided into several branches.

❸ A manifestation become stone: It was Gaudí's wish that the interior of the Sagrada Familia always be illuminated at night so that the light could shine outwards through the open masonry – as a stone symbol of the words of Christ.

❹ Choral galleries: The galleries opposite each other are intended to be reserved for choirs.

❺ Gaudí's chain model: A hanging rope or chain represents the optimal force progression of an arch or dome; but, upside down. If the model is turned around,

you see the vaults, arches and tree structure of the Sagrada Família.

Sunlight floods through a stained glass window into the cathedral interior. The church was consecrated by Pope Benedict XVI in 2010 (above)

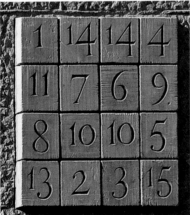

The numbers 12 and 16 are missing from the magic square (left) on the Passion facade but 10 and 14 are duplicated. The rows, columns and diagonals all produce the number 33, representing the age of Jesus Christ at the time of the crucifixion

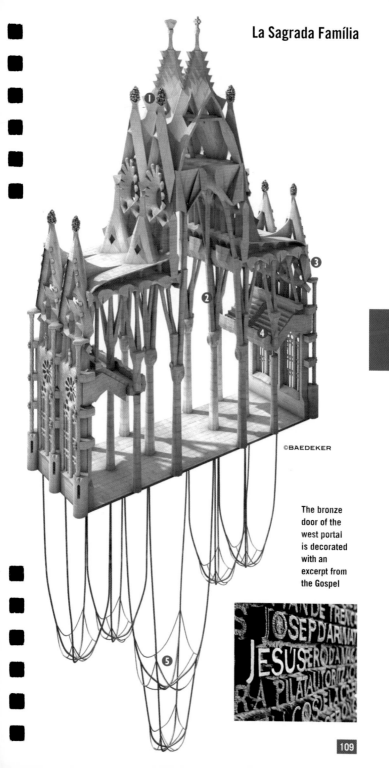

©BAEDEKER

The bronze
door of the
west portal
is decorated
with an
excerpt from
the Gospel

The towers
of the Passion
Facade are
built to
Gaudí's design

INSIDER INFO

- Do ⚡ **climb one of the towers,** either by lift or a long spiral staircase, for a close-up view of the spires. These multicoloured pinnacles have been compared to everything from hock bottles to billiard cues and are one of Barcelona's most emblematic sights.

- **Arrive early,** though, to have any chance of climbing the staircase in the Nativity Facade. Avoid the long queues by booking your tickets online.

- There are **two lifts,** one at either end of the building, though the views are better from the Nativity Facade.

- Don't forget to bring **binoculars** to get a better look at the finer detailing, especially the pinnacles of the spires.

- True to character, Gaudí slipped in hundreds of symbols and private jokes. Look at the base of the two main columns on the Nativity Facade; **a turtle** with flippers bears the seaward pillar and **a tortoise** with paws the landward one. **Chameleons,** among Gaudí's favourite creatures, can be seen carved in the stonework all over the cathedral.

Insider
Tip

⭐Park Güell

Built as part of an idealistic dream, Park Güell bristles with Gaudí's secretive symbolism and daring devices, a showcase for his inventiveness.

In 1900, Eusebi Güell, inspired by the garden cities that had sprung up in London's suburbs, commissioned Gaudí to work on a design for a new residential area away from the city centre. Güell's plan for an estate with recreational areas and 60 houses, the design of which was to be entrusted to other architects, was snubbed by wealthy locals. Only a couple of the proposed houses, including the one where Gaudí briefly lived (now the Casa Museu Gaudí), were ever built, leaving the park as an expensive ornament later bought by the city.

Inside the Walls

The 15ha (37-acre) park has several gates (the original intention was to have seven, like the ancient city of Thebes), but the most dramatic is the **main entrance** on Carrer d'Olot, most conveniently reached by buses 24 and 25. The tremendous iron railings of the gate are built to the same palm-leaf design as those at the Casa Vicens (▶ 121), and there are two fairy-tale **gatehouses** at the entrance: one is shaped like an elephant, with four thickset pillars for legs and a howdah of ceramic roof-tiles perched on top. One of its chimneys could be the elephant's trunk,

The wavy edge of the Sala Hipóstila's upper terrace forms a series of benches

L'Eixample & Gràcia

held upright, while another is modelled on a hallucinogenic toadstool, the fly agaric; other stacks are the spitting image of the morel, a delicacy in Catalonia.

Inside the gates, a **ceremonial staircase** leads up towards the **Sala Hipóstila**, the park's centrepiece. The brightly coloured, crenellated stairway is dominated by two colourful fountains: a salamander – symbolizing alchemy – dribbles water from its mouth while, above it, a bronze-horned serpent's head, representing the staff of Aesculapius, the Greek god of healing, leers out from the Catalan flag's red and yellow stripes. At the top of the staircase is a bench in the form of a tile-rimmed gaping mouth. Designed so that it is shady in the summer and sunny in the winter, it is the perfect place to stop and look down upon the park's incredible entrance.

Right: Gaudí's gurgling salamander fountain, an unmissable feature of the ceremonial staircase

Signs and Symbols

Gaudí intended the **Sala Hipóstila** to be the garden city's marketplace. Eighty-six Doric columns support the roof, which is decorated with four sun-shaped disks, composed of kaleidoscopic shards of tile, bits of bottle and fragments of stone, representing the four seasons. Encircling them are smaller circles representing the moon in various phases. Figures from Greek mythology, Christian emblems, Sanskrit script, Egyptian symbols and Old Testament characters are among the embellishments. Rainwater flows through the interior of the column into an underground water depot.

Forming a parapet around the edge of the open space above the marketplace are the distinctive **wavy benches**; their multicoloured curves form niches like theatre boxes, making a perfect spot to enjoy the fabulous views of the park and city stretching to the sea below.

Equally impressive is the labyrinth of **serpentine viaducts and porticoes** that hugs the wooded hills on which the park is built. The organic-looking columns holding them up are shaped like crinkly palm trunks or twisted-stemmed champagne glasses. Salvador Dalí once wrote: "At the Park Güell we entered grottoes through gates shaped like ox livers". He adored the surreal park and one of his favourite photographs of himself was taken in 1933 by the stupendous undulating bench. You'll want to follow suit.

Circular mosaics depicting the seasons decorate the roof of the Sala Hipóstila

TAKING A BREAK

The bar on the main terrace is an essential stop for a drink while you take in the fabulous view. For something more substantial it is worth taking a cab the short ride to **Can Travi Nou** (Carrer Jorge Manrique, tel: 9 34 28 03 01), an old Catalan farmhouse that is difficult to reach by public transport. Here you can enjoy traditional food in the shady garden or elegant interior: *mar i muntanya* dishes (meat and fish combined) are a speciality.

Insider Tip

➕ 201 off E5 ✉ Carrer d'Olot
🕐 25 Oct–23 Mar 8:30–6, 24 Mar–19 Oct 8am–9:30pm
Ⓜ Lesseps, Vallcarca 🚌 24

Casa Museu Gaudí
➕ 201 off E5 ✉ Park Güell, Carreterra del Carmel
☎ 9 32 19 38 11; www.casamuseugaudi.org
🕐 Apr–Sep daily 10–8, Oct–Mar 10–6 🎫 €5.50

INSIDER INFO

- **Avoid Sunday afternoons and public holidays**, when the park is jam-packed.
- Views from the park are superb, so try to go on a **clear day**.
- The park is hard work for anyone with **mobility problems** – there are lots of steps and it's very steep.
- The **Capelya**, part Mallorcan watchtower, part Druids' shrine, is a typical Gaudíesque folly. It lies slightly off the beaten track, to the left from the main entrance. You can't go inside but it's worth taking a look.

In more depth Unless you are a Gaudí fan or have plenty of time, don't bother with the **Casa Museu Gaudí**. It houses some Gaudí memorabilia and a few examples of his own furniture.

⭐6 Casa Milà

This other-worldly apartment block designed by Gaudí is officially called the Casa Milà, after the dilettante politician Pere Milà, who commissioned it nearly a century ago. More commonly known as La Pedrera (the Quarry), it has become one of the icons of the city.

The undulating forms of La Pedrera's cliff-like silhouette dominate a corner of the elegant Passeig de Gràcia. The strange but beguiling exterior, remarkable for its creamy limestone curves, tangled wrought-iron balconies and spider's-web main doorway, caused much controversy when it was completed in 1912. The building was described variously as a petrified aquarium, a hangar for airships and even an earthquake preserved in sculpture. In the 1920s, French president Georges Clemenceau was said to have been so disturbed by the sight of the building that he cut short a lecture tour of the city; back in Paris he was quoted as claiming that in Barcelona they were building homes for dragons.

The apartment block was one of Gaudí's final works before he dedicated himself to La Sagrada Família (▶ 104), and its sleek lines, smooth surfaces and curvaceous forms go beyond pure Modernisme. It is a triumph of aesthetics over practicality. When one of the tenants complained that it was hard to fit a piano into

At night, Casa Milà's exterior is beautifully lit: a sight not to be missed

the curved rooms, Gaudí is reputed to have advised them to take up the violin instead. The building was also far bigger than had originally been envisaged. Barcelona City Council ordered Milà to knock down the top floor or pay a 100,000-peseta fine, a sum now roughly equivalent to a million dollars. Milà could not afford to pay the fine but was let off the hook; the city authorities eventually caved in, acknowledging that the building was a work of art. In 1984, UNESCO declared it a World Heritage Site – it was the first 20th-century building to be awarded this honour.

Exhibitions and the Roof

On the first floor, reached from the entrance on Passeig de Gràcia 92, excellent **temporary art exhibitions** are run by the CatalunyaCaixa savings bank (entrance is free). The staircase rises from one of the fabulous inner court-yards, with its grotto-like decoration.

Insider Tip

The other entrance, at Carrer de Provença 261–5, takes you to the **Espai Gaudí**, an exhibition about the origins of Casa Milà with a film, a reconstruction of a 1920s apartment and explanations of the architecture. From here, stairs lead to the fantastic brick-lined **attic**, with its labyrinth of elegant parabolic arches. Here you can see an interesting display of models of Gaudí buildings. The grand finale to any visit, however, is step-

Even the roof terrace design reflects Gaudí's committment to Modernisme

ping out onto the wonderful undulating **roof** (reached from the attic), with its forest of shard-encrusted chimney stacks. The vistas of the city from here are breathtaking.

Originally, a huge statue of the Virgin Mary was to have perched on the top of the building but this idea was vetoed by Milà, who was wary of attracting

anti-religious attacks by the Anarchists then dangerously active in the city.

Sleek lines and curved forms characterize the interior

TAKING A BREAK

La Bodegueta (Rambla de Catalunya 100, tel: 9 32 15 48 94) serves some of the best tapas and wines in the neighbourhood as well as cava by the glass. Ham, charcuterie, cheese and *pa amb tomàquet* (➤ 39) are all excellent and prices are reasonable. You may find you have to eat standing up as it is always crowded.

➕ 200 B3
✉ Passeig de Gràcia 92 and Carrer de Provença 261–265
☎ 9 02 40 09 73; www.lapedrera.com
🕐 Mar–Oct daily 10–8; Nov–Feb 9–6:30 💶 €16.50
🚇 Diagonal, Passeig de Gràcia

INSIDER INFO

- The **temporary art exhibitions** run by the CatalunyaCaixa on the first floor are free.
- **One ticket** purchased at the Carrer de Provença 261–5 entrance includes the Espai Gaudí, the attic and the roof.
- It is worth coming back to **see the building at night**, when it is beautifully lit.
- During the summer (Fri, Sat 9pm–midnight) you can lounge on the **tiled steps of the amazing rooftop** while sipping a glass of ice-cold cava.
- Some of the **original furniture** from Casa Milà is on display at the Museu Nacional d'Art de Catalunya (MNAC, ➤ 136).

⭐ Manzana de la Discordia

Casa Lleó Morera, Casa Amatller and Casa Batlló stand almost side-by-side in a single block on the Passeig de Gràcia, forming one of the most famous architectural ensembles in Barcelona. Built by three leading Modernist rivals, the houses are wildly disparate in style – hence the name.

A riot of detail, Casa Lleó Morera was the work of architect Lluís Domènech i Montaner

Casa Lleó Morera

At the corner of Carrer del Consell de Cent (Passeig de Gràcia 35) is Casa Lleó Morera, Lluís Domènech i Montaner's 1905 ornate remodelling of an existing building, commissioned by Albert Lleó i Morera. The stone carvings on the **facade** reveal infinite symbolism, but the lion *(lleó)* and mulberry tree *(morera)* and its leaves are recurring themes. The **main entrance** on the side street is decorated with exquisite green ceramics and, inside the **circular oriel** at the corner, is a marble column – in fact only the visible section is marble: the rest is of cheaper stone. The building is closed to the public.

Casa Amatller

Undergoing restoration until late 2012, Casa Amatller at No 41, built in 1900, predates Casa Lleó Morera by five years; its architect Josep Puig i Cadafalch took quite a

different approach. He attempted to create for his client, Antoni Amatller, a fanciful version of a Dutch or Flemish step-gabled house. He threw in fashionable Gothic details, such as gargoyles, twisted columns and coats of arms carved in stone, plus a fake marble column

The facade of Casa Amatller is decorated with sgraffito decoration, ceramics and symbolic carvings

later copied in the Casa Lleó Morera. Catalonia's nationalism is symbolized by a carving of *St George slaying a dragon*, clinging to a column by the medieval-looking doors. The subtle **sgraffito decoration** (made on wet plaster to show a different surface underneath) on the main facade is set off by extravagant ceramic motifs. The windows and shape of the house itself form stylized letter As, which were Antoni Amatller's initials.

Casa Batlló

Finally, you come to Casa Batlló, one of the city's Modernist gems. The awe-inspiring building was designed by Gaudí for the textile industrialist Josep Batlló i Casanovas. The design deliberately clashes with that of other buildings in the block, jutting out several metres above them, and when it was built in 1907 it exceeded the official height limit in the area.

The **exterior** illustrates the legend of St George (Catalonia's patron saint). The blue-and-green ceramic cladding on the walls is reminiscent of a dragon's scaly skin, the curved roof-top its crested back, the balcony railings and pillars the bones of its victims – earning it the nickname the House of Bones.

In the **interior**, you can admire more undulating forms – the mushroom-shaped fireplace is a marvel. Telephone-style audio guides (in several languages) are included in the price, though the cascade of excited superlatives can become tiresome.

BLOCK OF DISCORD

The name Manzana de la Discordia is a clever play on words. Manzana means both "block" and "apple" in Spanish, so the name means both Block of Discord and Apple of Discord (a reference to Greek mythology).

The play on words doesn't translate well into Catalan as the words for block and apple differ. In Barcelona you may see references to the Illa de la Discordia – the official Catalan name.

Detail of Gaudí's Casa Batlló, a building which has been dubbed the House of Bones

The elliptically arched attics and the **roofs**, adorned with multicoloured, tile-coated chimney stacks, are usually included in the visit. For a bigger fee, you can enjoy a drink and live music on the rooftop on summer evenings (mid-Jun to early Sep Wed–Sun 9pm–midnight).

TAKING A BREAK

Cervecería Catalana (➤ 126) is one of the best tapas restaurants in the area.

🔁 200 B2 ✉ Passeig de Gràcia 35–45
🚇 Passeig de Gràcia 🅱 Casa Lleó Morera closed to the public

Casa Amatller
☎ 9 34 96 12 45; www.amatller.org
🕐 Mon–Sat 10am–3pm;
closed for renovations due to be completed in Jan 2015.

Casa Batlló
☎ 9 32 16 03 06; www.casabatllo.es
🕐 Daily 9–8 💶 €20.35. Tickets available online or at the ticket office

INSIDER TIP

- **Avoid high noon on sunny days** – you'll be blinded by the sun when trying to take in the detail of the buildings.
- The **Ruta del Modernisme** (www.rutadelmodernisme.com), with offices at the main tourist information office (➤ 35; Plaça de Catalunya), arranges tours of the Manzana.
- Take time to admire the **lift in the Casa Batlló** – another Modernist wonder in shiny wood.

Insider Tip

㉜ Gràcia

Gràcia is Barcelona's bohemian quarter; artists, writers and students have long been drawn to its narrow streets and shady squares. Once a separate township with a reputation for radical politics, it has even been known to declare itself an independent republic. Although Gràcia has seen gentrification in recent years, it remains a place apart, with low-rise buildings and a villagey feel that contrasts sharply with the grid plan of the Eixample.

Gràcia is above all a place for strolling, pausing to shop at local markets or to absorb the atmosphere of the lively little squares. It begins at the top of Passeig de Gràcia, just beyond Avinguda Diagonal. This is where you will find **Casa Fuster**, a Modernist apartment block built by Lluís Domènech i Montaner and his son Pere; it has a Venetian-style white marble facade and now functions as a five-star hotel. There are more Modernist houses as you continue up the hill along the main street of the district, Carrer Gran de Gràcia.

Gràcia's Plaças

Carrer Moya to your right leads to **Plaça de la Vila de Gràcia**, Gràcia's unofficial heart. The square is popularly known as Plaça del Rellotge, after the attractive mid-19th-century clock tower that dominates the square. During the 19th century the tower was a symbol of liberty and a rallying point for revolutionary demonstrations. The former town hall nearby is a reminder that Gràcia was Spain's ninth largest city until it was annexed by Barcelona in 1897.

Across Travessera de Gràcia, **Plaça del Sol** is another typically lively, friendly plaça, successfully remodelled in the 1980s. There are several bars and nightspots. One of the prettiest squares is the **Plaça de la Virreina** with a small church and terrace cafes.

Insider Tip

Plaça del Sol is a lively place to stop for a drink

The Moorish-style Casa Vicens was one of Gaudí's first commissions in the city

Not far from here, reached across Carrer Gran de Gràcia, is **Mercat de la Llibertat** (1893), a magnificent Modernist market hall designed by Gaudí's assistant Francesc Berenguer.

Casa Vicens

Gràcia's most celebrated sight, **Casa Vicens** (Carrer de les Carolines 24), is situated a little way up the main street. It was one of Gaudí's first commissions in Barcelona, built between 1883 and 1888 as a summer house for the tile manufacturer Manuel Vicens. When Gaudí first visited the site, he found a yellow zinnia flower and adopted it as the motif for the thousands of tiles that clad the exterior of the Moorish-style building. A palm leaf, also discovered on the ground, inspired the fantastic iron railings that fence in the courtyard (and which were also used to great effect in Park Güell). The house is now privately owned and the interior cannot be visited, though you may be able to peek through the windows at the lavish smoking room.

TAKING A BREAK

The food is as no-nonsense as the formica-and-leatherette decor at the extremely popular **Envalira** (Plaça del Sol 13, tel: 9 32 18 58 13. Closed Aug and Mon, Sun evening). Fish and seafood cooked to Catalan, Basque and Galician recipes loom large on the reassuringly predictable menu. The generous portions of rice-based dishes come highly recommended, as do the salads and sausages. Prices are moderate and service brisk.

■ 200 C4
◎ Fontana, Joanic

INSIDER INFO

- If you want an itinerary to see the Highlights of Gràcia, follow our walk through the quarter (➤ 179).
- The ⚄ **Festa Gran de Gràcia**, a week-long festival, starts on 15 August. The streets are decked out with thematic decorations and Graciencs party the night away. The opening ceremony is a colourful and noisy spectacle of *castells* (where young men stand on each other's shoulders to create a human tower), giants and other traditional Catalan festivities.

At Your Leisure

Above: Tàpies's *Nuvol i Cadira* crowns the Fundació Antoni Tàpies; below: The splendid staircase at the Fundació Francisco Godia

🔢 Fundació Francisco Godia

Housed in Casa Garriga Nogués, a fine refurbished Eixample mansion, the Fundació is a small gem. Francisco Godia (1921–90), a local playboy as well as a Formula One racing driver, thought "driving fast was the most beautiful thing in the world", but he also had a keen eye for paintings and sculpture. The result is this impeccably displayed collection.

On the ground floor there is a short video about the man dubbed "Paco, the Gentleman Driver", as well as a collection of memorabilia, including cups and his driving gloves, plus a collection of paintings to whet your appetite.

Exhibits upstairs are arranged chronologically, beginning with Romanesque religious sculptures and spanning the centuries with works by Zurbarán, Rusiñol and Picasso, plus many more. The 15th-century Islamic-influenced plates from Manises, near Valencia, dominate the cabinet of Spanish

ceramics, while outside on the terrace stands a tantalizing work by contemporary sculptor Cristina Iglesias.

🔢 200 B2 ✉ Carrer de la Diputació 250
☎ 9 32 72 31 80; www.fundacionfgodia.org
🕐 Wed–Mon 10–8, Sun 10–3.
Guided visits noon Sat and Sun
💶 €5.50 Ⓜ Passeig de Gràcia, Catalunya

FIVE BEAUTIFUL MODERNIST DOORWAYS *Insider Tip*

- **Casa Comalat** at Avinguda Diagonal 442 (corner of Carrer de Còrsega).
- **Casa Jaume Forn** at Carrer de Roger de Llúria 52 (corner of Carrer de València).
- **Casa Ramon Casas** at Passeig de Gràcia 96.
- **Farmàcia Bolós** at Rambla de Catalunya 77 (corner of Carrer de València).
- **Farmàcia Puigoriol** at Carrer de Mallorca 312.

34 Fundació Antoni Tàpies

This wonderful red-brick building, built for the Montaner i Simon publishing house in the 1880s by Modernist master Lluís Domènech i Montaner, houses the contemporary art foundation set up by Barcelona-born artist Antoni Tàpies. The ornate facade is crowned by one of his sculptures, *Nuvol i Cadira* (Cloud and Chair), which looks as though he went berserk with a tonne of barbed wire. Inside, the immaculate galleries are hung either with Tàpies's own paintings – he has dominated Catalan art ever since Miró's death – or temporary exhibitions of guest artists. Tàpies

The collection at the Museu Egipci spans some 4,000 years of Egyptian history

himself favours huge canvases, mostly painted in earthy colours.

🚹 200 B3
✉ Carrer d'Aragó 255
☎ 9 34 87 03 15; www.fundaciotapies.org
🕐 Tue–Sun 10–7
🎫 €7 🚇 Passeig de Gràcia

35 🚻 Museu Egipci

The treasures at Spain's only museum devoted to Egyptian art span more than 4,000 years, from simple Predynastic vases to the striking *Golden Lady*, a stucco-and-gold-leaf artefact dating from Roman times. Statuettes are the privately owned museum's forte, made of a variety of materials including wood, bronze and limestone. They depict a pantheon of deities and sacred mammals and birds such as jackals, ibises and baboons. The mummy collection features cats, falcons

Stone hieroglyphs at the Museu Egipci

and a baby crocodile as well as humans, while a set of wooden and terracotta funerary masks and sarcophagi will no doubt catch your eye. Among the gorgeous jewellery on show, the fabulous golden head of Osiris stands out – a bronze statue of the same goddess is equally remarkable.

The museum has an excellent shop, a bright terrace cafe and interesting temporary exhibits. The host of activities it organizes include evening animations in which costumed actors bring the whole place to life.

➕ 200 C3
✉ Carrer de València 284
☎ 9 34 88 01 88; www.museuegipci.com
🕐 Mon–Sat 10–8, Sun 10–2.
Tours only in Spanish
💶 €11
🚇 Passeig de Gràcia

🔢 A CHANGE OF TEMPO...

...in the centre of several Eixample blocks, including the small **playground** at Carrer d'Aragó 299 or **Torre de les Aigües**, Carrer de Roger de Lluria 56 (which becomes an urban beach in the summer holidays; open daily 10–8).

36 Fundació Suñol

Catalan businessman Josep Suñol's contemporary art collection is shown in rotation at this relatively new gallery. Housed in the sleek lines of a refurbished Eixample apartment, the beautifully presented collection changes twice a year. It includes modern works from a range of artists from Dalí to Sean Scully, Giacometti to Anthony Caro, with a slight Spanish/Catalan bias. The spaces are thoughtfully curated, juxtaposing colours or themes rather than using a simple chronological order. Downstairs with a small outside courtyard there is a double-height space dedicated to promoting new artists and showing unusual works. From the terrace and courtyard you get a wonderful view of the more private face of the surrounding apartment blocks.

➕ 200B3
✉ Passeig de Gràcia 9 ☎ 9 34 96 10 32; www.fundaciosunol.org 🕐 Mon–Fri 11–2, 4–8, Sat 4–8
💶 €4 🚇 Diagonal

37 Hospital de la Santa Creu i Sant Pau

Definitely in the running for the world's most beautiful hospital, this marvellous garden-city infirmary was begun by Lluís Domènech i Montaner in 1901 and was eventually completed

The chapel-like entrance of the Hospital de la Santa Creu i Sant Pau

by his son Pere in 1930. The concept behind the design was that hospitals could be functional without being depressing or uncomfortable. It replaced the Antic Hospital de la Santa Creu in El Raval, where Gaudí died in 1926. Each of the 30-odd mosaic-covered pavilions is unique in design and designated as a specialist ward. The main reception building is a masterpiece of stone, ceramics and stained glass; wander around the park, admiring the Modernist craftsmanship and incredible detail.

Since the hospital doesn't meet the requirements of 21st-century medicine, departments are gradually being relocated to a new building. However, given its UNESCO World Heritage Site status, the building's future is guaranteed. Once refurbished it will become the headquarters of the International Centre of the Mediterranean.

➕ 201 off F4
✉ **Carrer de Sant Antoni Maria Claret 167**
☎ **9 32 91 90 00; www.visitsantpau.com**
🕐 **Guided tours daily 10, 11, noon and 1 (English) and 10:30 (French and Spanish)**
💶 **Guided tours: €10** 🚇 **Hospital de Sant Pau**

OFF THE BEATEN TRACK

A luxuriant cypress maze, with a statue of Eros at its centre (above), is the central element of romantic **Parc del Laberint**, tucked away in the northwestern Horta district of the city. Begun at the end of the 18th century by the eccentric Marquis of Llúpia, the park was designed to symbolize the game of frivolous love. The crumbling neo-Mozarabic mansion, an unusual moss garden, a romantic canal with a rustic bridge, and a magnificent panorama of the city add to the appeal of the gardens.

➕ 201, off E5 ✉ **Carrer del Germans Desvalls** ✉ **Daily 10–dusk**
💶 **€2.20. Free on Wed and Sun** 🚇 **Mundet** 🚌 **27, 60, 73, 76**

Where to...
Eat and Drink

Prices
Expect to pay per person for a three-course meal, excluding drinks:
€ under €25   €€ €25–€50   €€€ over €50

Botafumeiro €€€
Mariscos are an unforgettable experience at this legendary and madly expensive old-school Galician seafood restaurant. Plate after plate of the best shellfish in Spain are placed before you by the white-jacketed staff, who wait on tables both in the bar and in the series of elegant dining rooms to the rear. Patronized by the international business community and by Spanish royalty, the establishment prides itself on the quality and freshness of its fish and seafood, much of which is flown in daily from Galicia and stored live in holding tanks near the restaurant's entrance. There is a lengthy list of fish dishes on the menu, plus a few token meat dishes.
✚ 200 B5 ✉ Carrer Gran de Gràcia 81
☎ 9 32 18 42 30; www.botafumeiro.es
🕐 Daily noon–1:30am. Closed three weeks in Aug 🚇 Fontana

Cervecería Catalana €€
Enjoy a tasty selection of tapas in this popular corner bar – they also serve *montaditos,* warm bite-sized sandwiches – and if you are lucky, you might even get one of the rare outside spots.
✚ 200 B3 ✉ Carrer de Mallorca 236
☎ 9 32 16 03 68 🕐 Daily 8–1:30am
🚇 Passeig de Gràcia

Flash Flash €
Students of 1960s design will be in their element at Barcelona's pioneer designer bar. The decor is still all-white with leatherette booths and curvaceous corners. Tortillas (omelettes) are the house speciality, available in more than 50 varieties, savoury and sweet. A choice of burgers, salads and sandwiches completes the menu.
✚ 200 B4 ✉ Carrer de la Granada del Penedès 25 ☎ 9 32 37 09 90; www.flashflashbarcelona.com
🕐 Daily 1:30pm–1:30am 🚇 Diagonal

Gat Blau €/€€
A very pleasant restaurant serving meals made with organic ingredients – the young team place a lot of importance on using locally sourced produce – and is part of the Slow Food movement. The seasonal dishes are simple but varied and delicious. Daily lunch menu.
✚ 199 E2 ✉ Consell de Cent 139
☎ 9 33 25 61 99; www.gatblau.com
🕐 Tue–Sat 1–4 and Thu–Sat 9–11 🚇 Rocafort

Hàbaluc €€
Vegetarians and meat lovers can sit down together and enjoy some creative Catalan cuisine. Everything is tasty and healthy, from the salad with fresh figs through to the organic veal carpaccio with mango and Parmesan. Relaxed atmosphere, tranquil terrace.
✚ 200 A3 ✉ Carrer Enric Granados 41,
☎ 9 34 52 29 28; http://restaurantehabaluc.com
🕐 Daily 8–1am 🚇 Diagonal

Moments €€€
Come here to indulge in some innovative, Michelin-starred cuisine. The menu has a selection of sublime dishes created by Carme Ruscalleda – the only female chef in the world with a total of five

Michelin stars – and her son Raul Balám. Using seasonal and regional produce they put their own spin on traditional local dishes. The restaurant is exclusive and stylish. There is a lunch menu Tue–Fri.

➕ 200 B2 ✉ Passeig de Gràcia 38–40, ☎ 9 31 51 87 81, www.mandarinoriental.es, 🕐 Tue–Sat 1:30–3:30, 8:30–11:30. Closed in Aug 🚇 Passeig de Gràcia

Roig Robí €€€

Mercè Navarro is not just one of Barcelona's few women chefs, and a self-taught one at that, she is one of the best in a city. She serves imaginative food in a pair of flower-filled dining rooms. In summer, the glass doors open onto a shady courtyard, a perfect place for outdoor eating. Writers, artists and politicians are among the regulars who come to eat seasonal, market-fresh dishes such as lobster with rice and chicken, stuffed with foie gras.

➕ 200 B4 ✉ Carrer Sèneca 20 ☎ 9 32 18 92 22; www.roigrobi.com 🕐 Mon–Fri 1:30–4, 8:30–11:30, Sat, Sun 8:30–11:30pm 🚇 Diagonal

Tapas 24 €€

This venture by Carles Abellan, one of Barcelona's many Michelin-starred chefs, addresses the poor quality of tapas in so many of Barcelona's bars. Tapas 24 serves mouth-watering traditional tapas and seafood alongside playful takes on bistro favourites, including his signature ham-and-cheese toastie. The cool decor and open kitchen are complemented by friendly, helpful service.

➕ 200 C2 ✉ Carrer de la Diputació 269 ☎ 9 34 88 09 77; www.carlesabellan.com 🕐 Mon–Sat 9am–midnight 🚇 Passeig de Gràcia

BARS AND CAFES

Bar Calders €

Modern version of a traditional bodega, they serve authentic Catalan vermouth, snacks and tapas. The pavement terrace is very popular.

➕ 199 E1 ✉ Carrer del Parlament 25 ☎ 9 33 29 93 49 🕐 Mon–Fri 5pm–2am, Sat 11am–2:30am, Sun 11am–0:30 🚇 Sant Antoni

Dry Martini €

Pull up a stool at the bar or sink into one of the comfy leather couches at this world-renowned cocktail bar and let the friendly staff serve up a Martini in one of the myriad versions, or request any other cocktail that takes your fancy. The relaxed contemporary soundtrack mixes well with the traditional decor.

➕ 200 A4 ✉ Carrer d'Aribau 162–166 ☎ 9 32 17 50 72 🕐 Mon–Fri 1pm–2:30am, Sat–Sun 6:30pm–2:30am 🚇 Hospital Clinic

La Gran Bodega €

At this inexpensive, popular tapas bar you can enjoy a range of tempting traditional tapas. Test your hand-eye coordination by drinking from the *porrón*, a glass jug with a long spout, which (if you are lucky or if your aim is good) pours the wine down your throat.

➕ 200 A3 ✉ Carrer de València 193 ☎ 9 34 53 10 53 🕐 Daily 8:30am–1am 🚇 Passeig de Gràcia

Laie Llibreria Café €

This casual cafe was Barcelona's first literary cafe (► 128); a great place to sit and read or enjoy some cake, coffee or their daily lunch menu. In fine weather you can sit on the veranda.

➕ 200 C2 ✉ Carrer de Pau Claris 85 ☎ 9 33 02 73 10 🕐 Mon–Fri 9–9, Sat 10–9 🚇 Urquinaona

La Valenciana €

This famous *orxateria* and *torroneria* (nougat shop) is one of the few places left which serves *orxata*, a cold drink made with crushed tiger nuts. Choose from a selection of light snacks, then indulge in excellent home-made ice creams.

➕ 200 A4 ✉ Carrer d'Aribau 16 bis ☎ 9 33 17 27 71 🕐 Mon–Sun 8:30am–10:30pm, Fri–Sat 9am–2am. Opening times may vary 🚇 Universitat

Where to...
Shop

The Eixample – in particular the Passeig de Gràcia, and the Rambla de Catalunya, running parallel to it – is *the* place to come for a truly extravagant shopping session. International designer showrooms stand beside pavement cafes along the Passeig de Gràcia, while the leafy Rambla de Catalunya retains some of its older specialist shops. The bohemian Gràcia neighbourhood is full of small, multicultural, offbeat shops and designers selling organic and sustainable wares. For those looking for a bargain, the outlet stores in the streets east the Passeig de Gràcia – especially around Carrer Girona south of Gran Via de les Corts Catalanes – sell good-quality clothing at discounted prices.

FASHION AND ACCESSORIES

The Passeig de Gràcia is lined with all the big names in international fashion; the further towards Avinguda Diagonal you go, the smarter things get. High-street stores like Zara, Mango and H&M are located at the bottom reaches near Plaça de Catalunya, while Hermès, Jimmy Choo, Chanel and their ilk are several blocks to the north. Some of the shops are located in stunning Modernista buildings: note particularly **Bagués**, the art nouveau jewellers in Casa Amatller at Passeig de Gràcia 41 (tel: 9 32 16 01 73; www.bagues.com, Metro: Passeig de Gràcia).

Halfway up Passeig de Gràcia at numbers 55 to 57, **Bulevard Rosa** (tel: 9 32 15 83 31, Metro: Passeig de Gràcia), is a warren of smart little shops selling everything from baptismal outfits to one-off silver-

ware, handmade chocolates to stylish bikinis.

Trendy **Camper** shoes are now popular around the world, but in Barcelona you can still them slightly cheaper (Carrer València, 249, Metro: Passeig de Gràcia; El Triangle shopping complex, Plaça Catalunya). Save up to half price on shoes at the outlet store of the renowned Catalan shoe chain **Casas** (Gran de Gràcia, 239, Metro: Lesseps), they sell both their own models as well as brands such as Moschino and Miss Sixty. Those who prefer to browse in little boutiques rather than shopping for famous labels should head for the area around the Travessera de Gracia, the Gran de Gràcia and the lively squares in the Gracia neighbourhood.

The rows and rows of mismatched stock at discounted prices at **Mango** (Carrer de Girona 37, tel: 9 34 12 29 35, Metro: Tetuan, Girona) and **Desigual** (Carrer de la Diputació 323, tel: 9 32 72 00 66, Metro: Girona) are popular hunting grounds for many shoppers.

BOOKS

If you fancy reading more about Barcelona, try the comprehensive travel bookstore **Altaïr** (Gran Via de les Corts Catalanes 616, tel: 9 33 42 71 71, Metro: Universitat, until 9pm). All manner of publications are sold alongside records and endless cups of cappuccino at **Laie Llibreria** (➤ 127). The store stays open until 1am and sometimes hosts evening jazz sessions. Seek out the other browser-friendly branch at the CCCB (➤ 64).

Casa del Libro (Passeig de Gràcia 62, tel: 9 32 72 34 80, Metro: Passeig de Gràcia) is a huge multi-floored bookshop selling some English-language titles, especially guidebooks.

In the **Bulevard dels Antiquaris**, a cavernous mall (Passeig de Gràcia

Insider Tip

55, www.bulevarddelsantiquaris. com, Metro: Passeig de Gràcia), you'll find everything from stylish art nouveau furniture to shimmering crystal chandeliers.

FURNITURE AND DESIGN

For all those even vaguely interested in design, **Vinçon** (Passeig de Gràcia 96, tel: 9 32 15 60 50; www.vincon.com, Metro: Passeig de Gràcia) is an essential stop. Inside this splendid Modernista building you'll find contemporary classics beside fair-priced designer homeware and furniture, plus a well-chosen seasonal range of gadgets and decorative items.

Bd Ediciones de Diseño (Carrer de Mallorca 29, tel: 9 34 58 69 09; www.bdbarcelona.com, Metro: Passeig de Gràcia, Diagonal, Provença) is a classic of Barcelona contemporary design housed in a fabulous building by Domènech i Montaner.

FOOD AND DRINK

Colmado Quílez (Rambla de Catalunya 63, tel: 9 32 15 23 56, Metro: Passeig de Gràcia) is a fabulous grocer. If you are buying food for a picnic, come here for wine, ham and cheese.

The charming art nouveau **Queviures Murria** stocks delicacies such as oils, hams, cheeses and their own cava (Roger de Llúria, 85, www.murria.cat, Metro: Passeig de Gràcia).

Equally luxurious are the delicatessen, cakes and ice-creams tempting you at **Pastisseria Maurí** (Rambla de Catalunya 102, tel: 9 32 15 10 20, Metro: Diagonal, Provença).

Last but not least, **Vinus & Brindis** (Carrer del Torrent de l'Olla 147, tel: 9 32 18 30 37, Metro: Fontana) is the place to go for friendly, knowledgeable advice on Catalan and other Spanish wines.

Where to...
Go Out

While some of the legendary designer bars in Eixample are now passé, the nightlife here (despite its outwardly staid appearance) still has a lot to offer. This is where the city's vibrant gay scene is focused, especially around the Carrer Consell de Cent (between Muntaner and Casanova). There are so many gay venues here that Eixample has been dubbed "Gayxample". For the latest information about what's on, check out *Nois* magazine (www.revista nois.com), available at any of the kiosks along the Ramblas. In the evenings the Gràcia district, with its small bars, pavement cafes and simple eateries is characterized by a more offbeat and multicultural atmosphere.

NIGHTCLUBS

For nearly three decades the Kiosko General de Barcelona, **KGB**, (Carrer Alegre de Dalt, 55, tel: 93 2 10 59 09, http://sala-kgb.com, Thu–Sat, Metro: Joanic) has held on to its reputation as one of the hottest clubbing venues. Housed in a converted warehouse, the club regularly hosts DJ sessions and live concerts.

A hip, perennial favourite is the **Otto Zutz Club** (Carrer Lincoln, 15, www.ottozutz.com, Wed–Sat, Metro: Fontana) which spans three floors of an old converted factory. The club is well known for its DJ sessions featuring house, hip hop and R&B music.

If Cuban's more your thing, try **Antilla BCN**. In fact you'll find merengue and salsa, too, and other Latin beats, with some free tuition thrown in.

A big name in Eixample night-life is **Luz de Gas** (Carrer de Muntaner 246, tel: 9 32 09 77 11, buses: 6, 7, 15, 58, 64, NitBus 8). This club is set in a grand theatre where the music varies according to the night. Whatever the night it's where the beautiful people hang out. It is also a venue for live concerts.

The very central **City Hall** (Rambla de Catalunya 2–4, tel: 9 33 17 21 77; www.ottozutz.com, Metro: Catalunya) has various different dance floors, playing a pleasing mix of tunes, and a relaxing out-door terrace.

The **Astoria Club** (Carrer Paris, 193, Wed–Sat, Metro: Diagonal) is housed in a beautiful old cinema that has been converted into an exclusive lounge club and restau-rant. The club's three spacious bar counters, small dance floor and film projections make it a hit with the more upmarket, fashion-conscious crowd.

Located in the basement of the luxurious Hotel Omm (►38), **Ommsession** is one of the most fashionable nightspots in the city and is well worth checking out. Join the city's beautiful people for live music and DJ sessions.

Another popular nightclub is **Luz de Gas** (Carrer de Muntaner 246, www.luzdegas.com, Metro: Diagonal). Set in a grand music hall the club has some delightfully decadent belle époque decor. It has some good live concerts, especially during the jazz festival from October to December.

GAY NIGHTLIFE

Punto BCN (Carrer de Muntaner 63, tel: 9 34 53 61 23, Metro: Universitat) is a good place to start the evening.

Later, head for **Arena Madre** (Carrer de Balmes 32, tel: 9 34 87 83 42, Metro: Universitat), a fun, popular gay venue, or its more mixed sibling **Arena VIP** (Gran Via de les Corts Catalanes 593, tel: 9 34 87 83 42, Metro: Universitat) for a young, partying crowd.

Metro (Carrer de Sepúlveda 158, tel: 9 33 23 52 27, Metro: Universitat) is another megadisco, with two dance floors and three bars. It's open all night, every night until the early morning. **Salvation** (Ronda de Sant Pere 19–21, tel: 9 33 18 06 86; www.matinee group.com, Metro: Urquinaona) offers a mix of house music and DJ choices.

The drag-show restaurant is a quintessentially Barcelona ex-perience. Of several dotted around the Eixample, the two best are the **Ne Quid Nimis** (Carrer de Casanova 30, tel: 9 32 18 30 00, Metro: Universitat) – the Latin name means "nothing in excess" – and the **Diva** (Carrer de la Diputació 172, tel: 9 34 54 63 98, Metro: Universitat).

CINEMA

Gràcia's **Verdi** remains one of the city's leading movie houses. The original branch (Carrer de Verdi 32, tel: 9 32 38 79 90, www.cines-verdi.com, Metro: Fontana) and the newer four-screen **Verdi Park** (Carrer Torrijos 49, tel: 9 32 38 79 90, Metro: Fontana) show a blend of golden oldies and recent re-leases, with a high proportion of English-language films.

At the **Melies** (Carrer de Villarroel 102, tel: 9 34 51 00 51, www.meliescinemes.com, Metro: Urgell) you can catch a variety of foreign arthouse films with subtitles.

OTHER ENTERTAINMENTS

If you're in the city in the summer months, don't miss **La Pedrera de Nit**; you can admire the cityscape and drink *cava* on the rooftop of the Casa Milà (►114).

Montjuïc & Poble Sec

 **Little Treats**

Magical fountain spectacle

Enjoy the **La Font Màgica** (➤ 147) a sound-and-light show from the terrace of the Las Arenas shopping mall on Plaça Espanya.

Swimming pool with a view

The public pool, Piscina Municipal de Montjuïc, near the **Fundación Joan Miró** (➤ 144) has a panoramic view of Barcelona.

A Mediterranean cultural experience

In summer there are al fresco films and concerts under the stars at the Festival Sala Montjuïc in the **Castell de Montjuïc** (➤ 146).

Getting Your Bearings

Montjuïc, a steep, landscaped bluff looming to the south of the city, revels in the nickname of Magic Mountain – a survivor from Celtiberian and Roman times when a fort and temple to Jupiter crowned its heights. For centuries Montjuïc isolated Barcelona from the rest of the world and, with its cemetery and awe-inspiring castle from which Spanish troops subjugated their colony, it had grim associations. Since the 1929 International Exhibition and the upgrade for the 1992 Olympics, its outlook has been far brighter: designer pavilions stand cheek-by-jowl with exhibition palaces, and Olympic stadiums with concert halls.

One of the finest approaches to Montjuïc is by funicular railway, accessed from the Avinguda del Paral.lel metro station. The Drassanes, the city's medieval shipyards, lie to the east of Montjuïc at the port end of the Ramblas, close to the station, and make a convenient place to start your day's sightseeing. The Drassanes have been transformed into Barcelona's highly acclaimed Museu Marítim, which provides a fascinating testimony to the city's seafaring past.

View of the Museu Nacional d'Art de Catalunya

Once on Montjuïc, you'll find two of the city's greatest art museums, one dedicated to Joan Miró and his colourful works, the other showing off a world-renowned collection of Catalan Romanesque frescoes, rescued from decaying Pyrenean churches.

Nestling at the foot of Montjuïc, Poble Sec is a narrow warren of streets slightly removed from the city with its own special atmosphere. Although there are no sights as such, a wander around the traditional working-class neighbourhood makes for a gentle reintroduction from the green of the mountain back into the bustle of the city. Especially around the Carrer Blai where a new pub and restaurant scene has developed, also in close proximity is La Ciutat del Teatre, a theatre complex that includes the Teatre Lliure, the Mercat de les Flors and the Institut del Teatre.

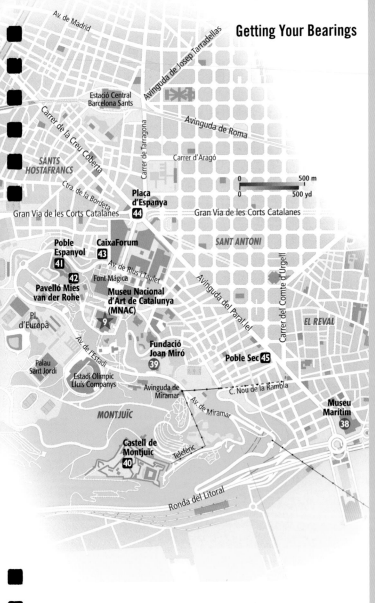

TOP 10
⭐ Museu Nacional d'Art de Catalunya (MNAC) ➤ 136

Don't Miss

At Your Leisure

Perfect Days in....

The Perfect Day

If you're not quite sure where to begin your travels, this itinerary recommends a practical and enjoyable day in Montjuïc and Poble Sec, taking in some of the best places to see. For more information see the main entries (➤ 136–147).

⊛ 9:30am

After a leisurely start, wander down to the Drassanes (medieval royal ship-yards) and the delightful museum cafe (➤ 141) for a coffee-and-croissant breakfast. Then visit the outstanding ㊳ **Museu Marítim** (➤ 140), where Barcelona's seafaring history is laid out.

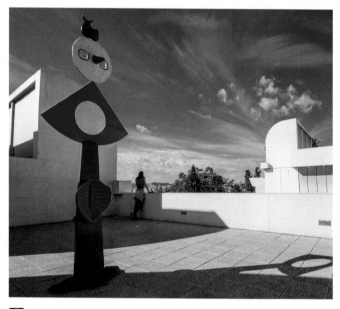

⊛ 11:30am

Walk a few steps up the Avinguda del Paral.lel to the Paral.lel metro station where you can take the funicular to the ㊴ **Fundació Joan Miró** (above, ➤ 144). The visit to the museum is a must.

⊛ 1:30pm

The cafe at the Fundació Joan Miró is ideal for a midday snack, after your lunch you can take the Telefèric de Montjuïc cable car up to the fortress (Castell) for some breathtaking panoramic views. Or you can go up on foot, just follow the signs. The descent to the ☆ **Museu d'Art de Catalunya** (MNAC, ➤ 136) is via some delightful Mediterranean gardens, but you can also take the bus (50, 51).

🕒 3:00pm

MNAC houses five major art collections: the pride and joy are the Romanesque frescoes. Leave time for the Gothic masterpieces, the Cambó Bequest, the Thyssen-Bornemisza Collection, or the modern section of 19th- and 20th-century artwork. It's impossible to see the whole lot in one go, so choose what takes your fancy.

🕒 6:00pm

If you are interested in arts and crafts, or are still looking for souvenirs, then make a little detour to the workshops of the ㊶ Poble Espanyol (► 146). Escalators lead down to the ㊷ Pavelló Mies van der Rohe (► 146).

🕒 8:00pm

At the ㊹ Plaça d'Espanya (► 147) the Art Deco Font Màgica (ill. below, ► 147) offers an impressive spectacle of water and lights, colour and music. Then head via the Carrer Lleida to the ㊺ Poble Sec (► 147) neighbourhood, where the atmospheric warren of streets are full of pubs, tapas bars, outdoor cafes and restaurants, for a great finish to the day.

9 MNAC

The Museu Nacional d'Art de Catalunya (MNAC), housed in the 1929 mock-baroque Palau Nacional, has one of the finest collections of medieval art in Europe. In 2004 the museum's already impressive holdings were extended when two major art collections moved here from other venues in the city. Its exhibits include the Thyssen-Bornemisza collection of European masterpieces and a huge display of 19th- and 20th-century Catalan paintings, sculptures and furniture.

Together with some fine examples of Catalan Gothic art, two priceless collections of old European masterpieces, and an exhibition of more modern creations, vivid Romanesque frescoes salvaged from crumbling Pyrenean churches are displayed in the museum's great galleries. These were stunningly laid out by Gae Aulenti – the Italian architect who transformed an old Paris train station in 1986 into the acclaimed Musée d'Orsay. An added attraction is the breathtaking view from the terrace, across Plaça d'Espanya and the city roofs to the mountain of Tibidabo.

The Palau Nacional's central hall is capped by a magnificent dome

Romanesque Galleries

You should start chronologically with the Romanesque galleries, divided into **ambits**, or areas, rather than rooms. In each *ambit* is an informative plan locating each church, with scale models, photos and ample explanations in English and Catalan.

Romanesque art is remarkable for its simplicity. In medieval times, many people were illiterate and the church walls would become a colourful story book, a "poor man's Bible" adorned with childlike images. Take, for example, the **apse from Santa Maria d'Àneu** (Ambit III), recovered from a remote Pyrenean valley: the all-knowing eyes on the stylized angel's wings are powerful symbols of God's power. The undoubted highlight, though, is the **set of murals**

from Sant Climent de Taüll (Ambit V), which date from 1123 but remain as vivid as when they were painted. The figure of Christ in Majesty in the central apse is wonderfully expressive, with wide eyes, flowing hair and a book in his left hand, inscribed with the words *Ego Sum Lux Mundi* (I am the light of the world).

Gothic Galleries

On the opposite side of the central hallway are the Gothic galleries, also divided into *ambits*. First are some colourful murals, akin to medieval comic strips, recording the Catalan capture of Mallorca in 1229. They

The retable of St Barbara, part of the museum's Gothic collection

were rescued from several palaces along Barcelona's Carrer Montcada, now home to the Museu Picasso (►80). The subsequent rooms contain items ranging from chests and statues to coins and cabinets, along with a fine collection of mostly religious paintings from Catalonia and elsewhere in Europe.

One of the highlights, the *retable of St Barbara*, attributed to Gonçal Peris Sarrià (Ambit VIII), is a magical riot of colour and gold leaf, with fairy-tale castle turrets adding to its charm. The saint's quill pen and delicate crown are portrayed with the finest of brush strokes. In Ambit XII, look for

The 12th-century apse mural from Sant Climent de Taüll

Jaume Huguet's *retable of St Michael*, regarded as one of the finest examples of Gothic art. The richness of the archangel's attire and his insect-like wings make him a striking if somewhat disturbing figure. In the lower right-hand corner, you can make out bits of the dragon he's just killed.

Insider Tip

MUST-SEES

The five outstanding exhibits in this treasure-trove of a museum are:

- The **apse from Santa Maria d'Àneu** (Romanesque, Ambit III).
- The **paintings from Sant Climent de Taüll** (► left, Romanesque, Ambit V).
- Fra Angelico's tempera **Madonna of Humility** (Thyssen-Bornemisza collection).
- Jaume Huguet's **retable of St Michael** (Ambit XII).
- **Furniture** designed by Gaudí (19th- and 20th-century art, Rooms X–XIII).

Montjuïc & Poble Sec

Thyssen-Bornemisza Collection and Cambó Bequest

During the 1920s and 1930s, German industrialist Baron Heinrich Thyssen-Bornemisza de Kaszon amassed an outstanding collection of European art. In 1993, the Spanish State acquired the collection from his son, the Baron Hans Heinrich. Most of it went to Madrid, but part was kept in Barcelona, at first at the Monestir de Pedralbes (➤ 156) from where it was moved in 2004.

The most important paintings – along with a few choice Gothic sculptures – belong to the Italian Trecento (14th century), though there are also some fine examples from the 15th and 16th centuries. Fra Angelico's majestic yet delicate **Madonna of Humility** (*c.*1435) is notable; the harmony of the composition, Mary's blue robes and the fine lily offered to her by the infant Jesus are simply perfect. The **Nativity** (1325) by Taddeo Gaddi, and the **Madonna and Child** (1340–5) by Bernardo Daddi, a pupil of Giotto, are both wonderful examples of the simplicity of 14th-century Italian art, albeit with the lavish use of gold paint. Lorenzo Monaco's harmonious tempera panel **Madonna and Child Enthroned with Six Angels** (1415–20) conveys intense emotion, while Veronese's **Annunciation** (1570) is a decoratively lyrical work that sums up the

The 15th-century *Madonna and Child Enthroned with Six Angels* by Lorenzo Monaco

triumphant monumentalism of the 16th century. Among the handful of baroque paintings by artists from Italy, Holland, Flanders and Spain, Francisco de Zurbarán's intense *Christ on the Cross* (1630) stands out.

A smaller, but no less significant collection of paintings was bequeathed to Barcelona by the influential **Cambó** family, and includes works by *Tiepolo, Goya and Rubens*. The collection is housed in its own galleries at the end of the Gothic galleries.

Art of the 19th and 20th centuries

This spans the period from 1800 to the Spanish Civil War, and ranges from neoclassicism to Modernisme and Noucentisme, which was a return to classical forms as a backlash against the decadence of Modernisme. The collection includes paintings by great Catalonian artists such as bohemian Santiago Rusiñol (1861–1931) and Ramon Casas (1866–1932), who led the early Modernist painters with their evocative Parisian works, *Laboratory at La Galette* (1890) and *Plein Air* (1890), respectively (Room VI). Casas's beige-toned painting of himself and Pere Romeu *On a Tandem* (1897) has become an icon of late 19th-century art in Barcelona. Josep Clarà (1878–1958) was the finest exponent of Noucentiste sculpture. His *Repose*, a marble with the purest of forms, was sculpted for the International Exhibition in 1929 (Room XIX). There are also some fabulous pieces of furniture and ornaments by Gaudí and Puig i Cadafalch that once graced the interiors of Casa Milà (► 114) and the Manzana de la Discordia (► 117) (Rooms X–XIII). Don't miss Gaudí's undulating wooden sofa from the Casa Batlló.

TAKING A BREAK

MNAC's lunchtime restaurant **Òleum** (tel: 9 32 89 06 79, Tue–Sun 1–4, Tue–Sat 7:30–11:30pm), set in the Throne Room with fine views over the city, serves contemporary cooking with a Catalan twist. Alternatively there's Cúbic cafeteria-bar downstairs by the Oval Floor serving sandwiches and cakes.

➕ 202 C4
✉ Palau Nacional, Parc de Montjuïc ☎ 9 36 22 03 76; www.mnac.cat
🕓 Oct–Apr Tue–Sat 10–8, May–Sep Tue–Sat 10–8
💶 €12. Free first Sun of the month and Sat after 3pm 🚇 Espanyav

INSIDER INFO

It is impossible to see this huge mass of great art all in one visit. Especially if time is short, concentrate on the **Romanesque frescoes**, which can be described as the truly world-class element of the museum. The **temporary art exhibitions** sometimes held downstairs are worth investigating if you have time.

③⑧ Museu Marítim

This museum, housed in the former royal shipyards, is worth a visit for the building alone. Built in the 13th century at the height of Catalonia's maritime power, the Drassanes Reials are both a triumph of civic Gothic architecture in Barcelona and the best surviving example of a medieval shipyard anywhere in the world. These remarkable medieval warehouses, with soaring arches, elegant aisles and cavernous stone vaults, have all the appearance of a secular cathedral.

The yards were built to supply ships for the Catalan-Aragonese fleet when the Crown of Aragón was expanding into a major Mediterranean empire. While other great seafaring cities such as Venice and Palermo destroyed their medieval shipyards, Barcelona continued to use them right up until the 18th century. Even as late as the Civil War, the yards were put to use as an arsenal. Repeatedly restored and currently being painstakingly modernized,

The museum is housed in the city's 13th-century royal shipyards

Caravels such as these were used in the voyage to the Americas in 1492

the shipyards have housed the city's maritime museum since 1941.

Modernization

The whole museum will be undergoing modernization until 2015. The beautiful three-masted schooner *Santa Eulàlia* and part of the permanent exhibitions may be open occasionally, for a reduced entrance fee.

The Collection

The items on display cover the full history of seafaring, from ancient maps and compasses to models of fishing boats and actual vessels. There is a replica of *La Real*, the royal galley built here for John of Austria in 1568. It was this vessel, the flagship of the Christian fleet, that enabled the Holy League (Spain, Venice, Malta and the Papal States) to defeat the Ottoman Turks at the critical Battle of Lepanto on 7 October, 1571 – a battle which is seen as a turning point in the fortunes of the various Mediterranean empires. The replica, built in 1971 on the 400th anniversary of the battle, measures 60m (200 feet) in length and includes lifesize models of the 236 oarsmen needed to power the original. With its golden figurehead depicting Neptune astride a dolphin and its lavish gilt decoration, *La Real* looks more like a baroque altarpiece than a battleship.

Included in the entry price for the museum is a visit to the *Santa Eulàlia,* which was launched in 1918 and is now, after restoration, moored in the water at the Port Vell.

TAKING A BREAK

The **museum's cafe** is a good bet for a drink and a snack or for the tasty lunchtime three-course *menú*. There are outside tables in the shade of the plane trees.

⊞ 203 F2
✉ Avinguda de les Drassanes s/n
☎ 9 33 42 99 20; www.mmb.cat
🕐 *Santa Eulàlia:* Apr–Oct Tue–Fri noon–7:30, Sat 2–7:30, Sun 10–7:30 (tours Sat 10–1); Nov–Mar Tue–Fri noon–5:30, Sat, Sun 10–5:30 (tours Mon 10–1)
💷 €5 (interim admission charge until re-opening)
Ⓜ Drassanes
🍴 Cafe-restaurant

INSIDER INFO

Come here **early in the morning** before the museum gets crowded out by parties of school children, or visit later in the day. Don't miss the dozen or so carved **figureheads**, mostly from the 18th and 19th centuries.

The Legacy of a Seafaring Nation

The Drassanes Reials (royal shipyards) were established in the 13th century and continued to be expanded until well into the 18th century. The buildings themselves provide an unusual example of civic Gothic architecture, while their sheer size and spaciousness – with soaring arches, vaults and niches – all have the appearance of Gothic churches. This is where the galleys and caravels of the Crown of Aragón were built, serviced and repaired. However, when maritime interests became focused on the Atlantic following the discovery of America, the importance of the shipyards decreased and the buildings were used as storehouses and for other purposes. In 1936, the decision was made to install a museum here. The complex has been a protected monument since 1976; the museum is currently undergoing extensive renovation work planned to last until early 2015 and only parts of the exhibition are open to the public.

❶ La Real: The main hall is dominated by a full-sized reproduction of the galley, La Real, the flagship of the fleet, from which John of Austria defeated the Turks at the Battle of Lepanto on 7 October 1571. 236 rowers were needed to move the 60m (200 foot) long galley. With its lavish gold ornamentation and figurehead (Neptune astride dolphin) it hardly looks like a battleship at all.

❷ Figureheads: The exhibition of carved figureheads from the 18th and 19th centuries on the upper floor of the museum is also extremely impressive.

❸ Steam navigation: Among the exhibits in this section are the replicas of sections of a transoceanic steamship from around 1900 and the reproduction of Narcis Monturiol's submarine.

❹ Documentation centre: Archives providing information on shipping (Centre de Documentació Marítima) and teaching materials about the sea, particularly aimed at students.

❺ Cafeteria and Museum Shop

La Real's lavishly decorated stern

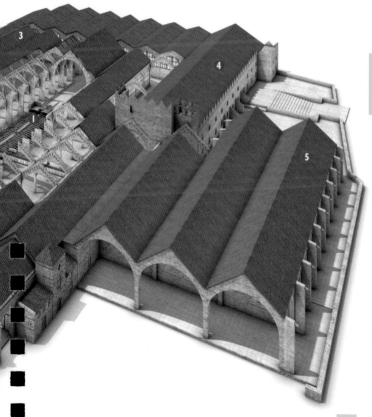

㊱ Fundació Joan Miró

Joan Miró's playful sculptures and brightly coloured paintings are given the perfect setting in this purpose-built gallery. The building commands dreamy views across the city, and its white walls, terracotta flagstones and elegantly curved roofs lend it a pleasing Mediterranean aspect that complements Miró's work.

With his simple, bold designs and childlike use of primary colours, Joan Miró (1893–1983) seems to embody the artistic spirit of Barcelona. His works can be seen all over the city, from the mural at the airport to the pavement mosaic on the Ramblas (►52) and the sculpture that dominates Parc de Joan Miró (►145). Catalans have taken him to their hearts, perhaps because unlike Picasso he was born in the city. His striking abstract images have become symbols of Barcelona, seen on everything from T-shirts and ashtrays to branches of La Caixa bank, for whom he designed the logo.

The outdoor sculptures are one of the Fundació Joan Miró's main attractions

A Spectrum of Work

This extensive collection, much of it donated by Miró himself, provides an excellent introduction for anyone unfamiliar with his work. In addition to 200 paintings, 150 sculptures and a series of vivid tapestries, the collection includes more than 5,000 sketches and all of his graphic works. Although there are large gaps, especially around the mid-life period, it is possible to trace Miró's artistic development from his childhood etchings and youthful experiments with Cubism to the emergence of his highly personal and instantly recognizable style,

a blend of surrealism and abstract art.

The best of the early works are found in the **Sala Joan Prats**, named after Miró's friend and patron. These include *Street in Pedralbes* (1917) and *Portrait of a Young Girl* (1919), as well as the disturbing *Man and Woman Front of a Pile of Excrement* (1935). His familiar themes

L'estel matinal (Morning Star) characterizes Miró's work

start to emerge in paintings such as *Morning Star* (1940), though at the same time he was also working on *Barcelona* (1944), a powerful series of black-and-white lithographs inspired by the Civil War.

The **Sala Pilar Juncosa**, named after Miró's wife, contains many of his later works, produced after he moved to Mallorca in 1956. Among the paintings here are *Figure Before the Sun* (1968) and *Woman in the Night* (1973), large canvases with simple lines and bold yellows and reds. This gallery also contains some of his best-known sculptures, including *Sunbird* (1968), in sparkling white Carrara marble. There are more sculptures on the rooftop terrace and in an adjoining sculpture garden.

TAKING A BREAK

Most people head for the museum's shady courtyard cafe-restaurant. Alternatively, walk downhill to the **Miramar Bar** (Avinguda Miramar 93, tel: 9 34 42 31 00) by the cable car that goes across the harbour. It serves pricey snacks, but it has great views.

✚ 202 C3
✉ Plaça Neptú, Parc de Montjuïc
☎ 9 34 43 94 70; www.fundaciomiro-bcn.org
🕐 Jul–Sep Tue–Sat 10–8, Sun and public holidays 10–2:30; Oct–Jun Tue–Sat 10–7; (also Thu till 9:30pm all year round). Guided tours 12:20 Sat and Sun
💶 €11 🚇 Paral.lel plus Funicular de Montjuïc 🚌 50, 55, Bus Turístic (blue)
🍴 Cafe-restaurant, excellent bookshop and giftshop

INSIDER INFO

One of Miró's most famous sculptures can be seen in **Parc de Joan Miró**, across the Plaça d'Espanya at the foot of Montjuïc. On the site of the former *escorxador* (slaughterhouse) – hence the square's other name, Parc de l'Escorxador – the park is dominated by the gigantic ***Dona i Ocell*** *(Woman and Bird)*, a tile-encrusted obelisk that has become one of the city's landmarks.

At Your Leisure

40 Castell de Montjuïc

The trip to the 18th-century castle by 🚡 *telefèric* (cable car) is exhilarating and the views from its battlements are splendid. The fortress has a sinister history that many Catalans would prefer to forget. It was here that Catalan president Lluís Companys was executed by one of Franco's firing squads in 1940.

The castle is gradually being remodelled as the Military Museum is turned into a Peace Centre, but you can still wander around the battlements. In summer, outdoor cinema and concerts are arranged in the grassy moat; check with the tourist office for details.

➕ 202 C2
✉ Carretera de Montjuïc 66
☎ 9 32 56 44 45
🕐 Apr–Sep daily 9–9, Oct–Mar 9–7 💶 Free
🚇 Paral.lel, also Funicular and Telefèric de Montjuïc (➤ 187) 🚌 50

41 Poble Espanyol

There are more than 100 buildings illustrating Spain's architectural and cultural diversity in the Poble Espanyol. The "village" was built for the 1929 International Exhibition but, long resented by Catalan nationalists, it went into decline until an admirable refurbishment in the 1990s revived its fortunes.

Some of the Poble Espanyol's finest buildings are replicas of houses and palaces from around Catalonia, with examples from Gerona, Lleida and the Pyrenees. Shops on the site sell high-quality crafts produced by resident artisans. You can also eat well in the variety of bars and restaurants: choose from Andalucian or Basque, Castilian or Galician specialities. At night, entertainments are plentiful.

Insider Tip

➕ 202 B4
✉ Avinguda del Marquès de Comillas 13
☎ 9 35 08 63 00; www.poble-espanyol.com
🕐 Mon–Thu, Sun 9–midnight, Fri till 3am, Sat till 4am
💶 €11
🚇 Espanya 🚌 13, 50, 61

42 Pavelló Mies van der Rohe

Pioneering modern architect Mies van der Rohe designed this functionalist structure (also known as the Pavelló Barcelona) as the German pavilion for the 1929 International Exhibition. The pavilion was reconstructed in the 1980s as a tribute to the architect on the centenary of his birth. The building is characterized by

The sleek Pavelló Mies van der Rohe

clean lines and simple forms, and its combination of sleek marble, granite and glass, and still pools of water create a calm, meditative atmosphere.

Among the exhibits of the architect's life and work on display is the Barcelona Chair, which he designed especially for the King and Queen of Spain's visit to the pavilion during the Exhibition. The much-copied leather-and-steel seat is still a favourite in office waiting rooms.

✚ 202 B4 ✉ Avinguda
Francesc Ferrer i Guàrdia 7
☎ 9 34 23 40 16;
www.miesbcn.com
🕐 Mon 4–8, Tue–Sun 10–8.
Guided tours Wed, Fri 5–7
💶 €5 🚇 Espanya

43 CaixaForum

Casaramona, a
whimsical brick
textile mill built
in 1911 by Puig
i Cadafalch, stood
empty for decades
until it reopened as
Fundació La Caixa's
new arts centre in 2002.
Japanese architect Arata
Isozaki turned it into one of
Barcelona's most rewarding
exhibition spaces. In addition
to the permanent collection of
contemporary art – with works
by, for example, Miquel Barceló,
Anish Kapoor, Tony Cragg, Joseph
Beuys and Jannis Kounellis – outstanding temporary exhibits are
held. A 👫 **children's section**, workshops, concerts, an excellent gift
shop and a smart cafeteria and
restaurant are added attractions.

✚ 202 B4
✉ Avinguda Marquès de Comillas 6–8
☎ 9 34 76 86 00; www.fundacio.lacaixa.es
🕐 Mon–Fri 10–8, Sat, Sun till 9;
Jul–Aug Wed till 11 💶 Free 🚇 Espanya

44 Plaça d'Espanya

This monumental "square",
guarded by two majestic red-brick
Venetian- style campaniles, was
designed as a grand entrance to
the 1929 International Exhibition.
Your gaze is drawn upwards by a
series of staircases and escalators
towards the ostentatious Palau
Nacional. On summer evenings,
the row of fountains in the middle
of the staircase come to life as
👫 **La Font Màgica**, a spectacular
but tacky sound-and-light show
that delights both adults and
children alike.

✚ 202 C5 🚇 Espanya

La Font Màgica
🕐 Thu–Sun 9pm–11:15pm, every 30 mins

45 Poble Sec

Covering the steep network of
streets from the northern foot of
Montjuïc to Avinguda del Paral.lel,
Poble Sec is a small workaday
neighbourhood with a laid-back
feel. It was never included inside
the city walls because, as its name
suggests, there were no water
sources here, and its atmosphere
remains one apart from the city
centre. At the end of the 19th century the Avinguda del Paral.lel was
lined with theatres and cabaret
bars, including the legendary
El Molino, which emulated the
Moulin Rouge in Paris. There
are still some clubs in the area
(▶ 150), but it is Poble Sec's
small bars and restaurants that
draw visitors these days.

✚ 203 F3 🚇 Poble Sec, Paral.lel

Where to...
Eat and Drink

Prices
Expect to pay per person for a three-course meal, excluding drinks:
€ under €25   €€ €25–€50   €€€ over €50

Quimet & Quimet €/€€
This special little bodega in the heart of the Poble Sec serves tapas prepared before your eyes. The quality of the ingredients is superb – try the cured shoulder of pork, air-dried tuna or tiny sardines. Wine is sold by the glass, and there are up to a dozen special beers. The house vermouth is served in the traditional way, with soda water.

Insider Tip

✚ 203 E3 ✉ Carrer del Poeta Cabanyes 25
☎ 9 34 42 31 42
🕐 Mon–Fri 2–4, 7–10:30, Sat 2–4 🚇 Paral.lel

Restaurant Miramar €€€
With splendid views over the port and harbour, this minimalist restaurant serves slightly formulaic modern Mediterranean cuisine in elegant surroundings. There are also tables outside in the garden. The bar and cafeteria above the restaurant serve over-priced basic food, but they have excellent views (open 10–10).

✚ 203 E3 ✉ Carretera Miramar 40, in the Montjuïc telefèric station for the harbour cable car from Barceloneta
☎ 9 34 43 66 27; www.club-miramar.es
🕐 Tue–Sat 1–4, 8–11, Sun 1–3:30
🚇 Paral.lel, Funicular de Montjuïc, harbour cable car

La Tomaquera €€
It gets noisy and service can be brusque but La Tomaquera provides authentic Catalan home cooking in a no-nonsense setting – the very essence of Poble Sec. There's a great selection of grilled meats and *cargols* (snails), the

house speciality. Credit cards are not accepted and you can't reserve ahead; you need to arrive early or be prepared to wait for a table.

✚ 203 D3 ✉ Carrer de Margarit 58
🕐 Tue–Sat 1:30–4:30, 8:30–10:45; Closed Aug
🚇 Poble Sec, Paral.lel

Tickets €€€
Ferran Adrià's world-famous gourmet restaurant El Bulli may have closed its doors but it lives on in his new Michelin-starred tapas restaurant. The decor is flamboyant, with film posters and theatre lights, while the miniature dishes all bear the signature of the master – just far simpler and more affordable. Relaxed atmosphere, professional service. Online reservations essential, at least a month (or two) in advance!

✚ 203 D4 ✉ Avinguda Paral.lel 164
☎ 93 2 92 42 53, www.tickestbar.es
🕐 Tue–Sat 7pm–11pm, Sun 1pm–3pm
🚇 Poble Sec

BARS AND CAFES

Bar Primavera €
This shady, outdoor bar halfway up Montjuïc provides a convenient recuperation point for a drink or sandwich for those who have chosen

✚ 203 D3 ✉ Carrer Nou de la Rambla 192
☎ 9 33 29 30 62 🕐 Apr–Oct Tue–Sun 9am–10pm; Nov–Mar Tue–Sun 8–7
🚇 Paral.lel

Bar Seco €
With an emphasis on eco-friendly and fair-trade ingredients, this

cafe-bar provides a welcome alternative for a snack – organic tapas, vegetarian dishes and sandwiches – or a drink – fresh juices and small-brewery beers.

➕ 203 E3

✉ Passeig de Montjuïc 74

☎ 9 33 29 63 74

🕐 Summer: Mon 8am–5pm, Tue–Fri 8am–2am, Sat 10–2am, Sun 10–1am; Winter Mon–Wed 8–5 or, Thu–Fri 8–2am, Sat 10–2am, Sun 10–1am

🚇 Paral.lel

Where to...
Shop

Montjuïc and Poble Sec are not the most fertile shopping districts in the city. However, the museum shops sell imaginative gifts and good reproductions to take home.

MUSEUM SHOPS

The **gift shops** at the Museu Marítim (➤ 140), Fundació Joan Miró (➤ 144), MNAC (➤ 136) and Poble Espanyol (➤ 146) are places to find unique items. In addition to directly related souvenirs – model ships, Miró reproductions and signed prints, books on Gothic painting and crafts from the regions of Spain – you'll find a great range of postcards, illustrated books, stylish jewellery and quirky designer gifts.

At the **Museu d'Arqueologia**, on the way up the hillside from the Poble Sec (Passeig de Santa Madrona 39–41, tel: 9 34 23 21 49; www.mac.cat, Metro: Poble Sec) you can buy reproductions of ancient artefacts. You don't have to visit the museum to shop here.

CRAFTS

The workshops at the **Poble Espanyol** (➤ 140) produce a comprehensive range of goods, including stained glass, pewterware, lace and jewellery. Top craftspeople make high-quality goods here right before your eyes, but prices tend to be higher than elsewhere in the city. Be warned – there are also outlets here selling overpriced inferior products.

Where to...
Go Out

Poble Sec was once synonymous with entertainment. Most of its cabaret clubs have now closed, but several venues here, and on Montjuïc, are worth a detour.

SPORT

Spectator and participatory sports are the principal entertainments in Montjuïc, a legacy of the 1992 Olympic Games. The **Piscines Bernat Picornell** swimming pool (Avinguda de l'Estadi 30–38, tel: 9 34 23 40 41, Metro: Espanya) is part of the Anella Olímpica complex. Unless the pool is being used for a competition, it is open to the public daily 7am–midnight on weekdays; it closes at 9pm on Sat, Sun at 7pm.

Nearby **Palau Sant Jordi**, a masterly feat of modern architecture, doubles up as an indoor sports venue, used for basketball and athletics, and a giant concert hall; it hosts most of Barcelona's mega rock and pop concerts and sporting events.

The **Estadi Olímpic de Lluís Companys**, which incorporates a stadium built in 1929 by Mila and Correa, was the major venue for the 1992 Olympics. It is open to the public daily 10–6, or until 7pm in the summer.

THEATRE

The annual **Festival del Grec** (http://grec.bcn.cat) takes place from the end of June to mid-August. Events are staged at venues throughout the city, including the **Teatre Grec**, the elegant Greek-style amphitheatre on Montjuïc. Theatre, both mainstream and avant-garde, dominates, but there's also dance, jazz, flamenco and rock. If you can, try to catch a performance at the Teatre Grec itself (Metro: Poble Sec). Here, against a fabulous backdrop of cypress trees, you can see the festival's major dance spectacles, plays and concerts; the seats are uncomfortable, though.

The **Teatre Mercat de les Flors** (Plaça Margarida Xirgu, Carrer Lleida 59, tel: 9 34 26 18 75; www.mercatflors.org, Metro: Poble Sec) lies not far away. The massive hangar-like halls of this converted flower market lend themselves to large-scale productions of a less conventional kind. Next door the *Teatre Lliure* (tel: 9 32 89 27 70; www.teatrelliure.com) occupies a futuristic space designed by Fabià Puigserver, inside the 1929 Palace of Agriculture, part of the Ciutat del Teatre. Drama and dance of a very high standard alternate here.

CONCERTS AND SHOWS

For flamenco, look no further than **El Tablao de Carmen** (Carrer dels Arcs 9, tel: 9 33 25 68 95; www.tablaodecarmen.com, Metro: Espanya), up at the Poble Espanyol. Pretty authentic shows take place from Tuesday to Sunday at 7:45pm–9pm and 10pm–11:15pm. It's not cheap, but you can choose between the dinner, tapas and glass of champagne options, and the quality of the musicians, singers and dancers is invariably high.

From late June to September, Thursday to Sunday and public holidays, from 9pm–11:15pm (earlier during the rest of the year), you can witness the astounding spectacle of **La Font Màgica** (➤ 147), a free sound-and-light show. It takes place along the stepped avenue linking the Plaça d'Espanya to the Palau Nacional.

NIGHTCLUBS AND BARS

Amid a pine grove just behind the Poble Espanyol lies **La Terrrazza** (Avinguda Marquès de Comillas 13, tel: 9 34 23 12 85; www.laterrrazza.com, Metro: Espanya). The legendary (and crowded) open-air club on the hillside of Montjuïc attracts guests with up-to-date sounds, DJ sessions and live concerts (summer Thu–Sat).

Housed in what was once an elegant ballroom **Club Apolo** (Carrer Nou de la Rambla, 113, www.sala-apolo.com, Metro: Paral.lel), is one of the hippest places in town to enjoy live music, DJs and dance parties. On weekends the Apolo becomes the **Nitsa Club**, well known far beyond the city limits for its sessions.

If you are looking for a congenial local pub then head for the 100-year-old **Gran Bodega Saltó** (Blesa 36, tel: 93 4 41 37 09, http://bodegasalto.net, Mon–Sat after 7pm, Sun after 1pm, Metro: Paral.lel). The interior is eclectic, quaint and cosy and the proceeds from the pub's cultural program go towards a neighbourhood support initiative.

Finally, **Tinta Roja**, a late-night bar just off Avinguda del Paral.lel (Carrer Creu dels Molers 17, tel: 9 34 43 32 43; www.tintaroja.net, Metro: Poble Sec), is a small atmospheric tango haunt doubling up as an art gallery.

Pedralbes & Tibidabo

 Little Treats

Musical dolls at the press of a switch
The vintage fairground machines of the
Museu d'Automates in **Tibidabo** (➤ 160) are
among the most beautiful in the world.

Mountain views
The observation deck of the **Torre de Collserola**
(➤ 160) offers panoramic mountain views.

Demigods in blue and red
At **Camp Nou** (➤ 162) you can wait at
Entrance 9 (before or after a match) to see
Lionel Messi and teammates to arrive in
their sports cars.

Pedralbes & Tibidabo

Getting Your Bearings

Barcelona's outlying districts lay claim to some of its top destinations. Beyond walking distance they may be, but the city's efficient public transport will whisk you there in no time.

In the smart western neighbourhood of Pedralbes sits the splendid royal monastery of the same name. The monastery's cool cloisters, resounding with the trickle of a fountain and the gentle murmur of nuns singing in the chapel, are the perfect place to escape the bustle of the city.

South of the monastery, just off the Avinguda Diagonal, lies the Palau Reial de Pedralbes, currently home to the three collections that comprise the Museu de les Arts Aplicades: the Museu de la Ceràmica, the Museu de les Arts Decoratives and the Museu Textíl i Indumentària. The section of the Avinguda Diagonal that cuts through the district of Les Corts, between the Palau Reial de Pedralbes and Plaça de Francesc Macià, is mostly lined with offices, banks and apartment buildings, though there are also several megamalls, making it a popular place for one-stop shoppers.

To the south is FC Barcelona's mammoth stadium, Camp Nou, where football fans flock to see their team in action. To the west are Barcelona's excellent science museum, CosmoCaixa, and Tibidabo, where you can ride on roller coasters with the whole city laid out spectacularly before you.

Ronda de Dalt Carre

Universitat Politèc
de Catalunya

Avinguda Diagonal

COLLBLANC

Zona
Universitària

Carrer de Sants

Museu
FC Barcelona   **4**

0   500 m
0   500 yr

Glass and metal prevail at CosmoCaixa, Barcelona's superb science museum

Tibidao 48   Tibidabo

51
**Parc de
Collserola**

Funicular del Tibidabo

Plaça del
Funicular

CosmoCaixa
Ronda de Dalt Carretera   47

SARRIÀ

46 **Monestir
de Pedralbes**

*SANT GERVASI
DE CASSOLES*

RALBES   Av. de Pedralbes

Passeig de la Bonanova

*LES TRES
TORRES*   Via Augusta

50 **Pavellons de
la Finca Güell**

Plaça
Pius XII

Via de Carles III

**Camp Nou-
FC Barcelona**

Don't Miss

At Your Leisure

**Mount Tibidabo
is the highest
peak in the
Collserola
range and from
its summit on
a clear day
you can make
out the island
of Mallorca in
the distance**

The Perfect Day

If you're not quite sure where to begin your travels, this itinerary recommends a practical and enjoyable day in Pedralbes and Tibidabo, taking in some of the best places to see. For more information see the main entries (➤ 156–164).

🕘 9:00am

This day needn't be rushed. Linger over breakfast wherever you choose, and then make your way out to the **46 Monestir de Pedralbes** (left; ➤ 156) by metro, FGC, regular bus or maybe the Bus Turístic. Be warned: there are no cafe facilities to speak of there. Be at the gates of the convent when it opens at 10am, to enjoy the cloisters (left) in the gentle morning sunlight.

🕚 11:00am

Go down the sloping Avinguda de Pedralbes, either by bus (the Bus Turístic comes this way) or on foot, past the magical entrance to the **50 Pavellons de la Finca Güell** (below; ➤ 163); pause to look at Gaudí's wrought-iron dragon, half-horror, half-wonder.

🕛 12:00 noon

Next, join the crowds of football pilgrims at **49 Camp Nou** (➤ 162). Cross Avinguda Diagonal at Plaça de Pius XII and go down Avinguda de Joan XXIII. Alternatively, go on a shopping spree along Avinguda Diagonal (➤ 166).

🕜 1:30pm

Enjoy a picnic in the gardens of the **Palau Reial de Pedralbes**, which adjoins the Pavellons de la Finca Güell, or take a taxi to have lunch at La Balsa

restaurant (➤ 159). Then find your way to Barcelona's excellent science museum, **47 CosmoCaixa** (➤ 158).

🕔 5:00pm

This is the time to set your sights on **48 Tibidabo** (➤ 160). Public transport will get you there easily – the museum heritage Tramvia Blau (Blue Tram) runs daily in summer until 8pm, otherwise often only on weekends (www. tmb.cat), the No 196 bus runs every day. To go higher up you can then take the cable car – the views over the city are marvellous.

🕗 8:00pm

You can stay up here all evening. Pre-dinner drinks are top-rate at the Mirablau (➤ 165), next to the tram terminus – either on the garden-terrace or inside the bar. Alongside, on the Plaça del Doctor Andreu, is the fabulous La Venta restaurant (➤ 165), which doesn't take advantage of its location with high prices. Elephant (➤ 166) is one of the city's most exclusive nightclubs.

Tibidabo **48**

51 Parc de Collserola

CosmoCaixa **47**

46 Monestir de Pedralbes

50 Pavellons de la Finca Güell

Camp Nou-
49 FC Barcelona

46 Monestir de Pedralbes

This 14th-century monastery was built for a Catalan queen. Its exquisite cloisters and garden retain their regal majesty 700 years later.

The Monestir de Pedralbes (from the Latin *petrae albae*, meaning white stones) was founded in 1326 for the nuns of the Order of St Clare by Elisenda de Montcada, second wife of King Jaume II. The Montcadas were one of the most powerful noble families in 14th-century Catalonia and Montcada women in particular played a significant role in the kingdom's history. Widowed just two years after her marriage, Elisenda withdrew to the convent and most of what you see there was built through her generosity. A small community of Poor Clare nuns still live here in separate, specially built quarters.

The elegant, three-tiered Gothic cloisters surround a peaceful court-yard garden

Exploring the Monastery

The elegant **cloisters** consist of three tiers of galleries each supported by slim stone pillars. In the far left-hand corner of the central garden a Plateresque wellhead, built around 1500, stands discreetly behind trees and beds of medicinal herbs. Walk around the cloisters counterclockwise to the **Capella de Sant Miquel** (St Michael's Chapel), lined with frescoes executed in the 1340s by Ferrer Bassa, a student of Giotto di Bondoni. Oils and tempera depict the life of the Virgin and the Passion.

As you explore the cloisters you'll also see exquisitely painted **prayer cells** from the 14th century. The Cell of St Francis, the Cell of St Alexius and the Cell of St Joseph are on the ground floor, while the Cell of Our Lady of Montserrat, the Cell of Our Lady of the Snows and the Cell of the Holy Entombment are on the upper floor. The finest of all is the Cel.la de la Pietat on the ground floor, with its 16th-century retable of Mary as a child.

Don't forget to go down to see some of the **living quarters** of the monastery: the cells and cellars, the kitchen and the infirmary give a real insight into how the nuns once lived. In the refectory, the Mother Superior would break her vow of silence with Bible readings from the pulpit while the nuns ate in silence around her.

 Insider Tip

The monastery museum provides an insight into the daily life of the nuns and includes displays of religious art from the 14th–20th century

TAKING A BREAK

Vivanda (Carrer Major de Sarrià 134, tel: 9 32 05 47 17), by the Sarrià neighbourhood market, serves delicious Catalan food, inside or on a garden terrace.

➕ 198 off B5 ✉ Baixada del Monestir 9
☎ 9 32 56 34 34; www.museuhistoria.bcn.cat
🕐 May–Oct Tue–Fri 10–5, Sat 10–7, Sun 10–8, holidays 10–2; Nov–Apr Tue–Sat and holidays 10–2, Sun 10–5
💶 €7; Free first Sun of the month 🚇 FGC Reina Elisenda 🚌 22, 63, 64, 75

INSIDER INFO

- In winter, the monastery is open **mornings only**, except on Sundays; save yourself a wasted trip in the afternoon.
- Although the adjacent **church** (daily 10–1, 5:30–8) is a simple edifice, far less impressive than the monastery, it is worth visiting for the effigy **tomb of Queen Elisenda** – she died in 1364, and this alabaster masterpiece, to the right of the main altar, was made soon afterwards.

47 CosmoCaixa

Housed in an early 20th-century building, CosmoCaixa is definitely a science museum for the 21st century. Laying strong emphasis on evolution and ecology, it is designed to arouse interest in the world around us. Its innovative layout, interactive displays and fun activities will be a hit with younger visitors especially.

CosmoCaixa ambitiously sets out to trace the history of existence from the Big Bang to modern telecommunications. Applying the motto "From a Quark to Shakespeare", its whole ethos is based on universality and environmental concerns. Language, writing and the whole complexity of human culture are also addressed in depth.

The Building

The museum's humanistic ethos is reflected in the building. Constructed as an asylum for the insane to an ornate Modernist design, it was completed by Josep Domènech i Estapà in 1909. Seven decades later the abandoned edifice was converted into Barcelona's Science Museum, but more than 20 years further on the Fundaciò La Caixa called on architects the Terradas brothers to thrust the museum firmly into the new millennium.

In doing so they provided the city with Europe's most up-to-date museum of its kind – in 2006 it won the EuroPean Museum of the Year Award. Shiny glass and metal prevail in the new structure, while all exhibits are accessible to young and old alike.

The Foucault's pendulum is a graphic representation of Earth's rotation

The Collection's Highlights

You can wander around a permanent display on the **History of Matter**. Divided into four parts – Inert, Living, Intelligent and Civilized Matter – it traces the development of planet Earth, explaining all phenomena from gravity to electricity by means of sophisticated hands-on exhibits. The **Geological Wall** looms over surrounding exhibits like a hi-tech cliff. Seven slices of rock – quarried around Spain and Brazil – help to interpret the world's geology, again thanks to graphic information panels (in English, Catalan and Spanish) and ingenious machines.

You can walk both through and beneath the centrepiece **Flooded Forest**. It recreates an Amazonian rainforest habitat complete with enormous fish, turtles and anacondas, in a huge glasshouse-cum-aquarium whose steamy atmosphere, full of jungle smells, transports you to northern Brazil. More than 50 species of amphibians, insects, reptiles, mammals and birds have their home here – don't worry, though, none of the creatures you can come into contact with is harmful.

Two further dimensions are provided by a working **Foucault's pendulum** and a 136-seat **Planetarium** in which you can go on a journey through the history of the Universe. An excellent **bookshop** by the entrance, specializing in all things scientific, is a great place for souvenir hunting.

Vistors using the spiral ramp enjoy a close-up view of the tree suspended by cables in the central well

TAKING A BREAK

The museum has an attractive cafeteria serving snacks. Conveniently close by, however, is **La Balsa** (Carrer Infanta Isabel 4, tel: 9 32 11 50 48), in an attractive wooden building surrounded by lush gardens. Catalan fare includes hake in squid-ink sauce, and prawn and salt cod croquettes in a tarragon sauce, which will set you back about €50 per head. In August it is closed at lunchtime.

✚ 198 off B5 ✉ Carrer de Teodor Roviralta 47–51
☎ 9 32 12 60 50; www.cosmocaixa.com
🕐 Tue–Sun and most public holidays 10–8 💶 €4. Free first Sun of the month
🚇 FGC Avda Tibidabo 🚌 17, 22, 58, 60, 73, 75, 196

INSIDER INFO

- You will find 👪 **several sections specially for kids**: their names – Touch Touch!, Clik and Flash, and Bubble Planetarium – speak for themselves.
- Lifts take you up and down, but don't miss the stylish **spiralling ramp** for alternative inter-floor access. In its well dangles the desiccated trunk of an Amazonian tree, which looks like a giant loofah.

④⑧ Tibidabo

There are two main reasons for making your way to the summit of Mount Tibidabo, the highest peak of the Collserola range that looms behind Barcelona: the stunning views and the old-fashioned fairground, the Parc d'Atraccions. The journey up, by tram and funicular, is part of the enjoyment.

🎠 Parc d'Atraccions

Few amusement parks in the world can claim better views from their helter-skelters, carousels and Ferris wheel than this one. Located near the top funicular station, the park is set in landscaped gardens spread over different levels on the mountainside. A highlight is the Hotel Krueger, a house of horrors of which even Alfred Hitchcock would have approved.

Views of the city from the Ferris wheel at the Parc d'Atraccions are simply breathtaking

Torre de Collserola

On a nearby ridge rises the elegant glass-and-steel Torre de Collserola, a impressive example of modern architecture. The 268m (880-foot) tower was built by British architect Norman Foster as a telecommunications tower for the 1992 Olympics. From the top, reached by a glass lift, you can see back towards the mountains, as well as across the city and out to sea.

TAKING A BREAK

The **Mirablau** (Plaça del Doctor Andreu, tel: 9 34 18 58 79), at the end of the tram line, has the finest view in Barcelona; the entire port and city are seemingly at your feet. Enjoy drinks on the garden terrace or in the bar, which has huge floor-to-ceiling windows. Drinks are expensive and it can become very crowded, but a stop here is an essential Barcelona experience.

➕ 198 off B5 🚉 FGC Avda Tibidabo, Tramvia Blau and Funicular 🚌 17, 22, 58, 73, Tibibus

Parc d'Atraccions
✉ Plaça del Tibidabo 3–4
☎ 9 32 11 79 42; www.tibidabo.cat
🕐 Jul–Sep Wed–Sun noon to at least 8, times vary on Sat, Sun (check website) 💶 €28.50

Torre de Collserola
☎ 9 34 06 93 54; www.torredecollserola.com
🕐 Aug Wed–Aug noon–2, 3:30–8; rest of year variable (check website) 💶 €5.60

GETTING THERE

Every bit as much fun as Tibidabo itself is the journey to get there. First take a No 17 bus or the FGC train from Plaça de Catalunya to Avinguda del Tibidabo. Look for the tram tracks, and you'll see the stop for the **Tramvia Blau** (Blue Tram) that trundles up to Plaça del Doctor Andreu (pay the conductor on entering). The tram runs daily the week before Easter, late June to mid-September and around Christmas 10–6 (8, in summer); Saturday and Sunday only rest of year (10–6). Otherwise (or for quicker access) take **Tibibus** from Plaça de Catalunya or the No 196 bus from Avinguda del Tibidabo. At Plaça del Doctor Andreu, take the funicular railway to the top of Tibidabo. From June to September it runs daily every 20 minutes from 10:45am to just after the attractions close (last bus half an hour before the park closes). In winter, Friday and Saturday only 10:45 to 7:15.

INSIDER INFO

- Come only when **the weather is good**, preferably when there's not too much haze or smog.
- Time your visit for the early evening as the **sunsets** are unforgettable (double check transport times so you are not stranded).
- In the Tibidabo amusement park there is the **Espejos Mágicos**, a distorting mirror that is over 100 years old, as well as a popular mirror maze which was remodelled and equipped with new technology. You will find them in front of the roller coaster in the **MiraMiralls**, which was awarded an architecture prize in 2009.
- Funfair fans in search of more modern, more extreme rides should visit **🏨 Port Aventura**, near Tarragona (ask at the tourist offices ➤ 35 for more information).

In more depth Above the fairground is the huge basilica of **Sagrat Cor** (the Church of the Sacred Heart), modelled on the Sacré-Coeur in Paris. Topped by a huge statue of Christ, it is a clearly visible landmark from nearly everywhere in the city.

At Your Leisure

49 🏟 Camp Nou – FC Barcelona

If football is your thing, then you should do your utmost to see a match at Camp Nou, home to FC Barcelona. However, it is difficult to get tickets: the stadium seats just under 100,000 but there are around 130,000 club members and many more fans of the Blaugrana. Unless you book tickets in advance, your best bet is to turn up for a match and see if there are any spare tickets *(reventa)*.

Entrance 9 will also get you into the **Museu FC Barcelona** (Barça Museum), one of the city's most popular museums with more than half a million visitors every year. Cups, trophies, photographs and posters are displayed alongside all kinds of memorabilia, with big names from the past

Camp Nou stadium: hallowed ground for Barça supporters

such as Johan Cruyff and Maradona looming large. Informative exhibits trace the club's history back to 1899, when it was co-founded and chaired by Englishman Arthur Witty and fielded four British players. The high point of the tour is going on to the pitch through the tunnel

Ronda de Dalt Carretera
46 Monestir de Pedralbes
Av. de Pedralbes
Avinguda Diagonal
Av. de Doctor Marañon
Pavellons de la Finca Güell 50
Zona Universitària
Plaça Pius XII
Camp Nou- 49 FC Barcelona

and gazing up at the rows upon rows of red seats; you also get to visit the president's box.

🔢 194 A2

✉️ Carrer d'Aristides Maillol 7–9

☎️ 9 34 96 36 00 (for ticketing enquires); www.fcbarcelona.es

Museu FC Barcelona

☎️ 9 34 96 36 00

🕐 Summer, Easter holidays: daily 9–7:30, Jan–Mar, Nov–Dec Mon–Sat 10–6, rest of year: 9:30–7, Sun and holidays 10–2:30

💶 €23 🚇 Collblanc

🚌 15, 54, 56, 57, 7 51 13, 158

50 Pavellons de la Finca Güell

The Moorish pavilions (gatehouses) of the Finca Güell (the Güell estate) were designed by Gaudí. Among his earliest achievements, they point to some of the extraordinary concoctions he dreamed up for the Park Güell (➤ 111). But the *pièce de résistance* is without doubt the gate to the estate, which was inspired by the mythical dragon in the epic poem *L'Atlàntida* by nationalist hero Jacint Verdaguer. It was finished during a stay on the estate. Gaudí literally stretched the use of wrought iron beyond

anyone else's imagination, and here the 🔢 **taut forms of the dragon**, with its horrific jaws, make it look as though it is about to spring off the frame towards you.

🔢 194 B4

✉️ Avinguda de Pedralbes 7

☎️ 9 33 17 76 52; www.rutadelmodernisme.com

🚇 Palau Reial

🚌 7, 33, 63, 67, 68, 74, 75, 78

51 Parc de Collserola

Bordering the city is the Serra de Collserola reserve, 8,000ha (19,770 acre) of natural paradise with extensive pine and oak woods, poplar groves and Mediterranean shrubs. With **Mount Tibidabo** (➤ 160) as its highest peak, the mountain range acts a "green lung" for the residents as Barcelona, which has more air pollution than any other city in Europe. The park is rich in **fauna** with boars, foxes, squirrels, weasels, rabbits, hedgehogs as well as many species of birds

Gaudí used a mosaic of tile fragments, a technique known as *trencadí*, to decorate the gatehouses at Finca Güell

Pedralbes & Tibidabo

such as hawks and tawny owls. In the autumn there are huge flocks of migratory bird on route to the south. The park also has some archaeological sites, including **Ca'n Oliver** at Cerdanyola, the remains of a settlement that was inhabited between 500 and 300 BC by the Iberians. The built heritage further includes castle ruins and the remains of medieval fortresses, such as the castle of **El Papiol** – perched on a rocky peak overlooking the city – its oldest parts dating back to the 11th and 12th century. Hermitages, Romanesque and Gothic churches and typical Catalan farms (*masías*) dot the landscape. The most striking building in recent times is the **Torre de Collserola** (➤ 160).

The picturesque surroundings of the Serra de Collserola are a popular **recreation destination** for stressed city dwellers who come out here on weekends to hike, cycle, jog, bird watch or just relax. For tourists it is an ideal day trip, with easy walks and superb views. The park's **information centre** has maps and route suggestions and on certain days there are themed tours and ornithological excursions (see website for details). The best way to get to the park is to take

The Parc de Collserola is ideal for a bike ride near the city

the Ferrocarriles from Plaça Catalunya to the Peu de Funicular station; from there you take the rack railway on to the Parc de Collserola.

➕ 194 B4
✉ Information Centre: Carretera de Vallvidrera–Sant Cugat (BV1462), at 4.7 km
☎ 9 32 80 35 52;
www.parcnaturalcollserola.cat
🕙 Daily 9:30–3
🎟 Free

View from the basilica Sagrat Cor across to the Serra de Collserola

Where to...
Eat and Drink

Prices
Expect to pay per person for a three-course meal, excluding drinks:
€ under €25   €€ €25–€50   €€€ over €50

ABaC €€€

Located in a stunning, contemporary building, ABaC is one of Barcelona's top restaurants, with young chef Jordi Cruz garnering many coveted awards for his creative cooking. Opt for the taster menu, which might include *foie gras* steamed in bamboo or mushroom, crab and avocado tartare. The restaurant is formal, decorated in soft, neutral shades, with a large glass window through which you can watch the chefs at work. There are also tables outside on the decked terrace for good weather. Upstairs is an exclusive 15-roomed hotel and downstairs a luxury spa.

+ 198 off B5 B5 ☒ Avinguda del Tibidabo 1
☎ 9 33 19 66 00; www.abacbarcelona.com
◷ Tue–Sat 1:30–3:30, 8:30–midnight
▣ FGC Avda Tibidabo

L'Illa Food Hall €/€€€

Pull up a chair at one of the many outlets in the basement of L'Illa shopping mall – for example, Fishhh!, with market-fresh fish and seafood; Bovinum, with Spanish classics; L'Angolo Italiano, with fresh pastas and cold cuts, or Araguil, with Middle-Eastern specialities. It's also a perfect place to put together your own picnic or buy ready-made salads and meals.

+ 200 A4 ☒ L'Illa, Avinguda Diagonal 557
☎ 9 34 44 00 00; www.lilla.com
◷ Mon–Sat 9:30–9:30 ▣ Maria Cristina

L'Oliana €€

Understated refinement sums up this neighbourhood restaurant specializing in Catalan cuisine, with the emphasis on fish. The weekday set menu is unbeatable value.

+ 200 A5
☒ Carrer de Santaló 54
☎ 9 32 01 06 47; www.oliana.com
◷ Mon–Sat 1–4 and 8:30–midnight, Sun 1–4
▣ Muntaner

La Venta €€

This colourful restaurant in the square by the funicular up to Tibidabo serves innovative dishes either on the attractive terrace or in the glass conservatory. Booking is recommended.

+ 198 off B5
☒ Plaça del Doctor Andreu s/n
☎ 9 32 12 64 55; www.restaurantelaventa.com
◷ Mon–Sat 1:30–3:15, 9–11:15, Sun 1:30–3:15
▣ FGC Avda Tibidabo

BARS AND CAFES

Bar Tomás €

This unassuming neighbourhood bar is renowned as the best place in Barcelona for *patatas bravas* (chunks of potato spiced up with a paprika sauce). Other options include tasty *croquetas* (croquettes) and *boquerones* (anchovies in vinegar). Service is speedy and no-nonsense.

Insider Tip

+ 198 off B5
☒ Carrer Major de Sarrià 49
☎ 9 32 03 10 77
◷ Thu–Tue 8am–10pm. Closed Aug
▣ FGC Sarrià

Mirablau €

Sip a cocktail and drink in the breathtaking views of the whole city from this idyllic hillside bar. There are snacks available in the daytime and at 11pm a nightclub opens downstairs. The drinks' prices are on the high side, but it's worth a splurge for the view.

✚ 198 off B5
✉ Plaça del Doctor Andreu 2
☎ 9 34 18 58 79; www.mirablaubcn.com
🕐 Sun–Thu 11–4:30am, Fri, Sat till 6am
🚋 Tramvia Blau

Where to…
Shop

In the upper reaches of the Avinguda Diagonal you'll find some fashionable malls where you can shop at national and international chains.

DEPARTMENT STORES

El Corte Inglés has two mammoth branches at Avinguda Diagonal – Nos 471–473 (tel: 9 34 93 48 00) and 617–619 (tel: 9 33 66 71 00); they're both reliable for clothing and shoes. Metro: Maria Cristina, www.elcorteingles.es.

SHOPPING MALLS

L'Illa (Avinguda Diagonal 545–557, tel: 9 34 44 00 00, www.lilla.com) is a vast mall, with international stores including many well-known fashion chains. Don't miss the food hall (► 165) in the basement (Metro: Maria Cristina; bus 6, 7, 33, 34, 63, 66, 67, 68, 78 and the Bus Turístic).

The **Pedralbes Centre** (Diagonal 609, tel: 9 34 10 68 21, www.pedralbescentre.co), farther away from the city centre, is where you'll find **Be** and **Furest**, for her and his fashion, die Schuhmode der Firma **Tascón**, and **Gocco** for children's clothes.

SPECIALIST STORES

The **Barça shop** (tel: 9 34 92 31 11) at Camp Nou stadium (► 162) sells the team's latest kit and accessories.

Where to…
Go Out

These uptown areas are home to a selection of slick bars and see-and-be-seen clubs.

NIGHTCLUBS

Bikini (Avinguda Diagonal 547, tel: 9 33 22 08 00, www.bikinibcn.com, late Wed to Sun nights, Metro: Les Corts), renowned for rock and South American gigs, opens. At weekends it stays open to daybreak.

Relatively new lounge club **Up and Down** (Avinguda del Doctor Marañón 17, tel: 9 34 47 02 45, Metro: Zona Universitària) offers upmarket clubbers a varied diet of guest DJs. The **Elephant** nightclub (Passeig dels Til.lers 1, tel: 9 33 44 02 58; www.elephantbcn.com, Metro: Palau Reial), in a lavishly decorated Pedralbes mansion, is the popular uptown choice for a drink and mixed tunes. At the foot of the funicular to Tibidabo is **Merbeyé** (Plaça del Doctor Andreu, tel: 9 34 17 92 79, www.merbeye.net, Metro: FGC Avda Tibidabo) a cocktail bar and club where a fashion-conscious and moneyed clientele relax to laid-back jazz.

CINEMA

Renoir (**Les Corts**, Carrer Eugeni d'Ors 12, tel: 9 34 90 55 10; www.cinesrenoir.com, Metro: Les Corts) screens English-language classics and current films in their original version with subtitles.

Excursions

Excursions

Barcelona is not just a great city, it also enjoys a fantastic location wedged between magnificent mountains and the Mediterranean. Should you feel like a break from the city itself, you could take advantage of the highly efficient regional transport network to get away and see a bit more of what Catalonia has to offer. To avoid the worst of the crowds head inland or try to avoid summer weekends or public holidays.

Whether you head south along the coast to the resorts of the Costa Dorada or north to those of the famed Costa Brava, you'll happen upon enticingly sandy beaches. Although parts of the Costa Brava have become over-developed, there are still some charming resorts. To the south lies the popular resort of Sitges, a picturesque fishing village with a very lively nightlife, especially for the gay scene.

Inland, there are just as many choices. The monasteries at Poblet and Santes Creus are outstanding, as is the holy site of Montserrat, set amid spectacular mountain scenery.

Southwest of the city lies the lush wine-growing region of Alt Penedès. Cava (sparkling white wine) is the speciality here, and you can enjoy free tastings at wineries in Vilafranca, the regional capital, and at nearby Sant Sadurní d'Anoia. The traditional market town of Vic, 70km (44 miles) north of Barcelona, gives one a taste of old Catalonia.

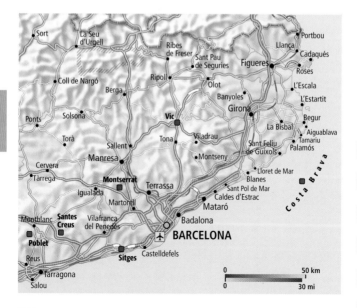

Sitges

Despite the fact that Barcelona has some wonderful beaches, it is worth taking a trip out to Sitges, a popular Costa Dorada resort some 30km (19 miles) to the southwest.

The town's beautiful beaches and laid-back atmosphere have ensured its popularity

The nine safe, sandy beaches here can get packed in the summer season, but that won't mar the friendly holiday atmosphere as locals mingle with the many visitors. Charming little hotels, fine restaurants and, above all, an unequalled nightlife are further reasons to visit Sitges.

Having started out as an artists' colony at the end of the 19th century, the town has always taken a tolerant, alternative view of life, and for years has been a favourite with gay tourists. Mardi Gras (February to March) is a time for outrageous dressing up and night-long raves in the picturesque whitewashed streets. If all this gets too much, there are plenty of cultural activities. The **Museu Cau Ferrat**, **Museu Maricel** and **Museu Romantic** are all worth a visit. Santiago Rusiñol, a local painter who made Sitges fashionable in the 1890s, used Cau Ferrat (currently undergoing refurbishment) as a hideaway. The nautical house, with superb sea views, displays an eclectic collection of paintings, religious artefacts and memorabilia. The Maricel, a sea-facing villa next door, is another collector's paradise, housing all kinds of antiques and curios. Here priceless objects mingle with amusing junk. The high point of the tour of the Museu Romantic, a rather camp aristocratic villa that was once home to a wine magnate, is an international collection of dolls and dolls' houses.

Excursions

🚊 Sitges station from Sants and Plaça de Catalunya

Explore the quieter side to Sitges among its whitewashed backstreets

Museu Cau Ferrat
✉ Carrer Fonollar 📞 9 38 94 03 64 🕐 Jun–Sep Tue–Sun 10–2, 5–9; Oct–May Tue–Fri 10–1:30, 3–6:30, Sat 10–7, Sun 10–3
🛈 currently undergoing renovations – probably until the end of 2014

Museu Maricel
✉ Carrer Fonollar 📞 9 38 94 03 64 🕐 See Museu Cau Ferrat

Museu Romantic
✉ Carrer Sant Gaudenci 1 📞 9 38 94 29 69 🕐 See Museu Cau Ferrat

---

THE COSTA BRAVA

If you're set on seeing the famous Costa Brava, to the north of Barcelona, or even considering basing yourself there for visits to the city, it's worth knowing what each resort offers.

Nearest to Barcelona, and strictly speaking on the Costa del Maresme, **Caldes d'Estrac** (popularly known as Caldetes) and **Sant Pol de Mar** boast some great beaches at great locations, with art nouveau architecture and quaint little fishermen's houses. Both can be reached by train from Plaça de Catalunya.

Blanes, which is easily accessible, including by train, and **Tossa de Mar** are both fine if a bit built-up, but avoid **Lloret de Mar** and **Palamós** if you can as they are overcrowded and polluted.

Sant Feliu de Guíxols is another picturesque little resort between Tossa and Palamós. The beach is sandy – whereas much of the coast is rocky – and the Museu de la Ciutat is worth a look.

Begur and **Sa Riera**, north of Palamós, reward the relative difficulty of getting there (roads can get congested and public transport is inconvenient), and are oases of good taste along a particularly nasty stretch of seaboard. **Aiguablava** (accessible from Begur) and **Tamariu** (reached from Palafrugell) each have a pristine sandy beach and the clearest water imaginable; their seafood restaurants are among the best along the coast.

The Cistercian Monasteries

The majestic monastic buildings at Poblet and Santes Creus monasteries combine Romanesque and Gothic architectural styles to fascinating effect, and their beautifully proportioned cloisters are near-perfect works of art. Both are idyllic havens of peace.

Monestir de Poblet

Poblet, around 110km (68 miles) from Barcelona, is one of Catalonia's most popular tourist destinations. The monastery was originally built to house the tombs of the Catalan and Aragonese kings and queens in the 12th century and was taken over by the Cistercian Order in the 15th century. The dissolution of the monasteries in the early 19th century and the Civil War both took their toll, and Poblet is now home to only a handful of monks. The buildings were stripped of many of their glorious decorations, but some fabulous lace-like stone carving and an evocatively meditative atmosphere linger on.

You can visit the monastery either individually or as part of an official tour (tours leave every 30 minutes or so). Highlights are the lavish high altar reredos – a miraculously preserved masterpiece finely carved in honey-hued alabaster – the gorgeous royal tombs with their lifelike effigies and the covered fountain in the middle of the lush garden-like cloisters.

Monestir de Santes Creus

Santes Creus, some 30km (19 miles) east of Poblet, tends to be far quieter and rather than being shepherded around on a guided tour, you're left to your own devices. The ornate baroque altarpiece, King Peter III of Aragón's tomb and some delicate frescoes remain, and many of the out-buildings are in an appealing state of semi-ruin.

The ornate baroque altarpiece at Monestir de Santes Creus

🚊 L'Espluga de Francolí from station Sants, then taxi or bus to Monestir de Poblet 🚌 No public transport to Santes Creus – access by car or excursion only

Monestir de Poblet
✉ Poblet at L'Espluga de Francolí
☎ 9 77 87 00 89; www.poblet.cat
🕐 Guided tours daily 10–12:45, 3–6 (till 5:30 Nov–Feb and Sun all year) 💰 €7

Monestir de Santes Creus
✉ Aiguamurcia, 95km (59 miles) west of Barcelona
☎ 9 77 63 83 29 🕐 Tue–Sun 10–7 (till 5:30 Oct–May)
💰 €4.50, free Tue

The Wineries of the Alt Penedès

Catalonia's main wine-producing area lies approximately 50km (30 miles) southwest of Barcelona. The vineyards are best visited with your own transport. However, the appealing regional centres of Vilafranca del Penedès and Sant Sadurní d'Anoia are easily reached by train from Barcelona.

Catalonia's best wines and, above all, *cava* (Spain's answer to champagne) are produced by big-name wineries such as Freixenet and Codorníu. All the bodegas open their doors to the public and conduct tours of the presses and cellars before the wine-tasting. If you go to only one, make it **Caves Codorníu** for its grotto-like Modernist building, designed at the end of the 19th century by Josep Puig i Cadafalch. For guided tours of the region, contact the Catalonia tourist office (► 35). Don't drink and drive – there are strict drink-driving laws.

Wine festivals are held in the region in late September and early October, coinciding with the grape harvest.

Sample some of Catalonia's finest wines at the Caves Codorníu bodega in Sant Sadurní d'Anoia

Vilafranca del Penedès
The regional capital, Vilafranca del Penedès is a pleasant place to wander around and has an informative tourist office (Carrer Cort 14). At the **Vinseum** you can learn all about wine-making.

www.turismevilafranca.com; www.santsadurni.org

🚆 From Plaça de Catalunya and Sants, hourly trains take 40–50 minutes to reach Sant Sadurní and Vilafranca. A hire car will be needed to visit the vineyards

Caves Codorníu
✉ Sant Sadurní d'Anoia ☎ 9 38 91 33 42; www.codorniu.es
🕐 Mon–Fri 9–5, Sat, Sun 9–1 💶 €9. Reserve in advance

Caves Freixenet
✉ Carrer Joan Sala 2, Sant Sadurní ☎ 9 38 91 70 96; www.freixenet.es
🕐 Mon–Thu 10–1, 3–4:30, Fri–Sun 10–1

Vinseum
✉ Plaça Jaume I, Vilafranca del Penedès
☎ 9 38 90 05 82; www.vinseum.cat
🕐 Tue–Sat 10–2, 4–7, Sun and holidays 10–2 💶 €7

Montserrat

The Monastery of Montserrat, high up in the mountains 40km (25 miles) northwest of Barcelona, makes a great day trip from the city.

Montserrat (meaning serrated mountain) has been a place of pilgrimage since a monastery was founded on the mountainside to house the "Black Virgin" of Montserrat (*La Moreneta*), a wooden statue of the Madonna and Child with a smoke-blackened face, which mysteriously turned up here in the 12th century. Today, *La Moreneta* is on display in the 16th-century basilica, the monastery's church – but be prepared for a long wait. In the nearby Museu de Montserrat, you can see a display of the many gifts left by pilgrims.

Dotted over the mountain are 13 hermitages, all still in use, and a signposted route takes you past them all with superb views along the way. Those that can be seen inside include the Hermitage of Sant Joan, which can be reached by funicular or a steep, 20-minute walk from the monastery, and the Hermitage of San Jeroni, at the mountain's peak.

Montserrat figures prominently in the Catalan psyche and gets crowded. Much of the appeal of Montserrat lies in the stunning mountain scenery and in the journey to get there, which involves a rack railway or a stomach-churning cable-car ride from the foot of the mountain.

The monastery lies high in the mountains to the northwest of the city, accessible only by cable car or rack railway

Getting to Montserrat

🚃 GC line R5 from Plaça d'Espanya every hour takes one hour to Aeri de Montserrat (for the cable car) or the next stop, Monistrol (for the rack railway or El Cremallera; www.cremalleradementserrat.com). Regular cable cars and trains will whisk you up the mountain to the monastery in 15 minutes. A Trans Montserrat card (available at Plaça d'Espanya) includes all transport and represents a saving on buying individual tickets; Tot Montserrat also includes museum entry and a buffet lunch.

Montserrat
☎ 9 38 77 77 77;
www.abadiamontserrat.net

Basilica
🕐 Jul–Sep daily 7:30–8:30;
Oct–Jun 8–6:30 💷 Free

Museu de Montserrat
🕐 Daily 10–5:45; July,
Aug till 6:45 💷 €7

Vic

The small city of Vic, 65km (40 miles) northwest of Barcelona, makes a refreshing contrast to the metropolis, and with direct train links it is easily accessible in an hour.

In the heart of the Catalan countryside, halfway between the Mediterranean and the Pyrenees, is Vic, a sophisticated city with a lively cultural agenda. The vibrant Saturday morning market is undoubtedly one of its main attractions. Vic is almost synonymous with sausages, especially its famous *fuet*, a mild salami-like creation, and its fat and juicy *botifarra*, grilled and served with white beans *(mongetes)*. Sample these delicacies in the beautiful Plaça Major, one of the finest main squares in the country.

The interior of the neoclassical cathedral is decorated with 20th-century murals by Josep Lluís Sert, and the rest of the town is scattered with curious little churches and convents. A fine collection of medieval religious art, mainly from the Romanesque and Gothic periods, at the **Museu Episcopal** and the remains of a Roman temple complete the picture; all of the central sights can be conveniently visited by following a well-signposted tourist route.

Frescoes adorn the interior of Vic's neoclassical 18th-century cathedral

🚆 From Plaça de Catalunya or Sants, direction Ripoll or Puigcerda, every 30 to 50 minutes; takes 1 hour to 1 hour 20 minutes
🛈 Carrer de la Ciutat 4, tel: 9 38 86 20 91; www.victurisme.cat

Museu Episcopal
✉ Plaça Bisbe Oliba 3 ☎ 9 38 86 93 60 🕐 Apr–Sep Tue–Sat 10–7, Sun 10–2; Oct–Mar Tue–Fri 10–1, 3–6, Sat 10–7, Sun 10–2 💶 €7

Walks

Walks

1 BARRI GÒTIC

DISTANCE 2.5km (1.5 miles)   **TIME** 2 hours
START POINT Plaça Nova ⓜ Liceu or Jaume I ✚ 204 B4
END POINT Plaça de l'Angel ⓜ Jaume I ✚ 204 C3

One of Barcelona's many slogans is "the past has a future". This walking tour takes you back to that past: shady little squares, quaint narrow streets, vestiges of Roman walls and Gothic churches galore.

The medieval streets of the Barri Gòtic

1–2

From the **Plaça Nova** – to the right of the **cathedral** as you face it – walk up Carrer del Bisbe in between two huge drum towers, remains of Barcelona's Roman walls. Take the first right, Carrer Montjuïc del Bisbe, to reach, through an archway, **Plaça de Sant Felip Neri**. This quiet, five-sided square was reputedly Gaudí's favourite Barcelona plaça, while the offbeat **Museu del Calçat** (► 51) lies just around to the left.

2–3

Exit along Carrer de Sant Felip Neri, turn right onto Carrer de Sant Sever and descend **Baixada de Santa Eulàlia**, down which the city's patron saint was rolled naked in a barrel of broken glass. Where you meet Carrer Banys Nous, you'll see a tiled mosaic in the wall ahead. The street curls to the left, past several antiques shops and Llibreria Rodes. Go left at Carrer del Call, and you're now at the heart of Barcelona's medieval Jewish quarter, the **Call**. Turn up this street, Carrer de l'Arc de Sant Ramon, and take the first right, Carrer Marlet. At the corner is a small **Hebrew inscription**, translated into Spanish. Just along Carrer Marlet is the Sinagoga Major, abandoned in the 14th century, but undergoing restoration. At Carrer Marlet 5 is the **Centre d'Interpretació del Call**, with useful information on Jewish culture in Barcelona.

3–4

At the crossroads with the very picturesque Carrer de Sant Domènec del Call turn right, then after 100m (330 feet) go right into Carrer de Ferran. Second on the left is Carrer d'Avinyó, the inspiration for Picasso's *Les Demoiselles d'Avignon* back in the days when prostitutes plied their trade here; now it is highly respectable. Make a small diversion to the right into **Plaça de George Orwell**,

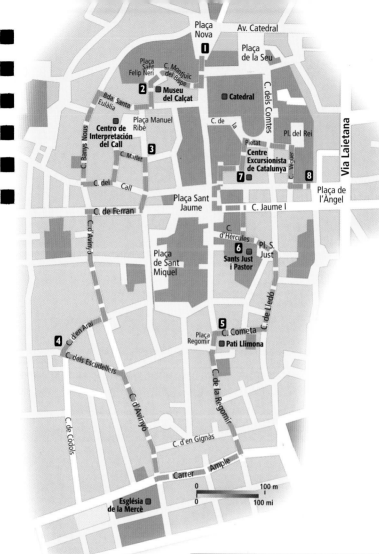

Plaça Nova

1

Av. Catedral

Plaça de la Seu

Plaça Sant Felip Neri

C. Montjuïc del Bispe

2 ■ Museu del Calçat

■ Catedral

Bda. Santa Eulàlia

Plaça Manuel Ribé

C. de la

C. dels Comtes

Centro de Interpretación del Call

3

C. Marlet

Pietat

Pl. del Rei

Centre Excursionista de Catalunya

C. Banys Nous

C. del Call

7

C. Veguer

8

Plaça de l'Àngel

Via Laietana

Plaça Sant Jaume

C. de Ferran

C. Jaume I

C. d'Avinyó

C. d'Hèrcules

6

Pl. S. Just

Plaça de Sant Miquel

Sants Just i Pastor

C. d'en Arai

C. de Lledó

C. dels Escudellers

4

5

C. Cometa

Plaça Regomir

■ Pati Llimona

C. d'Avinyó

C. de la Regomir

C. de Còdols

C. d'en Gignàs

Carrer   Ample

Església de la Mercè ■

0 ————— 100 m
0 ————— 100 mi

an attractive square with a modern sculpture, nicknamed "El Tripi".

4–5

Follow Carrer d'Avinyó down to **Església de la Mercè.** You can't miss the huge Virgin on top of the church. Turn left along Carrer Ample and continue to the crossroads. Turn left on to Carrer Regomir, heading up the road until you come to **Pati Llimona**, at No 3.

Plaça Sant Just, in the shadow of the Gothic church of Sants Just i Pastor, is a pleasant place to linger

Walks

5–6

Now go right along Carrer Cometa, and left along Carrer Lledó, lined with impressive stone buildings. You'll soon reach Plaça Sant Just: on the left-hand side, as you look at the church of **Sants Just i Pastor**, you'll notice a row of beautiful fountainheads still used by locals for their drinking water. The church has a fine, typically Catalan Gothic facade and a single, slender tower – but inside it's gloomy.

6–7

Turn left down Carrer d'Hèrcules, right into Carrer Arlet, and left again into **Plaça de Sant Jaume** (➤ 49). Head up Carrer del Paradis; the street slopes steeply upwards before a sharp right. Ahead of you at No 10 is the entrance to the **Centre Excursionista de Catalunya**; inside stand four fine Corinthian columns, all that remains of the **Temple d'August**, built at the highest point of the Roman city, 16.9m (55 feet) above sea level.

7–8

As Carrer del Paradis twists around and enters Carrer de la Pietat, you're treated to splendid views of the **Catedral** and its gargoyles. Carry on down Carrer de la Pietat, turn right into Carrer del Veguer, and left again into Plaça de l'Angel.

The drinking fountain on Plaça Sant Just is still on use today

PLACES TO VISIT

Centre d'Interpretació del Call
✉ Carrer Marlet 5
☎ 9 33 17 07 90; www.calldebarcelona.org
🕐 Mon–Fri 10:30–2, Sat–Sun 10:30–3

Centre Excursionista de Catalunya
✉ Carrer del Paradis 10–12
☎ 9 33 15 23 11; www.cec.cat
🕐 Mon–Sat 9–1, 4–9:30

TAKING A BREAK

If you're in need of some light refreshment the atmospheric *orxateria* (➤ 40) **La Granja** (Carrer Banys Nous 4) is the perfect place to stop. Alternatively, for something more substantial, try your luck at the ever-popular **Can Culleretes** (➤ 68), the oldest restaurant in the city. If you'd prefer to sit outside, head for the relaxed Plaça dels Traginers, a traffic-free square just behind the main post office, where there are a couple of informal cafes, including **El Salón** (➤ 70), serving the likes of nachos or gazpacho.

WHEN?

Go on a busy weekday or Saturday morning – otherwise the back streets are often quiet to the point of eeriness.

2 GRÀCIA

DISTANCE 3km (2 miles) **TIME** 2.5 hours
START POINT Plaça Joan Carles I 🅜 Diagonal ✚ 200 B3
END POINT Plaça de Lesseps 🅜 Lesseps ✚ 200 off B5

Enticing little squares and narrow streets characterize the neighbour-hood of Gràcia. Long a favourite haunt of artists and students, it has become smarter and more fashion-able in recent years, yet retains its special, bohemian charm.

1–2

The landscaped, open area in the middle of the Passeig de Gràcia, officially Jardins de Salvador Espriu, is popularly known as the **Jardinets**, or little gardens. On the right-hand side, where the street narrows to become Carrer Gran de Gràcia, is the **Casa Fuster** (Passeig de Gràcia 132), a Modernist masterpiece with lavish stone carving, built between 1908 and 1911 by Lluís Domènech i Montaner and his son, Pere. Immediately afterwards on the left, at Gran de Gràcia 15, is the superb **Casa Francesc Cama Escurra**, sport-ing beautiful stained-glass oriels. Opposite is Carrer de Gràcia, a typically narrow Gracienc alleyway; turn along it, past the stern 19th-century facade of the church of **Santa Maria de Jesús**. Turn left into Carrer Sant Pere Martir and left again into Carrer de Jesús, to rejoin Carrer Gran de Gràcia.

2–3

Up on the left-hand side is the gorgeous sgraffito facade of **Casa Elisa Bremon** (Gran de Gràcia 61), another Modernist house, dating from 1904. Go up to the corner of Carrer Santa Eugènia to take a peek at the equally fine **Casa Francesc Cama** (No 77). Its architect, Francesc Berenguer i Mestres, wasn't allowed to sign the facade when it was finished in 1905 as he had no university degree, so it bears his boss's signature: Miquel Pascual i Tintorer.

3–4

Now backtrack a few paces to **Travessera de Gràcia**, one of the neighbourhood's axes, lined with small shops, and turn left. Continue past a fine tiled drinking fountain, and then turn right down Carrer Matilde, which leads into **Plaça de la Vila de Gràcia** (➤ 120), an ideal place to stop for a coffee. The 19th-century clock tower standing at its heart gives the square its nickname, Plaça del Rellotge.

Casa Fuster, noted for its combination of neo-Gothic and classical styles

Walks

Plaça del Sol, a perfect place to take a break

4–5

Go up Carrer de M Pineda and head right, along the Travessera de Gràcia, until you come to the Mercat Abaceria Central, one of Gràcia's two markets (the other one, at Plaça de la Llibertat, has been handsomely refurbished). Go up Carrer Mare de Déu to **Plaça de la Revolució de Setembre de 1868**, another delightful open space with a bar or two tucked in its corners.

5–6

Gently amble along Carrer de Ramón y Cajal, which becomes Carrer Maspons just before you reach **Plaça del Sol** (➤ 120), with cafe-terraces for people-watching.

6–7

Walk up Carrer del Torrent de l'Olla, until you reach Plaça del Diamant. Cross the square and go along Carrer d'Astúries until you get to **Plaça de la Virreina**. It is home to the *barrio's* finest church, **Sant Joan**. On the opposite side is the handsomely ornate Modernist facade of **Casa Rubinat i Planas** (1906–09), at Carrer de l'Or 44.

7–8

Via the Plaça Manuel Torrente, head along Carrer del Robí and Carrer Tres Senyores before going up Carrer de Rabassa to the attractively shady **Plaça de Rovira i Trías**. Look for the statue of Antoni Rovira i Trías, who won the competition to design the Eixample but was pushed into second place by Madrid politicians. A bronze map at his feet shows what the city would have looked like if they had not chosen Ildefonso Cerdà's design.

8–9

From here carry on along Carrer de la Providència and Carrer Viada, then turn left on to Carrer del Torrent de l'Olla. Turn right on to Carrer d'Astúries, cross Carrer Gran de Gràcia, and wander along the Rambla del Prat, one of the noblest of Gracienc streets, lined with a serried rank of Modernist houses.

9–10

Go up wide Avinguda del Princep d'Astúries and turn right on to Carrer Breton de los Herreros. At the intersection with Carrer Gran de Gràcia, turn left. Climb a short stretch, then turn left on to Carrer Carolines to see **Casa Vicens** (➤ 121).

10–11

Finally, make your way up Avinguda del Princep d'Astúries to the major transport interchange, **Plaça de Lesseps**. On the corner of Carrer Gran de Gràcia, at Nos 30–32, you can admire three heavily ornamented houses called the **Cases Ramos i Carders**, built between 1905 and 1908 by the extravagant architect Jaume Torres i Grau. Their rich decoration and fantastic stained glass finish this walk around Gràcia with a flourish. Those who now still have enough time and energy can visit **Park Güell** (➤ 111).

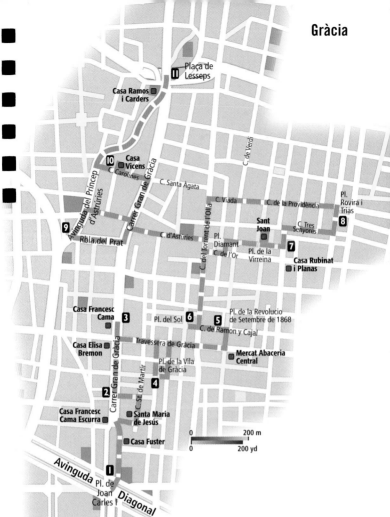

Gràcia

Plaça de Lesseps 11

Casa Ramos i Carders

Casa Vicens 10

C. Carolines

Carrer Gran de Gràcia

C. Santa Àgata

C. de Verdí

C. Viada

C. de la Providència

Pl. Rovira i Trias 8

Avinguda del Príncep d'Astúries

9 Rbla. del Prat

C. d'Astúries

C. del Torrent de l'Olla

Sant Joan

C. Tres Senyores

Pl. Diamant

C. de l'Or

Pl. de la Virreina

7

Casa Rubinat i Planas

Casa Francesc Cama 3

Pl. del Sol 6

5

Pl. de la Revolucio de Setembre de 1868

C. de Ramon y Cajal

Carrer Gran de Gràcia

Casa Elisa Bremon

Travessera de Gràcia

Mercat Abaceria Central

C. St de Martir

Pl. de la Vila de Gràcia

4

2

Casa Francesc Cama Escurra

Santa Maria de Jesús

Casa Fuster

0 — 200 m
0 — 200 yd

1

Avinguda Diagonal

Pl. de Joan Carles I

Modernist buildings line the Rambla del Prat, one of Gràcia's most enticing streets

Walks

3 MODERNIST GEMS

DISTANCE 4.5km (3 miles) **TIME** 3 hours **START POINT** Els Quatre Gats,
Carrer de Montsió 3 Ⓜ Catalunya ✚ 200 B1 **END POINT** Casa Pérez
Samanillo, Passeig de Gràcia & Avinguda Diagonal Ⓜ Diagonal ✚ 200 B3

Although Gaudí is Barcelona's most
famous Modernist architect, and
his buildings tend to steal the lime-
light, there is a great deal of art
nouveau architecture to be seen
in the city aside from his. Leading
names in the movement include
Lluís Domènech i Montaner, Puig
i Cadafalch and Jujol i Gilbert.

1–2

Begin at historic **Els Quatre Gats**
(►69). At the turn of the 20th
century, the cafe was a popular
place for Modernist artists to
meet. Picasso even designed
the menu. Built in 1896, it
was one of Puig i Cadafalch's
earliest achievements, an austere
red-brick facade embellished
with neo-Gothic sculpted oriels.
From the cafe, walk up Carrer
Magdalenes, cross Via Laietana
(at the crossroads you'll catch a
glimpse of the **Palau de la Música**

Catalana, ►78), and head
up Carrer Jonqueres to Plaça
Urquinaona. Go over the square
and turn right along Carrer d'Ausiàs
Marc, a smart street lined with
some beautiful Modernist houses
and shops at Nos 20, 31, 33 and
46; the last, **Casa Antonia Burés**,
is perhaps the finest. Stone trees
"grow" on the building's facade,
accurately imitating the plane trees
along the roadside.

2–3

Double back and head up Carrer
del Bruc, then turn left into Carrer
de Casp. **Casa Calvet** (No 48) is
one of Gaudí's earliest works
(1900). Although built to a surprisingly stark design, closer

**Casa Calvet, built in 1900, was
designed by Gaudí for textile
manufacturer Pere Calvet**

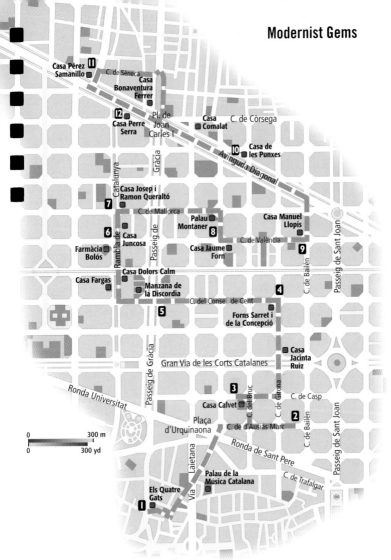

inspection reveals typically out-landish details such as the iron door knockers that look as though they have melted.

3–4

Rejoin Carrer de Casp and continue to the intersection with Carrer de Girona. Turn left, and continue to Carrer del Consell de Cent. On the way keep an eye out for **Casa Jacinta Ruiz** at No 54 and the charming **Forns Sarret i de la Concepció**, an art nouveau bakery at No 73.

4–5

Turn left along Carrer del Consell de Cent; you cross Passeig de Gràcia at a wonderful vantage point, with a side-on view of the **Manzana de la Discordia** (► 117).

Walks

Farmàcia Bolós on the Rambla de Catalunya

Notice also the street lamps with seats coated in white *trencadí* (ceramic shards). They were designed by Pere Falqués i Urpí in 1906.

5–6

After cutting across the Passeig de Gràcia, turn right after one block into the equally elegant Rambla de Catalunya, with its wide central pavement. Here you're treated to a trio of wonders. First, **Casa Dolors Calm** at No 54, by Josep Vilaseca i Casanovas (who built the Arc de Triomf, ➤ 87), has a striking five-storeyed gallery jutting out over the street, inspired by houses in Seville. **Casa Fargas** at No 47 echoes the Casa Dolors gallery with a stone oriel, but the overall style is eminently sober, not unlike the buildings along the grand boulevards of Paris. Last but not least is **Farmàcia Bolós** at No 77; the tree-of-life stained-glass window, laden with ripe oranges, is gorgeous.

Insider Tip

6–7

Cross the Rambla de Catalunya to **Casa Juncosa** (No 78). This is a more restrained affair, with its rough-hewn ashlars and symmetrical balconies, but the finely carved tympanum, with botanical motifs, gives it away as a Modernist building – it was built in 1909 to a de-

sign by Salvador Vinals i Sabater. Continue up the Rambla de Catalunya until you reach the intersection with Carrer de Mallorca.

7–8

Stop for a moment to look at **Casa Josep i Ramon Queraltó**, on the corner of the Rambla de Catalunya – the sgraffito work on the facade is particularly fine. Then continue down Carrer de Mallorca until you reach Carrer de Roger de Llúria. On the corner, to your right, stands **Palau Montaner** (Carrer de Mallorca 278), a masterpiece by Lluís Domènech i Montaner. The wrought-iron work in the gates and the glazed-tile mosaics are outstanding. Now turn right down Carrer de Roger de Llúria to reach Carrer de València.

8–9

You can't miss the flamboyant **Casa Jaume Forn** on the left-hand corner at Carrer de València 285. This tour de force by Jeroni Granell i Manresa, built in 1909, has an almost plain chamfered corner facade with edges softened by semi-cylindrical columns filled in with delicately decorated stained glass. The wood and wrought iron of the central doorway is outstanding. Count three blocks along Carrer de València to the left until you come to the corner with Carrer de Bailén. Here at No 339 stands the **Casa Manuel Llopis** (1903), by Antoni Gallissà i Soque, with sgraffito by Josep Maria Jujol, who also worked on several of Gaudí's projects.

9–10

Go up Carrer de Bailén to Avinguda Diagonal, turn left and go along two blocks. Wonderful **Casa de les Punxes**, once described as a cross between a Flemish guildhall and one of mad King Ludwig's Bavarian castles, stands at Nos 416–420, on the corner of Carrer del Rosselló. Its official name is **Casa Bartomeu**

Terrades i Brutau. It is really three houses in one: Terrades' three daughters each lived in one section. When it was built to a design by Josep Puig i Cadafalch in 1905 a pamphleteer described it as a "crime against the nation".

10 – 11

Continue along the avenue, past **Casa Comalat** (No 442), a "harlequin's hat set in stone" (take a look at the fabulous doorway), and turn right up the Passeig de Gràcia. On the left-hand side look for **Casa Bonaventura Ferrer** (Passeig de Gràcia 113), an unassuming house with subtle wrought-iron balconies by architect Pere Falqués i Urpí, dwarfed by the Deutsche Bank next door. Turn left along Carrer Sèneca then left again, down the lower reaches of Via Augusta, and turn right into Avinguda Diagonal. On the first corner is **Casa Pérez Samanillo**, a belvedere occupied by the Círculo Ecuestre (horse-riding club), with a wonderful large oval window on the Avinguda Diagonal facade.

11 – 12

Cross over Avinguda Diagonal and backtrack to the corner with Passeig de Gràcia, where the Diagonal metro station is located. On the way you'll recognize the exuberant style of Puig i Cadafalch in the splendid neo-Renaissance stone facade and mock-medieval turret of the **Casa Pere Serra** (Rambla de Catalunya 126).

Casa Juncosa, designed by Salvador Vinals i Sabater

The Modernist doorway to Casa Comalat

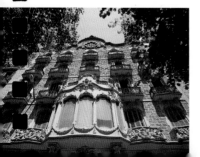

TAKING A BREAK

There is a wealth of cafes, tapas bars, restaurants and brasseries on the Passeig de Gràcia and the Rambla de Catalunya from which to choose; including **Pastisseria Maurí** (Rambla de Catalunya 102, tel: 9 32 15 10 20), which serves delicious cakes.

   De Tapa Madre (Carrer de Mallorca 301, tel: 9 34 59 31 34, www.detapamadre.com) is a great place to refuel with tasty tapas or a full three-course *menú*; unusually for this part of town it is open on Sundays too.

Insider Tip

WHEN?

Aim for Sunday afternoons or Monday mornings, when nearly everything else in the city is closed.

4 ALONG THE WATERFRONT

DISTANCE 5,5km (3½ miles), without cable car rides
TIME 3 hours **START POINT** Castell de Montjuïc ⓜ Paral.lel ➕ 202 C2
END POINT Port Olímpic ⓜ Ciutadella Vila Olímpica ➕ 205 F1

Since the 1990s, the city has made a feature of its waterfront. Starting from a vantage point that gives excellent views of the harbour and the sea, the walk will take you past luxury marinas and along waterside promenades to reach sandy beaches.

❶–❷

You don't need to go inside the forbidding **Castell de Montjuïc** (➤ 146) to enjoy spectacular views of the city's commercial harbour to the south, and of the old port, now a pleasure marina, to the north: the terraces in front of the fortified walls offer splendid panoramas for free. From the castle, either swing down on the **Telefèric de Montjuïc** cable cars and follow the signs along the Avinguda de Miramar to the **Miramar** (Sea Lookout) itself, or walk down the Carretera de Montjuïc.

❷–❸

From the Miramar you get closer views of the harbour and its maritime activity. If you have plenty of time and weather permits, amble around the delightfully landscaped **Jardins de Miramar** and wend your way down through the exotic cacti of the **Jardins de Mossèn Costa i Llobera**; otherwise catch

Transbordador cable cars arriving at Torre de Jaume I on the Moll de Barcelona the **Transbordador Aeri** cable car (► below) to the **Torre de Jaume I**, on the Moll de Barcelona. The views down onto Port Vell are breathtaking.

3–4

Head for the **Moll de la Fusta**, or Timber Wharf, by aiming for the landmark **Monument a Colom** (► 55) – the statue of Columbus atop his lofty column at the base of the Ramblas – surrounded by buildings such as the Duanes (Customs House), the **Museu Marítim** (► 140) and the Govern Militar (Military Governor's House). On the portside is the ticket office for the double-decker **Golondrinas** pleasure boats (► below); time permitting, take a ride around the harbour or even a short way along the coast.

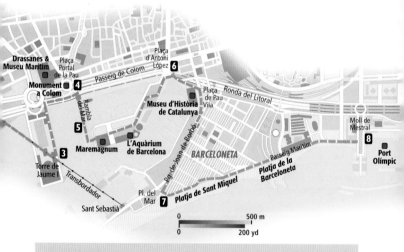

CABLE CAR AND GOLONDRINAS

Telefèric de Montjuïc
☎ 93 4 41 48 20, www.telefericodebarcelona.com
The cable cars run from 10am year round. Nov–Mar they close at 6pm, in April, May and Oct at 7pm and in Jun–Sep the last ride finishes at 9pm.
A good tip: The wait for the upward ride from the Estació Funicular can get quite lengthy in the summer; get there early or take a taxi up.

Transbordador Aeri
☎ 9 32 25 27 18
The cable cars across the harbour (often crowded) run Apr–Oct 10:15–7; May–Jun till 8; Nov–Mar 10:30–5:30 (always closed for lunch).

Golondrinas
☎ 9 34 42 31 06; http://lasgolondrinas.com
The boats run from 11:45 to 7:30 in the height of the summer, whittling down their hours to lunchtimes only in the winter. Closed 15 Dec to 1 Jan. The return trip to the breakwater takes 30 minutes, the voyage to the Port Olímpic and back 90 minutes.

Port Vell and the Monument a Colom at dusk

4-5

From the **Plaça del Portal de la Pau**, walk across the wooden **Rambla de Mar** swing bridge to the Moll d'Espanya.

5-6

Moll d'Espanya is home to the **Maremagnum** shopping and cinema complex, the IMAX movie-house and the **L'Aquàrium de Barcelona** (▶ 66). Where Moll d'Espanya joins the Moll de la Fusta is a busy traffic island, Plaça d'Antoni López, dominated by Roy Lichtenstein's unmistakable, extremely colourful *Barcelona Head* sculpture.

6-7

Weave your way eastwards to Plaça de Pau Vila, graced by the fine old warehouses now converted into the **Museu d'Història de Catalunya** (▶ 87). **Barceloneta** (▶ 88), with its tantalizing seafood restaurants and characterful narrow streets, stretches before you; either make your way through it or walk round the edge of the peninsula to reach the Passeig Marítim.

7-8

The **Passeig Marítim** takes you behind Barceloneta's beach to the ever-bustling **Port Olímpic** (▶ 97), a marina that was built specially for the 1992 Olympiad. It's still a very popular haunt with families and anyone looking for some frivolous fun or a tasty fish dinner. Beyond Port Olímpic is the seaside promenade where you'll compete for space with rollerbladers and cyclists. If you feel inclined, you could round off the walk with a dip in the Mediterranean. For more information on **Barcelona's beaches** ▶ 90.

TAKING A BREAK
Port Vell, Barceloneta and Port Olímpic are excellent places to sample seafood (▶ 93).

WHEN?
You can do this walk any day of the week, although the beaches get packed on summer weekends. To make the most of the views, the beaches and the bracing seaside air, go in fine weather.

Practicalities

Practicalities

WHAT YOU NEED

	USA	Canada	Australia	Ireland	Germany	Ireland	Netherlands
● Required Some countries require a passport to ○ Suggested remain valid for a minimum period ▲ Not required (usually at least six months) beyond the date of entry – check before you travel.							
Passport	●	●	●	●	●	●	●
Visa	▲	▲	▲	▲	▲	▲	▲
Onward or Return Ticket	▲	▲	▲	▲	▲	▲	▲
Health Inoculations	○	○	○	○	○	○	○
Health Documentation (► 194, Health)	●	●	●	●	●	●	●
Travel Insurance	○	○	○	○	○	○	○
Driver's Licence (national)	●	●	●	●	●	●	●
Car Insurance Certificate	n/a	n/a	n/a	○	○	○	○
Car Registration Document	n/a	n/a	n/a	○	○	○	○

WHEN TO GO

High season   Low season

JAN	FEB	MAR	APR	MAY	JUN	JUL	AUG	SEP	OCT	NOV	DEC
14°C	15°C	17°C	19°C	22°C	25°C	29°C	29°C	27°C	23°C	18°C	15°C
57°F	59°F	63°F	66°F	72°F	77°F	84°F	84°F	81°F	73°F	64°F	59°F

Sun   Cloud   Sunshine and showers   Wet

Temperatures are the **average daily maximum** for each month.

The best time to visit Barcelona is May to June or September to October, when the weather is fine but not too hot, and there is a lot going on in the city. July and August see an exodus of locals, and many museums, restaurants and shops either close or reduce their opening hours; day trippers from coastal resorts crowd the city, and the weather can be hot and sticky, with some violent thunderstorms. On the up side, there are plenty of fiestas and festivals to keep you entertained. Winters are cool but seldom cold, though it can snow; when skies are blue and visibility perfect, January and February can be good months of the year.

GETTING ADVANCE INFORMATION

Websites
■ City of Barcelona, www.bcn.es
■ Tourist Authority, www.barcelonaturisme.com

In Barcelona
Tourist Information Office Plaça de Catalunya
☎ +34 03 2 85 38 34 (from abroad);
   8 07 11 72 22 (in Spain)

GETTING THERE

By Air Barcelona has one intercontinental airport, El Prat, which lies 12km (7.5 miles) from the city centre.

From North America Non-stop flights are operated from New York by Iberia, in association with its partner in the Oneworld alliance, American Airlines. Other flights from North America involve a stop at Madrid or a change of planes, either at Madrid or another European airport, notably Amsterdam, Frankfurt, Lisbon, London, Milan or Paris.

From the UK and Ireland There is intense competition – especially from London. The lowest fares are often on the no-frills airlines easyJet and Ryanair, from Gatwick, Luton, Stansted and regional airports. British Airways and its alliance partner, Iberia, fly from Gatwick, Heathrow, Birmingham and Manchester. British Midland (bmi) flies from Heathrow, and easyJet also flies from Liverpool to Barcelona. Iberia flies from Dublin, in association with its Oneworld partner Aer Lingus.

From Australia and New Zealand There are no direct flights to Spain from Australia or New Zealand; connections via London, Frankfurt or Paris are the most common.

Approximate flying times to Barcelona: London (1.5 hours), Amsterdam (2 hours), New York (8 hours).

Ticket Prices Flight prices tend to be highest at weekends and in spring and summer (Easter to September). A good way to solve the problem of finding somewhere to stay, especially at busy times, is to buy a city-break package that includes flights and accommodation. Check with airlines, travel agents, specialist tour operators and the internet for current best deals.

By Rail The main regional, national and international rail station is Sants-Estació. Comfortable, fast, express trains connect the city to Paris, Madrid and Valencia.

TIME

Spain is one hour ahead of GMT in winter, one hour ahead of BST in summer, six hours ahead of New York and nine hours ahead of Los Angeles.

CURRENCY AND FOREIGN EXCHANGE

Currency Spain is one of the European Union countries to use a single currency, the euro. Coins are issued in denominations of 1, 2, 5, 10, 20 and 50 cents and €1 and €2. Notes are issued in denominations of €5, €10, €20, €50, €100, €200 and €500.

Exchange You can change **travellers' cheques** at banks and savings banks (caixes d'estalvis), at oficines de canvi (including late-night bureaux de change along the Ramblas) and at stations and airports. Bureaux de change don't charge commission, but apply (often far) less favourable rates.

Credit cards are widely accepted in shops, restaurants and hotels, although **proof of identity** (no copies), is usually required. VISA, MasterCard, AMEX and Diners Club are the preferred cards, and they can be used to withdraw cash from widespread ATMs for a fee.

In the UK	In the US (New York)	In the US (Los Angeles)
Spanish Tourist Office	Tourist Office of Spain	Tourist Office of Spain
79 New Cavendish Street	60 East 42nd Street	8383 Wilshire Blvd,
London W1W 6XB	53rd Floor	Suite 960
☎ 0870 850 6599	New York, NY 10165	Beverly Hills, CA 90211
	☎ 212/265-8822	☎ 323/658-7188

Practicalities

WHEN YOU ARE THERE

NATIONAL HOLIDAYS

1 Jan	New Year's Day	24 Sep	La Mercè
6 Jan	Epiphany	12 Oct	Discovery of Americas
Mar/Apr	Good Fri/Easter Mon	1 Nov	All Saints' Day
1 May	May Day	6 Dec	Constitution Day
May/Jun	Whit Monday	8 Dec	Immaculate Conception
24 Jun	St John's Day	25 Dec	Christmas Day
15 Aug	Assumption	26 Dec	St Stephen's Day
11 Sep	Catalan National Day		

ELECTRICITY

The power supply is 220 volts. Plugs have two round pins; visitors from the UK and North America will require an adaptor. A transformer is needed for appliances operating on 210/120-volts; these are hard to find in Spain so it's best to bring one with you.

OPENING HOURS

○ Shops ● Post Offices
● Offices ● Museums/Monuments
● Banks ● Pharmacies

8am 9am 10am noon 2pm 4pm 6pm 8pm 9pm

☐ Day ☐ Midday ☐ Evening

Most **shops** close from Sat afternoon until Mon or even Tue. Major stores and malls open all day, and some Sun. Many shops close in Aug.
Banks open 8:30–2 Mon–Fri. Many open Sat in summer. Savings banks open all day Thur.
Many **museums** close on Sun afternoons and all day on Mon

TIPS/GRATUITIES

- Most people round up **restaurant**, **bar** and **taxi** charges, and the more generous add on 5–10 per cent, but tipping is not expected.
- **Hotel porters** and **lavatory attendants** expect a small gratuity.
- **Tour guides** will appreciate a tip, particularly if they have been helpful.

SUNDAY TRADING

Traditionally only bakeries and cake shops traded on Sundays, but now shops may open on a few officially designated Sundays around summer and winter sales. Shops in the Maremagnum mall are permitted to open every Sunday.

TIME DIFFERENCES

Barcelona (CET)	London (GMT)	New York (EST)	Los Angeles (PST)	Sydney (AEST)
12 noon	11am	6am	3am	9pm

Practicalities

IN STAYING IN TOUCH

Post offices are identified by the yellow Correos sign and post boxes are yellow. The main post office at Plaça Antoni López opens Mon–Sat 8:30am–10pm, Sun 12–10pm. Stamps can also be bought from *estancs* (tobacconists).

Public telephones take coins and phonecards, which are available from *estancs* and kiosks. A few also accept credit cards. *Locutorios* (phone centres) are among the best places to make calls; there are lots in the Raval district. The cheap rate for international calls applies 8pm–8am and all day Sun.

International dialling codes
Dial 00 followed by
UK:	44
USA / Canada:	1
Irish Republic:	353
Australia:	61

Mobile providers and services Barcelona has excellent mobile-phone coverage including in the metro system. Network suppliers include Spain's own Movistar, as well as international names like Vodafone and Orange. 3G networks for mobile broadband are increasingly common. If you intend using your phone a lot, a local SIM card will avoid expensive roaming costs. They are available from *estancs*, newspaper kiosks, supermarkets and Fnac.

Many hotels offer broadband **internet** access including **WiFi**, as do some rental apartments. Increasingly, cafes around the city have WiFi areas, as does – rather surprisingly – Santa Caterina market. The Town Council is promising to enable all parks, markets and public libraries to offer free WiFi within the next few years. There are also internet cafes around the central section of El Raval (€1–€3 for 30 minutes).

PERSONAL SAFETY

■ Petty thefts are all too common in Barcelona, particularly close to the main sights. Pickpockets and bag-snatchers operate around the airport buses and trains in Plaça de Catalunya, Estació de Franca and Sants, and on buses (especially No 24 to Park Güell) and metros. Bag-snatching is also rife on the beaches.

■ In a busy place drawing attention to troublemakers may deter them but in quieter streets, although violent crime is rare, it is best not to struggle.

■ If the worst does happen, speak to a patrolling policemen or head for the special Guàrdia Urbana office at La Rambla 43 (tel: 93 2 56 24 30, Jul–Sep noon–2am; Oct–Jun daily 12–12). Here you'll need to get a *denuncia*, a certificate of the stolen items, for your insurance company. Take your passport or, if it has been stolen, a copy of it with you.

Police assistance:
☎ 091 from any phone

EMERGENCY 112
POLICE 091
FIRE 080
AMBULANCE 061

Practicalities

HEALTH

 Insurance EU citizens can get most medical treatment at reduced cost with the relevant documentation (EHIC card for UK and Irish nationals), although medical insurance is still advised. Health insurance is essential for non-EU nationals. If you need to see an English-speaking doctor, your hotel should be able to recommend one, or contact the tourist office.

 Dental Services Private dental care only is available and is not covered by EU agreements. The walk-in Centre Odontològic de Barcelona (Avinguda Madrid 141–45) tel: 93 439 45 00) is the most convenient place to go for help.

 Weather In hot weather, wear a hat and sunglasses, use sunscreen and drink plenty of fluids. Avoid alcohol during the day.

 Health Pharmacies (farmàcies), distinguished by a green cross (night pharmacies by a red cross), sell prescription and non-prescription drugs and medicines.

 Safe Water Tap and drinking fountain water are safe (unless it says no potable), but many prefer the taste of bottled water.

CONCESSIONS

Students and Young People An International Student Identity Card (ISIC), International Youth Travel Card or Euro<26 card entitles the holder to discounted admission to most museums and attractions.
Senior Citizens Over 65s can get free or discounted entrance to many sights; ID must be shown.
The Articket This covers MNAC, MACBA, Fundació Joan Miró, Casa Milà, Museu Picasso, Fundació Tàpies and the CCCB. It represents more than a 50 per cent saving if you go to all seven.
Barcelona Card (www.barcelonatourism.com) Free or discounted museum entry, unlimited use of public transport and special offers at shops and restaurants.

TRAVELLING WITH A DISABILITY

Public buses are wheelchair-friendly, as are some of the Metro lines. Most attractions lack special amenities, but newer museums, such as MACBA, do have facilities. Useful contact: Accessible Barcelona, tel: 93 428 52 27; www.accessiblebarcelona.com For taxis accessible with travel scooters and non-collapsible wheelchairs: **Taxi Amic** ☎ 93 420 80 88.

🧒 CHILDREN

Most hotels, restaurants and bars welcome children, but few have baby-changing facilities. In this guide special attractions for children are indicated by the icon above.

LAVATORIES

Public facilities are rare, but nearly all places of interest have modern, clean lavatories.

SMOKING

A strict ban on smoking in all enclosed spaces came into effect throughout Spain in 2011. Bars and restaurants no longer have designated smoking areas.

CONSULATES

UK	**USA**	**Ireland**	**Australia**	**New Zealand**
☎ 93 3 66 62 00	☎ 93 2 80 22 27	☎ 93 4 91 50 21	☎ 93 3 62 37 92	☎ 93 2 09 03 99

PRONUNCIATION

Catalan pronunciation differs considerably from Spanish. Catalan is more closed and less staccato in sound than its *Castilian* cousin but, like Spanish, is nearly always phonetic, albeit with a few special rules of its own, summarized below:.

au ow in wow
c ss or k (never th)
ç ss
eu ay-oo
g g or j (never h)
gu (sometimes) w
h silent
j soft j (never gutteral)
ig ch at the end of a word: vaig (I go)
  sounds like "batch"

ll lli in million
l.l ll in silly
ny ni in onion
r at beginning and rr heavily rolled
s z or ss, depending on position
tx ch in cheque
tg/tj dge in lodge (lotja sounds like
  "lodger")
v b (vi, wine, sounds like "bee")
x sh in shake

SURVIVAL PHRASES

Yes/no **Sí/no**
Please **Si us plau**
Thank you **Gràcies**
You're welcome **De res**
Goodbye **Adéu-siau**
Good morning **Bon dia**
Good afternoon **Bona tarda**
Good night **Bona nit**
How are you? **Com va?**
How much? **Quant és/val?**
Sorry **Ho sento**
Excuse me **Perdoni**
I'd like **Voldria…**
Open **Obert**
Closed **Tancat**
Today **avui**
Tomorrow **demà**
Yesterday **ahir**
Monday **dilluns**
Tuesday **dimarts**
Wednesday **dimecres**
Thursday **dijous**
Friday **divendres**
Saturday **dissabte**
Sunday **diumenge**

IF YOU NEED HELP

Help! **Ajuda!**
Could you help me, please? **Em podria
  ajudar, si us plau?**
Do you speak English? **Parla anglès?**
I don't understand **No ho entenc**

I don't speak Catalan **No parlo català**
Please could you call a doctor? **Podria
  avisar un metge, si us plau?**

DIRECTIONS

I'm lost **Estic perdut/a**
Where is…? **On és…?**
How do I get to…? **Per anar a…?**
  the bank **el banc**
  the post office **els correus**
  the telephone **el telèfon**
  the lavatory **els serveis**
  the station **l'estació**
Left **a l'esquerra**
Right **a la dreta**
Straight on **tot recte**
At the corner **a la cantonada**
At the traffic light **al semàfor**
At the crossroads **a la cruïlla**

ACCOMMODATION

Do you have a single/double room?
  Té alguna habitació senzilla/doble?
With/without bath/lavatory/shower
  amb/sense bany/lavabo/dutxa
Does that include breakfast?
  Inclou l'esmorzar?
Could I see the room?
  Podria veure l'habitació?
I'll take this room
  Ens quedarem aquesta habitació
Thanks for your hospitality
  Gràcies per la seva amabilitat

Useful Words and Phrases

NUMBERS

1 u/un/una	9 nou	17 disset
2 dos/dues	10 deu	18 divuit
3 tres	11 onze	19 dinou
4 quatre	12 dotze	20 vint
5 cinc	13 tretze	21 vint-i-un
6 sis	14 catorze	30 trenta
7 set	15 quinze	40 quaranta
8 vuit	16 setze	50 cinquanta

RESTAURANT

I'd like to book a table **Voldria reservar una taula**

A table for two, please **Una taula per a dos, si us plau**

Could we see the menu, please? **Podríem veure el menú, si us plau?**

A bottle of/a glass of… **Una ampolla/ copa (vas) de…**

Could I have the bill? **El compte, si us plau**

service charge included **servei inclòs**

breakfast **esmorzar**
lunch **dinar**
dinner **sopar**
table **taula**
waiter/waitress **cambrer/a**
starter **entrant**
main course **segón plat**
cover charge **cobert**
bill **compte**
VAT **IVA**

MENU READER

a la planxa grilled
aigua water
albergínia aubergine (eggplant)
all garlic
amanida salad
ànec duck
anxoves anchovies
anyell lamb
arròs rice
bacallà salt cod
bistec steak
bolets mushrooms
botifarra spicy sausage
bou beef
bullabesa fish soup
caça game
calamar squid
canelons Catalan cannelloni
carn meat
ceba onion
cervesa beer
cigrons chickpeas
coca cake
col cabbage

conill rabbit
cranc crab
cru raw
embotit sausage
enciam lettuce
ensaïmades pastry spirals
escopinyes cockles
escalivada roasted vegetable salad
escudella meat and vegetable stew
farcit stuffed
fetge liver
fideuà paella made from noodles
fideus spaghetti
formatge cheese
fregit fried
fruita fruit
fuet salami
gall d'indi turkey
gambes prawns
gel ice
gelat ice cream

julivert parsley
llagosta lobster
llet milk
llimona lemon
llonganissa salami sausage
mantega butter
marisc seafood
mel honey
mongetes beans
musclos mussels
oli oil
oliva olive
ostra oyster
ou egg
pa bread
pastanaga carrot
pastís cake
patata potato
pebre pepper
pebrot pepper (vegetable)
peix fish
pernil dolç cooked ham
pernil serrà cured ham

plàtan banana
pollastre chicken
poma apple
porc pork
postres dessert
raïm grapes
rap monkfish
rostit roast
sal salt
salsa sauce
salsitxa sausage
sec dry
sopa soup
suc de taronja orange juice
sucre sugar
tonyina tuna
tortilla omelette
truita omelette/ trout
vedella veal
verdura vegetables
vi blanc/negre white/red wine
xai lamb
xocolata chocolate

Street Atlas

For chapters: see inside front cover

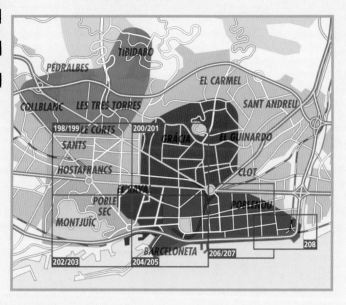

TIBIDABO
PEDRALBES
EL CARMEL
COLLBLANC · LES TRES TORRES
SANT ANDREU
198/199 · LE CORTS · 200/201
GRÀCIA · EL GUINARDÓ
SANTS
HOSTAFRANCS
CLOT
EL RAVAL
POBLE SEC · POBLENOU
MONTJUÏC
BARCELONETA · 206/207
202/203 · 204/205 · 208

Key to Street Atlas

Building of interest	Information
Public building	Museum
Water	Theatre / Opera house
Parc	Synagogue / Church
Forest	Post office / Police station
Cable car	Hospital / Library
Aerial raillway	Monument / Bus station
Rapit transit train	Place of interest
Underground	Ainternational airport
TOP10	Zoo / Beach
26 Don't Miss	Parking house
22 At Yout Leisure	Indoor swimming pool

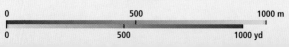

1 : 14.000

0	500	1000 m
0	500	1000 yd

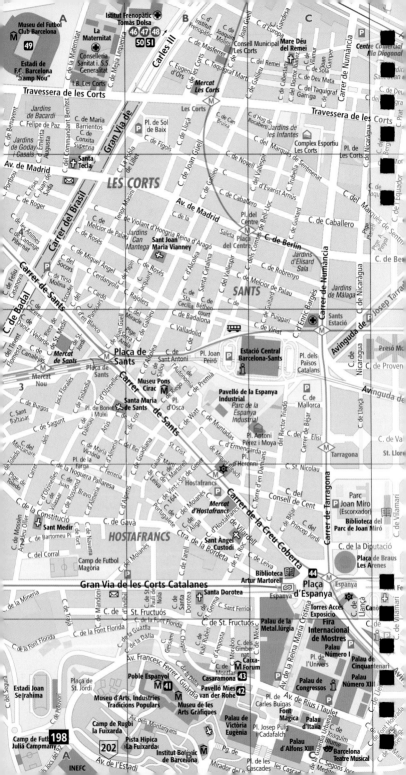

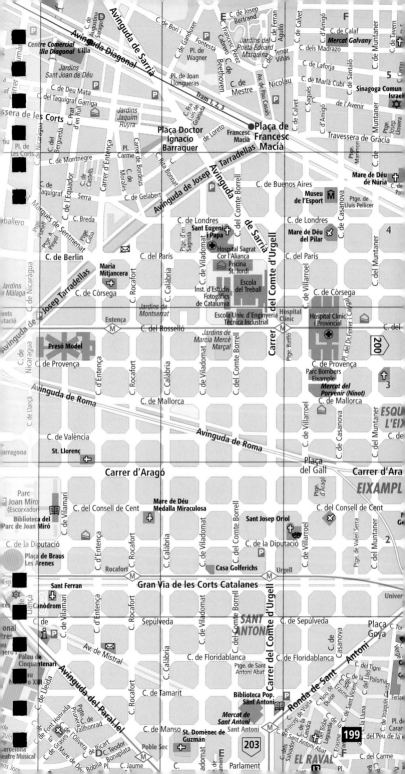

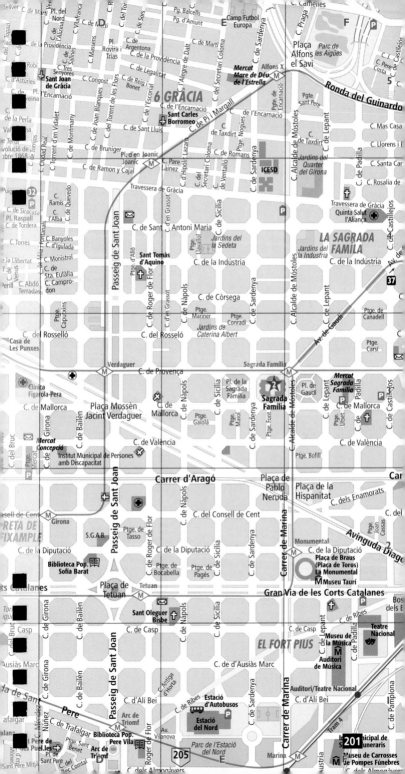

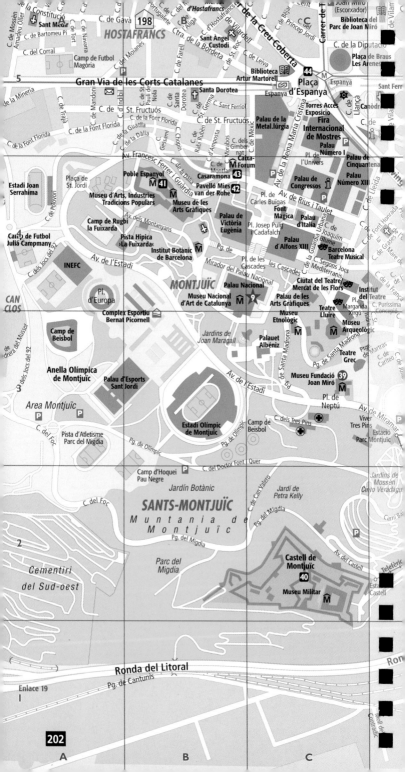

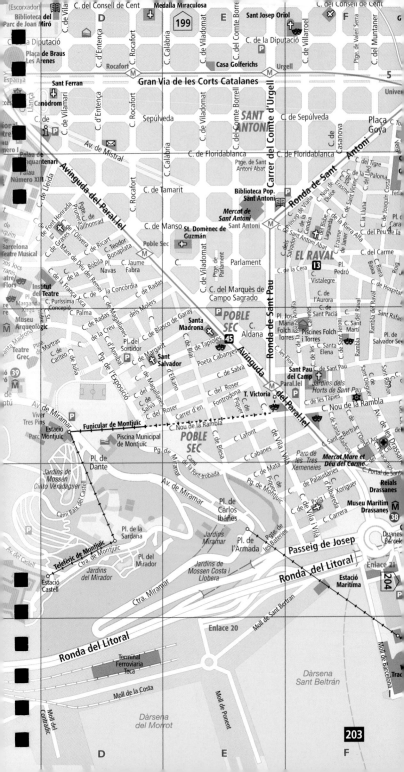

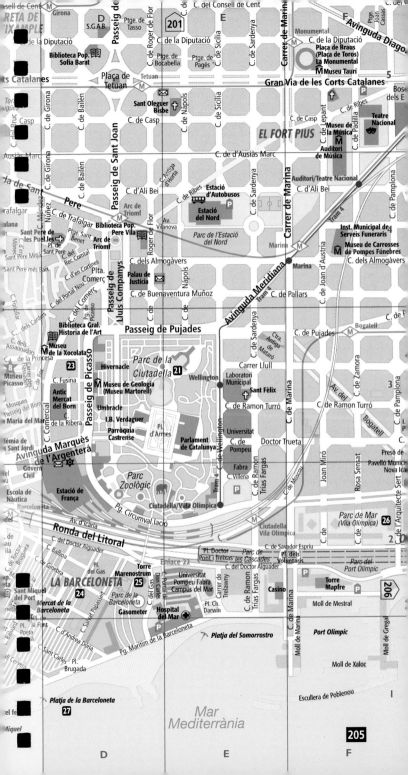

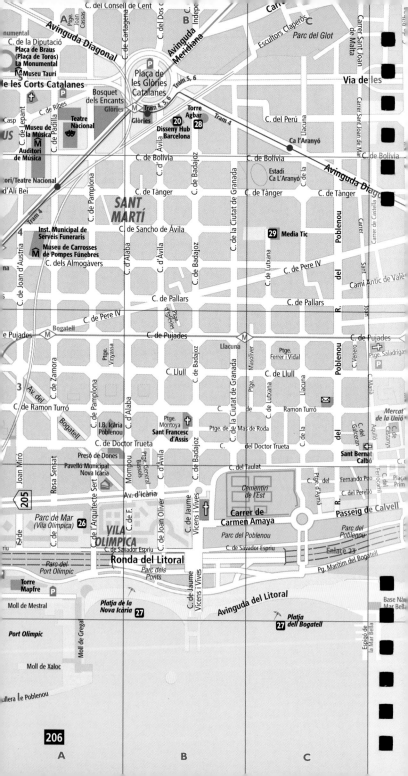

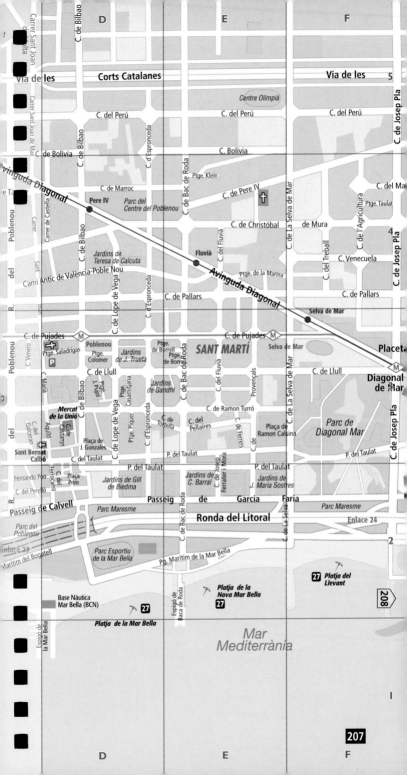

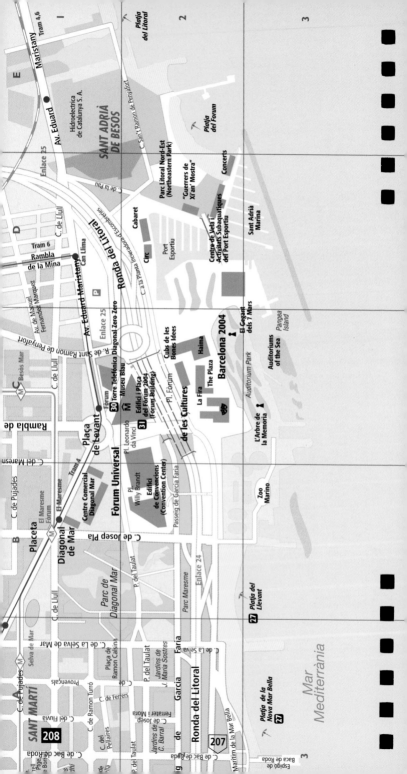

208

SANT MARTÍ

Tram 4,6

I

E

2

3

C. de Pujades

C. del Fluvià

C. de Ramon Turró

C. de Ferrers

C. del Pelaires

C. de Bac de Roda

Selva de Mar

Provençals

Plaça de Ramon Calsina

C. de La Selva de Mar

Plaça de
J. Maria Sostres

Jardins de
J. Maria Sostres

P. del Taulat

P. del Taulat

Jardins de
C. Barral

Garcia
Faria

C. de La Selva de Mar

Ferrater i Mora

Passeig de Garcia Faria

Ronda del Litoral

Marítim de la Mar Bella

Espigó de
Baca de Roda

207

Platja de la
Nova Mar Bella

27

Platja del
Llevant

27

Mar
Mediterrània

Besòs Mar

C. de Llull

C. del Maresme

Rambla de

Placeta

El Maresme
Fòrum

Diagonal
de Mar

Plaça
de Llevant

Centre Comercial
Diagonal Mar

Fòrum Universal

El Maresme

Pl.
Willy Brandt

Edifici
de Convencions
(Convention Center)

Pl. Leonardo
da Vinci

Torre Telefònica Diagonal Zero Zero

Edifici i Plaça
del Fòrum 2004
(Forum Building)

30

Museu Blau

31

Pl. Fòrum

Cubs de les
Bones Idees

La Fira

The Plaza

Haima

Barcelona 2004

El Gegant
dels 7 Mars

de les Cultures

L'Arbre de
la Memòria

Zoo
Marino

Auditorium Park

Auditoriums
of the Sea

Pangea
Island

Av. de Manuel
Fernàndez Màrquez

Can Llima

Tram 6

Rambla
de la Mina

R. de Sant Ramon de Penyafort

Enllaç 25

Av. Eduard Maristany

C. a la Planta Incineradora d'Escombraries

Ronda del Litoral

C. de Llull

C. de la Pau

SANT ADRIÀ
DE BESÓS

Hidroelèctrica
de Catalunya S. A.

Av. Eduard

Maristany Tram 4,6

Platja
del Litoral

Platja
del Fòrum

C. Sant Ramon de Penyafort

Parc Litoral Nord-Est
(Northeastern Park)

"Guerrers de
Xi'an' Mostra"

Concerts

Sant Adrià
Marina

Cabaret

Circ

Port
Esportiu

Centre de Vela i
Activitats Subaquàtiques
del Port Esportiu

Enllaç 25

Enllaç 24

Street Index

Street Index

Index

Notes

Picture Credits

Credits

1st Edition 2015

Worldwide Distribution: Marco Polo Travel Publishing Ltd
Pinewood, Chineham Business Park
Crockford Lane, Chineham
Basingstoke, Hampshire RG24 8AL, United Kingdom.
© MAIRDUMONT GmbH & Co. KG, Ostfildern

Authors: Andrew Benson (assisted by Teresa Fisher, Clarissa Hyman,
Lucy Ratcliffe), Dorothea Massmann
Editor: Frank Müller, Anja Schlatterer, Anette Vogt (red.sign, Stuttgart)
Revised editing and translation: Margaret Howie, www.fullproof.co.za
Program supervisor: Birgit Borowski
Chief editor: Rainer Eisenschmid

Cartography: © MAIRDUMONT GmbH & Co. KG, Ostfildern
3D-illustrations: jangled nerves, Stuttgart

Printed in China

Despite all of our authors' thorough research, errors can creep in.
The publishers do not accept any liability for this. Whether you
want to praise, alert us to errors or give us a personal tip –
please don't hesitate to email or post:

MARCO POLO Travel Publishing Ltd
Pinewood, Chineham Business Park
Crockford Lane, Chineham
Basingstoke, Hampshire RG24 8AL
United Kingdom
Email: sales@marcopolouk.com

FSC
www.fsc.org
MIX
Papier aus ver-
antwortungsvollen
Quellen
FSC® C020056

10 REASONS
TO COME BACK AGAIN

1. Barcelona has it all: **sightseeing, beaches** and **mountains.**

2. There are **more than 50 museums** and collections – far too many to visit in a single trip.

3. The outdoor **Mediterranean lifestyle** is wonderful for visitors from cooler climes in the north.

4. Where else can you find **Gothic, art nouveau** and **postmodernist** architecture side by side?

5. You will keep remembering the tempting displays of **tapas.**

6. There are still so many charming areas waiting to be discovered on **Montjuïc.**

7. **Pleasure and conviviality** – a meal in a restaurant is so much fun in Barcelona.

8. From classic to cult, from techno to taverns – there are no boundaries to Barcelona's **nightlife.**

9. This is the only place where you can climb on **human towers** (*castells*).

10. Quirky boutiques, creative fashions, trendy shops, design – **shopping** is a very special experience in Barcelona.